# The Conservation Revolution

## Radical Ideas for Saving Nature beyond the Anthropocene

Bram Büscher and Robert Fletcher

**VERSO**

London • New York

First published by Verso 2020

1 3 5 7 9 10 8 6 4 2

**Verso**
UK: 6 Meard Street, London W1F 0EG
US: 20 Jay Street, Suite 1010, Brooklyn, NY 11201
versobooks.com

Verso is the imprint of New Left Books

ISBN-13: 978-1-78873-771-5
ISBN-13: 978-1-78873-770-8 (LIBRARY)
ISBN-13: 978-1-78873-772-2 (UK EBK)
ISBN-13: 978-1-78873-773-9 (US EBK)

**British Library Cataloguing in Publication Data**
A catalogue record for this book is available from the British Library

**Library of Congress Cataloging-in-Publication Data**
A catalog record for this book is available from the Library of Congress

Typeset in Minion Pro by Hewer Text UK Ltd, Edinburgh
Printed and bound by CPI Group (UK) Ltd, Croydon, CR0 4YY

# Contents

# Acknowledgements

This book almost wrote itself. Not quite, of course. But somehow, from the start, we felt that this book had to be written. The seemingly sudden explosion of the Anthropocene conservation debates formed the initial impetus. It contained all the themes and issues we have both been thinking and writing about since the start of our academic lives and allowed us to revisit, rethink and update these in relation to new developments. The call for a new vision for conservation became the book's central drive. While trying to critically reflect on contemporary conservation, both of us have often been asked 'so what is the alternative?' This book is the start of an answer. Or rather: the start of a journey to join all those also seeking transformative ways forward, away from the capitalist mess we are all in. This, we believe, is (or *should be*) the new critical realism: to study, acknowledge and critically debate the messiness of the structures and lived realities of our contemporary political economy; and, on that basis, to contribute to imagining, envisioning and practising alternative ways forward. In a nutshell, this is the content of the book.

In the process, we were helped, supported and encouraged by many colleagues and friends. Special thanks, first, to Sebastian Budgen at Verso Books. His faith in the project and support through the whole process has been invaluable. Thanks also to all other colleagues at Verso for their support in the publishing process. Many thanks to Dan Brockington, Rosaleen Duffy and Wolfram Dressler for astute comments on (parts of) the manuscript and being a crucial part of the discussions contained in it. (More-than) academic friendships like these are what keep us going. Special thanks to Chris Sandbrook and Kevin Surprise for reviewing the manuscript for Verso. Your comments, critiques and suggestions were critical and helped to bring the manuscript to the next level.

Many other colleagues and friends read parts of the book, attended presentations where ideas in this book were presented and formed part of the networks that carried the ideas in the book forward. Thanks to Sian Sullivan, Jim Igoe, Scott Prudham, Frank Matose, Bill Adams, Lisa Campbell, Catherine Corson, Noella Gray, George Holmes, Alice Kelly, Elizabeth Lunstrum, Maano Ramutsindela, Kartik Shanker, Peter Wilshusen, Kenneth MacDonald, Murat Arsel, Danielle Hirsch, Zachary Anderson, Glenn Banks and many other colleagues and friends, including those in the amazing POLLEN network (politicale-cologynetwork.org). Thanks also to the CON-VIVA family, which will aim to explore, refine and concretize some of the ideas in this book in the next years: Mathew Bukhi Mabele, Wilhelm Kiwango, Anja Nygren, Sanna Komi, Dan Brockington, Rosaleen Duffy, Judith Krauss, Stasja Koot, Robert Coates, Katia Ferraz, Mariana Landis, Alexandre Reis Percequillo, Laila Sandroni, Ronaldo Morato, Rogerio de Paula, Silvio Marchini, Cíntia Angelieri, Peter Alagona, Alex McInturff, Kate Massarella, Coenraad Krijger, Gert Polet, Femke Hilderink-Koopmans, Amy Dickman and all other colleagues and partners who are part of and support the project. For those interested in knowing more and becoming a part of it, see: convivialconservation.com.

Within Wageningen University, thanks to our colleagues and friends in the Sociology of Development and Change group, the Rural Sociology group, the Centre for Space, Place and Society, the Forest and Nature Conservation group and others. Special thanks to the fantastic and inspiring postdocs, PhD and MSc students we have the pleasure to work with, and to the students who participated in the 2017 Wageningen Political Ecology summer school where the book was presented and discussed. Special thanks also to Nalini Gangabisoensingh, Marielle Takes and Sanne Hannink for support.

What makes this book truly revolutionary, in our eyes, is the love and support from our close friends and families, and especially Stacey and Arana, and Julia, Tenaya and Lori. You make all of this meaning-ful and possible.

# Introduction

A revolution in conservation is brewing. This is not necessarily an event that makes everything different. Rather, a growing urgency and pressure are building towards radical change. Even a cursory glance at conservation debates over the last decade shows that pressures on species and ecosystems – and hence the conservation community concerned with saving them – are extremely high and are certain to further increase. It has led to a growing realization that incremental, reformist change will not suffice to alleviate the pressure. The question for conservation is no longer whether we want or need radical change. It is brewing regardless. It is already happening. The question is how we understand the pressures and help direct imminent radical change towards something positive. This is the crossroads facing the conservation community today.

Now, the statement that conservation is at a crossroads has been true for a long time. Conservation biology, for example, has consistently portrayed itself as a 'crisis discipline'. Making 'hard choices' in complex contexts has always been part of the conservation equation. Yet the recent discussions concerning the advent of the Anthropocene seems to have upped the ante considerably, rendering already hard choices even more difficult. In this brave new world, ongoing debate concerning appropriate conservation strategies has moved beyond the longstanding 'people versus parks' dispute that had previously divided conservationists for decades. In the last decade, a number of radical alternate approaches to contemporary mainstream conservation have emerged. The two most prominent of these are 'new' or 'Anthropocene' conservation, on the one hand, and the 'neoprotectionist' or 'new back-to-the-barriers' movement, on the other. Together, these have caused quite a rift among conservationists.

According to new conservationists, life in the Anthropocene places an unprecedented and special burden on humans. *Homo sapiens* are seen to have changed global ecosystem functioning to such a degree that they now have to cultivate and manage the earth as one immense 'rambunctious garden'.[1] This is not necessarily something negative. Instead of only mourning biodiversity loss due to anthropocenic ecosystemic change, new conservationists believe we should switch focus to understanding and supporting the new and even potentially exciting possibilities that current global changes may bring.[2] Hence, what makes new conservation radical is that it aims to do away with conservation's long-standing infatuation with wilderness and associated ideas about 'pristine' nature as well as the conviction that these can be conserved as untouched protected spaces, away from humans. Nature and ecosystems always change, new conservationists argue. So why not embrace the 'new natures' that are currently evolving and use them to support human development?

To say that this perspective became a lightning rod is an understatement. After its opening salvos in 2011 and 2012, the new conservation proposal immediately provoked strong responses. Amongst these was a resurgence of 'neoprotectionism': a longstanding movement calling for a return to protected area expansion and enforcement. Unlike new conservationists, neoprotectionists do not believe that human-induced change is something (potentially) positive. Quite the contrary: they fear it will be the earth's undoing, precipitating the downfall of *Homo sapiens* and innumerable other species

---

1　Emma Marris, *Rambunctious Garden: Saving Nature in a Post-Wild World* (New York: Bloomsbury, 2011).

2　Fred Pearce, *The New Wild: Why Invasive Species Will Be Nature's Salvation* (Boston: Beacon Press, 2015); Chris Thomas, *Inheritors of the Earth: How Nature is Thriving in the Age of Extinction* (New York: Allen Lane, 2017); Menno Schilthuizen, *Darwin Comes to Town: How the Urban Jungle Drives Evolution* (London: Quercus, 2018).

in the process.[3] In the face of new conservation's bold acceptance of global human-centred conservation management, therefore, neoprotectionists have also upped their game considerably. Instead of putting humans in charge, they want to put nature back in charge. Many even argue that at least half the entire planet must be set-aside in a system of protected areas reserved for 'self-willed' nature. Only in this way, they assert, can an impending global ecological catastrophe be averted.[4] Instead of the radical mixing of people and nonhuman nature that new conservationists endorse, resurgent neoprotectionists call for a separation between people and nature on a scale hitherto never imagined.

These two radical proposals present far-reaching challenges to what we will refer to in this book as contemporary 'mainstream conservation'.[5] Mainstream conservation, many will agree, is not easy to define. In reality, it constitutes a very broad amalgam of different approaches, ideas and dynamics. Yet two key characteristics, we believe, based on our research over the last twenty years, can be singled out and generalized across this constellation for heuristic purposes. Mainstream approaches, first, still revolve very much around protected areas with strong links to broader participatory, stakeholder-focused approaches, including community-based conservation models. A second main characteristic of mainstream conservation is its capitalist character. This has been true for a long time but is increasingly focused on the idea that conserved nature can be turned into in situ 'natural capital' so that the creativity of the pursuit of profit can effectively and efficiently be linked to the protection of nature and the 'environmental services' it provides. The following chapter will expand on what we mean by mainstream conservation and relate this to the radical challenges brought by the emergence of the Anthropocene.

---

3   Edward O. Wilson, *Half-Earth: Our Planet's Fight for Life* (London: Liferight Publishing, 2016).

4   George Wuerthner, Eileen Crist and Tom Butler, eds, *Protecting the Wild: Parks and Wilderness, The Foundation for Conservation* (London: Island Press, 2015).

5   Daniel Brockington, Rosaleen Duffy and Jim Igoe, *Nature Unbound: Conservation, Capitalism and the Future of Protected Areas* (London: Earthscan, 2008).

## THE CHALLENGES OF THE ANTHROPOCENE

Popularized by geologist Paul Crutzen at the turn of the twenty-first century, the Anthropocene thesis is essentially the assertion that human influence has come to dominate all nonhuman processes to the point that it can now be identified as a distinct layer in the geological record.[6] The Anthropocene should thus designate our movement from the Holocene into a new epoch characterized by this pervasive human signature. The notion resonates with a similar contention by journalist Bill McKibben that expansion of human influence – particularly in terms of anthropogenic climate change – has precipitated the 'end of nature' as a distinct self-willed force altogether. Contemporary discussion of the Anthropocene contains quite similar proclamations that 'Nature is Over' or that 'Nature no longer runs the earth. We do'.[7]

The Anthropocene thesis, clearly, is a grand one. It is not surprising, therefore, that the concept and its implications have been and continue to be hotly debated, including among social scientists. Some, including many neoprotectionists, suggest that it exaggerates the extent of human control over the planet, proposing that nonhumans (from microbes to cereal grains) can instead be understood as colonizing and directing human processes.[8] Others worry that the concept conceals the reality that different groups of people have vastly different environmental impacts behind the image of a generalized 'humanity'.[9] Yet others, including some critical social scientists, have embraced the idea. They assert that this new reality completes the demise of the idea of an autonomous nature already initiated by critical perspectives in diverse scientific and philosophical traditions.

---

6   Paul Crutzen, 'Geology of mankind', *Nature* 415 (2002), 23; Paul Crutzen and Eugene Stoermer, 'The "Anthropocene"', *Global Change Newsletter* 41 (2000), 17–18.

7   Bryan Walsh, 'Nature is over', *Time Magazine*, 12 (March 2012), 83–5; Mark Lynas, *The God Species: Saving the Planet in the Age of Humans* (New York: National Geographic Books, 2011), 12.

8   Anna Tsing, *The Mushroom at the End of the World: On the Possibility of Life in Capitalist Ruins* (Princeton: Princeton University Press, 2015).

9   Andreas Malm and Alf Hornborg, 'The Geology of Mankind? A Critique of the Anthropocene Narrative', *The Anthropocene Review* 1, 1 (2014), 62–9.

Human geographer Jamie Lorimer thus states that 'diagnosis of the Anthropocene challenges the modern figure of Nature that has become so central to Western environmental thought, politics, and action.' Rather, 'the Anthropocene describes a very different world. This world is hybrid – neither social nor natural. It is nonlinear rather than in balance. Futures will not be like the past and will be shaped by human actions. Multiple natures are possible'.[10]

Social scientists who accept the Anthropocene see positive potential in how this new reality forces humans to acknowledge the extent to which their actions influence the planet and to therefore take their obligation to responsibly steward it more seriously. Lorimer asserts:

> The diagnosis of the Anthropocene and the popularization of the 'end of Nature' has the potential to value and catalyze modes of 'stewardship' based on diverse, reflexive awareness of the always-entangled nature of humans with their environments, the indeterminacy of ecology, and thus, the contested nature of any aspirations toward environmental management – from the local to the planetary scale.[11]

In this way, people may become 'aware of the impossibility of extricating themselves from the earth and start . . . to take responsibility for the world in which they live . . .'[12]

Taking heed of these different positions, the question of whether we should label our current era the Anthropocene is important. Later in the book, we will argue that a better descriptor for this new phase of human history is the 'Capitalocene', as argued by Andreas Malm, Jason Moore and others.[13] For now, however, we will continue to use

---

10   Jamie Lorimer, *Wildlife in the Anthropocene: Conservation after Nature* (Minneapolis: University of Minnesota Press, 2015), 2.

11   Lorimer, *Wildlife*, 4.

12   Lorimer, *Wildlife*, 4.

13   Alf Hornborg, 'Dithering while the Planet burns: Anthropologists' approaches to the Anthropocene', *Reviews in Anthropology* 46, 2–3 (2017), 61–77. We will come back to this discussion in chapter four.

the term since it has played such a pivotal role in the current conservation debate. Moreover, despite continuing debate concerning its validity as a scientific descriptor of the geological record, the last several years have seen the Anthropocene concept become increasingly used and accepted in both academic and popular media. The term, in short, has hit a raw nerve, prompting exploration of its grand implications.

Several of these implications present intriguing challenges for conservation, particularly for how to (re)interpret conservation science and what this says about our contemporary socio-ecological predicament. The dominant tenor from the scientific front is that the state of global biodiversity is dire, keeps getting worse and may soon surpass 'planetary boundaries' beyond which even more dramatic decline is inevitable. Some even argue that we are on the brink of 'biological annihilation'.[14] Yet, if the Anthropocene forces us to rethink basic assumptions of both the natural and social sciences – and hence the 'social' and the 'natural' more generally – it may also demand that we rethink this dominant position. This is something that the new conservation trend has taken to heart.[15]

The Anthropocene challenge is not just about how to act on what 'science' teaches us concerning the state of the global environment. Another equally fundamental challenge is that it has given massive impetus to long-standing discussions on how to (re)interpret the (role of) science in the first place.[16] These major challenges for conservation are at the centre of the current conservation debate, one that increasingly seems to demand radical choices.

---

14   Gerardo Ceballos, Paul Ehrlich and Rodolfo Dirzo, 'Biological annihilation via the ongoing sixth mass extinction signalled by vertebrate population losses and declines', *Proceedings of the National Academy of Sciences* 114, 30 (2017), 6089–6096.

15   Biologist and ecologist Chris Thomas explicitly argues that we need to 'throw off the shackles of a pessimism-laden, loss-only view of the world' and 'aspire to a world where it is as legitimate to facilitate new gains as it is to avoid losses'. Thomas, *Inheritors*, 9. For a critique, see Carl Safina, *In Defense of Biodiversity: Why Protecting Species from Extinction Matters*, (Yale Environment 360, yale.edu, 2018).

16   Esther Turnhout, 'The Politics of Environmental Knowledge', *Conservation and Society* 16, 3 (2018), 363–71.

## RADICAL CHOICES

Clearly, whatever the Anthropocene means, there is widespread consensus that our current reality of global, human-induced ecosystemic change presents stark challenges for conservation. It is concern for this dynamic that has led to the radical proposals now on the table. In this book, we critically examine these radical proposals within the context of the broader history of the conservation debate and propose our own alternative of 'convivial conservation'. For heuristic purposes, we deliberately start our presentation of these different approaches in a highly simplified manner, organizing the debate along two main axes: from capitalist to postcapitalist positions on one axis; and from positions steeped in nature–people dichotomies to those that aim to go beyond these dichotomies, on the other. As the book proceeds, we will problematize this simplistic picture to do more justice to the complexities of the current conservation debate and its participants, as well as to present a realistic and positive alternative.[17] If, for the moment, we stick to simplifying heuristics, however, we can identify four main positions along these two axes: mainstream conservation, new conservation, neoprotectionism and, finally, what we call 'convivial conservation'. The resulting schematic is depicted in Table 1.

Table 1. Four main positions on saving nature in the Anthropocene

|  | Nature/culture dichotomies | Beyond N/C dichotomies |
|---|---|---|
| **Capitalist** | Mainstream conservation | New conservation |
| **Beyond-capitalist** | Neoprotectionism | Convivial conservation |

---

17   We basically follow Henri Lefebvre's method here: 'reduction is a scientific procedure designed to deal with the complexity and chaos of brute observations. This kind of simplification is necessary at first, but it must be quickly followed by the gradual restoration of what has thus far been temporarily set aside for the sake of analysis.' Henri Lefebvre, *The Production of Space* (Malden: Blackwell, 1991), 105.

*Mainstream conservation*, we argue, is fundamentally capitalist and steeped in nature–people dichotomies, especially through its foundational emphasis on protected areas and continued infatuation with (images of) wilderness and 'pristine' natures. Phrased differently, mainstream conservation does not fundamentally challenge the hegemonic, global capitalist order and is firmly embedded in myriad 'dualisms' wherein humans, and their society or culture, are seen as (epistemologically and ontologically) distinct from 'nature'. As mentioned above, it is this latter element that new conservation targets and what makes it radical for many mainstream and other conservationists.[18] New conservationists portray nature and wilderness as an integrated element in a broader socio-natural 'rambunctious garden' to be managed by people. In effect, this seems to be the conservation biology version – and partial acceptance – of the idea advanced by critical social scientists that 'nature' is in reality always (plural) 'socionatures'.[19] This management, in turn, can (and for many should) be ardently capitalist. Many key new conservationists are, for example, staunch supporters of environmental service valuation and natural capital solutions to the environmental crisis.[20] These solutions not only leave growth and consumerism unproblematized but embrace these, albeit cloaked in a 'green' or 'ecologically modern' guise.

*Neoprotectionists* reject both these elements. As opposed to new conservationists, they are deeply and often consciously entrenched in nature–people dichotomies and believe that separation between people and nature is needed to stave off a collapse of all life-supporting ecosystems. At the same time, they have become increasingly – and often openly – critical of the continued faith in growth and consumerism shown by the new conservationists and those in the

---

18   Whether new conservationists actually succeed in overcoming the dichotomy is a question we will take up later, but see, for instance, Irus Braverman, *Wild Life: The Institution of Nature* (Stanford: Stanford University Press, 2015), 45–8. She argues that they do not and in chapter two we argue why we agree with this assessment.

19   Becky Mansfield et al., 'Environmental Politics After Nature: Conflicting Socio-ecological Futures', *Annals of the Association of American Geographers* 105, 2 (2015), 284–93.

20   Kareiva et al., 'Conservation in the Anthropocene. Beyond Solitude and Fragility', *Breakthough Journal* 2 (fall 2011).

mainstream.[21] In certain ways, with some important exceptions, many neoprotectionists are thus rather critical of contemporary capitalism, either explicitly or implicitly. However, one major problem in this stance, we will argue, is that this critique is often not based on a coherent theoretical or political frame, which leads to several intriguing and even disturbing contradictions in this position (as we discuss in the next chapters).

The two radical conservation approaches show that a conservation revolution might be brewing. Yet they cannot by themselves cause a revolution: neither is nearly radical enough and their contradictions, we will argue, cannot provide a realistic way forward. We see them, rather, as a prelude to the fundamental transformation that is needed. This is where *convivial conservation* comes in. The crucial difference between mainstream conservation, the two radical alternatives now on the table, and our own convivial conservation proposal is that we explicitly start from a political ecology perspective steeped in a critique of capitalist political economy. This critique is built on a rejection of *both* nature–people dichotomies *and* a capitalist economic system demanding continual growth via intensified consumerism. This probably makes it the most radical of the four proposals. But, we will argue in the conclusion, also the most coherent and realistic one. To put it bluntly: without directly addressing capitalism *and* its many engrained dichotomies and contradictions, we cannot tackle the conservation challenges before us. To take political ecology and a critique of capitalism seriously, therefore, means that we cannot rely on the current positions in the conservation debate, including their conceptualizations of nature and its relations to humans. This is why we will spend considerable time, in chapter five, developing our alternative proposal.

Convivial conservation might sound slightly awkward when suggesting a postcapitalist approach to conservation. Yet we have chosen the term deliberately. Most directly, because it is obvious that we need to find a better way to 'con vivire', 'live with' (the rest of)

---

21    Philip Cafaro et al., 'If we want a Whole Earth, Nature needs Half: A Response to Büscher et al.', *Oryx* 51, 3 (2017), 400.

nature. At the same time, the term was inspired by Ivan Illich's 1973 book *Tools for Conviviality*. In it, he acknowledges that he is 'aware that in English "convivial" now seeks the company of tipsy jollyness' but adds that this is 'opposite to the austere meaning of modern "eutrapelia," which I intend'.[22] Eutrapelia is generally defined as 'the quality of being skilled in conversation'. We believe that this is precisely what is needed in order to move the Anthropocene conservation debate forward: to skilfully and sensitively engage with the radical ideas now on the table and to imagine and enable a transition to a postcapitalist conservation. This, then, is how we understand and use 'conviviality', at least for now. In chapter five, we will develop further both Illich's and our own ideas of conviviality and why it makes sense to use this as a frame for a postcapitalist conservation paradigm.

These four main positions on 'saving nature in the Anthropocene' form a simplified heuristic characterization of the current conservation debates. As the book progresses, we will complicate this picture and offer necessary empirical, political and discursive nuances to the different approaches, including our own alternative of convivial conservation.

OUTLINE OF THE BOOK

The book's structure is straightforward. In the next chapter, we provide a brief recapitulation and an update of the 'great conservation debate' and how this now encompasses contemporary mainstream conservation as well as the two main radical alternatives of new conservation and neoprotectionism. This leads us to a more grounded appraisal of what we argue are the two foundational issues in the debate: the nature–culture dichotomy and our contemporary capitalist development model.

---

22    Ivan Illich, *Tools for Conviviality* (New York: Harper and Row, 1973), xxi. Illich even states that he had his doubts about the appropriateness of the concept: 'After many doubts, and against the advice of friends whom I respect, *I have chosen "convivial" as a technical term to designate a modern society of responsibly limited tools*.' Illich, *Tools*, xxiv (emphasis in original).

Next, in chapters two and three, we explore these two foundational issues in more depth in order to highlight and reflect on important nuances in the debate. Chapter two explains the problematic 'nature' and the origins of the nature–culture dichotomy. It focuses first on the dichotomy's central role in the Anthropocene conservation debate, especially in relation to central conceptions of 'nature', 'wilderness' and 'rewilding'. From there, the chapter turns to the first core argument of the book: the nature–culture dichotomy and our contemporary capitalist development model are historically deeply intertwined and continue to reinforce each other. Chapter three continues this analysis by delving more deeply into the close and long-standing linkages between capitalism and conservation. This leads to the second core argument of the book: conservation and capitalist 'development' have historically been closely intertwined but the nature of this relation is rapidly changing in ways that are important to understand.

Chapter four starts by discussing the consequences of the core arguments developed in chapters two and three. Here, we contend that both new conservation and neoprotectionism contain untenable contradictions in their common neglect of the close (historical) intertwining of capitalism and the nature–culture dichotomy. This, however, does not mean they lose all of their radical and political potential. The chapter argues that this potential is significant and that it needs to be harnessed by connecting it to other fields that have long engaged more radical ideas about conservation, especially political ecology. It concludes by developing a coherent set of theoretical premises on which to ground an alternative radical proposal. Chapter five is dedicated to developing this alternative and outlines its practical and political implications.

We conclude the book by arguing why we believe the alternative of convivial conservation is the most optimistic, equitable and, importantly, *realistic* model for conservation for the future. In doing so, we emphasize that while the term 'convivial conservation' may be new, many of its premises are not. Numerous indigenous, progressive, youth, emancipatory and other movements, individuals and organizations have long been working on, and engaged in, alternative conservation practices and ideas that include elements of what we propose here. We pay tribute to these in the intermezzo after chapter four. And while we may not be able to do justice to them all in a short book, we present convivial conservation as a scientifically grounded, *political* platform and paradigm that aims to build on, through and with these many past, current and no doubt future examples of alternative conservation practices and ideas.

The ultimate purpose of this platform and paradigm is to help make political choices clearer in this particular moment of time, what we will refer to as the 'Trump moment in conservation': a moment in which radical choices are no longer 'coming', but are being made all around us all the time.[23] Convivial conservation delves into this political fray with the hope of adding to others to (re)direct the choices that are being made in a more hopeful and just direction. And to be clear: these choices are foundational. As the following chapters show in detail, the anthropocene conservation debate touches on the foundations of the relations between humans and the rest of nature. This is why we need to go to their roots, as from these roots emerge the possibilities for hope.

---

23    Cf. Erik Swyngedouw and Henrik Ernstson, 'Interrupting the Anthropo-obScene: Immuno-biopolitics and Depoliticizing Ontologies in the Anthropocene', *Theory, Culture & Society* 35, 6 (2018), 3–30.

# 1

# Conservation in the Anthropocene

Much has been written about conservation over the last several decades. What we call the 'great conservation debate' is one with many nuances, contestations, contradictions and complexities. Numerous authors have produced sophisticated overviews of this debate along with some of its elements and its complicated histories. We do not wish to repeat them here. Our objective in this chapter is to investigate and discuss where the debate stands now and how it has changed – or is in the process of changing – with the advent of the Anthropocene and the fundamental debates this concept has unleashed.

We start the chapter with a (very) brief history of the 'great conservation debate' with special emphasis on its roots in the long-standing 'people-and-parks' discussion. This overview aims to develop an updated characterization of what political ecologists Dan Brockington, Rosaleen Duffy and Jim Igoe call 'mainstream conservation'.[1] Building on this characterization, the chapter moves on to discuss the two major radical challenges to mainstream conservation – the new conservation and the neoprotectionist positions – focusing on how they develop their particular solutions for reforming conservation in response to the Anthropocene. In the concluding sections, we provide a first evaluation of the debate, hinging on two main arguments: first, that the debate is currently hampered by the fact that neither alternative provides a coherent and logical frame or set of principles to adequately challenge and move beyond

---

1    Dan Brockington et al., *Nature Unbound*.

mainstream conservation; second, that only on the basis of a logical and coherent foundation can we come to a realistic and practical proposal for conservation in the future.

## A (VERY) BRIEF HISTORY OF THE 'GREAT CONSERVATION DEBATE'

Most overviews of the great conservation debate start with or lead to what is considered the epicentre of the conservation movement historically, namely the creation of protected areas (PAs). The way that PAs were originally understood and enforced was through an approach termed 'fortress' conservation, which in its ideal form sought to enclose a piece of wild terrain and prevent human disturbance therein. It often did so by removing human inhabitants, erecting fences around the newly cleared plots, and imposing fines or other forms of punishment for illegal entry. From this perspective, 'people in parks are a category error'.[2]

From the outset, this fortress model has coexisted with other competing approaches. Conservation in Western Europe, for example, has tended to operate quite differently than the wilderness preservation model prevailing in North America, the former emphasizing sustainable management of cultural and often agricultural landscapes.[3] Emma Marris glosses this distinction: 'while European conservationists focused on sustainable human use and avoiding extinctions, America perfected and exported the "Yellowstone Model," based on setting aside pristine wilderness areas and banning all human use therein, apart from tourism.'[4] Even in North America, moreover, a sustainable use paradigm has long competed with the

---

2   Dan Brockington, *Celebrity and the Environment: Fame, Wealth and Power in Conservation* (London: Zed Books, 2009), 133. Important to note is that this popular storyline is very western-centric, and that many different cultures in different places exhibited various forms of conservation prior to the focus on protected areas; Dan Brockington et al., *Nature Unbound*.

3   Marris, *Rambunctious*. William Sutherland, 'Conservation biology: Openness in management', *Nature* 418, 6900 (2002), 834–35; George Monbiot, 'The faith in the markets is misplaced: Only governments can save our living planet', *Guardian*, 22 April 2013.

4   Marris, *Rambunctious*, 17.

dominant preservationist approach, as symbolized by the famous battles between John Muir and Gifford Pinchot in the early twentieth century. Yet the wilderness preservation ideal has always stood at the centre of US conservation efforts, and even Europeans concerned with sustainable use sought their own wilderness in protected areas established both at home and in the colonies.[5] Thus the North American wilderness area stood as the main model for the global expansion of protected areas in the nineteenth and twentieth centuries.[6]

Beginning in the 1970s, the fortress conservation paradigm came under attack. Alongside broader decolonial and developmental shifts and associated challenges to belief in 'high modernism',[7] different actors, including indigenous peoples affected by conservation policies, start levelling fundamental critiques of the approach. First and foremost, the human costs of protected area creation, involving the expulsion of millions of conservation refugees globally, had become a growing cause for concern and pushback on the part of those expelled, who increasingly demanded compensation for their losses.[8] In addition to the social justice issues involved, this displacement was now seen as a threat to conservation itself due to concerns that angry people deprived of traditional livelihoods living on protected area boundaries posed a threat to conserved resources.[9] The status of most PAs as isolated islands further threatened the future of their resources due to lack of genetic flow across park boundaries.[10] In

5   Brockington et al., *Nature Unbound*; Paul Wapner, *Living Through the End of Nature: The Future of American Environmentalism* (Cambridge, MA: MIT Press, 2010).

6   Jim Igoe, *Conservation and Globalization: A Study of National Parks and Indigenous Communities from East Africa to South Dakota* (Belmont, CA: Wadsworth/Thompson, 2004); William Adams and Jon Hutton, 'People, parks and poverty: Political ecology and biodiversity conservation', *Conservation and Society* 5, 2 (2007), 147–83.

7   See, especially, Arturo Escobar, *Encountering Development: The Making and Unmaking of the Third World* (Princeton, NJ: Princeton University Press, 1995).

8   Mark Dowie, *Conservation Refugees: The Hundred-Year Conflict between Global Conservation and Native Peoples* (Boston: MIT Press, 2009); Igoe, *Conservation*, Brockington et al., *Nature Unbound*.

9   William Adams et al., 'Biodiversity conservation and the eradication of poverty', *Science* 36 (2004), 1146–9.

10   Monique Borgerhoff Mulder and Peter Coppolillo, *Conservation* (Princeton, NJ:

the 1980s and 1990s, moreover, social scientists seriously began to critique conceptual aspects of the fortress paradigm. They questioned, amongst others, the reality of the 'wilderness' it sought to defend and the nature of the 'nature' it contained.[11] Part of this critique entailed documentation of the immense human labour commonly involved in creating and preserving protected areas in a supposed 'pristine,' 'natural' state.[12]

All of this led to the rise of 'community-based conservation' (CBC) which, at the time, was a self-proclaimed 'new' conservation paradigm.[13] This paradigm asserted that development and conservation must be conjoined, and concerns for people's livelihood incorporated into protected area management.[14] Conservation, in this approach, would now be a fundamentally social endeavour. As Catherine Corson and colleagues describe, this perspective transformed PAs from a 'means to protect resources *from* people' to a 'means to protect resources *for* people'.[15] The degree to which this paradigm shift was successful in achieving conservation and development aims has been discussed intensely in literature on this topic, with some social scientists criticizing community-based conservation 'from within', with an

---

Princeton University Press, 2005).

11   William Cronon, 'The trouble with wilderness'. In *Uncommon Ground*, ed. William Cronon (New York: W.W. Norton 1996), 69–90; Bruce Braun and Noel Castree, eds, *Remaking Reality: Nature at the Millennium* (London: Routledge, 1998).

12   Roderick Neumann, *Imposing Wilderness: Struggles over Livelihood and Nature Preservation in Africa* (Berkeley: University of California Press, 1998); Karl Jacoby, *Crimes against Nature: Squatters, Poachers, Thieves and the Hidden History of American Conservation* (Berkeley: University of California Press, 2001); Dorceta Taylor, *The Rise of the American Conservation Movement: Power, Privilege, and Environmental Protection* (Durham: Duke University Press, 2016).

13   David Hulme and Marshall Murphree, eds, *African Wildlife and Livelihoods: The Promise and Performance of Community Conservation* (Oxford: James Currey, 2001); Harvey Locke and Philip Dearden, 'Rethinking protected area categories and the new paradigm', *Environmental Conservation* 32, 1 (2005), 1–10; Bram Büscher and Webster Whande, 'Whims of the Winds of Time? Contestations in Biodiversity Conservation and Protected Areas Management', *Conservation and Society* 5, 1 (2007), 22–43.

14   William Adams et al., 'Biodiversity conservation'.

15   Catherine Corson et al., 'Everyone's solution? Defining and redefining protected areas at the Convention on Biological Diversity', *Conservation and Society* 12, 2 (2014), 190–202.

eye to improving it, and others asserting that the approach was fundamentally flawed and must be abandoned altogether.[16]

At the time it was not only *social* scientists critically investigating this new conservation paradigm. From the outset, it also received strong criticism from more traditionalist conservationists concerned that community-based conservation would fail to adequately conserve the resources it was intended to protect. Their main response was to call for a return to strict fortress-style protection. This neoprotectionist or back-to-the-barriers position asserted, as biologist John Terborgh phrased it most forcefully, that protected areas constitute 'the final bulwark of nature in the Tropics and elsewhere'.[17] This backlash led to what has been labelled a 'people versus parks' debate between this position and defenders of a community-based conservation approach.[18] Subsequently, the neoprotectionist position was itself criticized severely on various grounds, being deemed an attempt to 'reinvent a square wheel' that never worked well in the first place.[19]

This discussion continues in the present and arguably still forms the backbone of the 'great conservation debate'. The many and sometimes complex positions adopted in this debate keep coming back in

16 See Adams and Hutton, 'People, parks and poverty'. Wolfram Dressler et al., 'From hope to crisis and back again? A critical history of the global CBNRM narrative', *Environmental Conservation* 37, 1 (2010), 5–15, for overviews. See Hulme and Murphree, *African Wildlife* for the former approach and Piers Blaikie, 'Is Small Really Beautiful? Community-based Natural Resource Management in Malawi and Botswana', *World Development* 34, 11 (2006), 1942–57 for the latter approach.

17 John Terborgh, *Requiem for Nature* (Washington, DC: Island Press/Shearwater Books, 1999), 20; See also David Ehrenfeld, 'Why put a value on biodiversity?' In: *Biodiversity*, ed. E.O. Wilson (Washington, DC: National Academy Press, 1988), 212–16; Bill Willers, 'Sustainable development: A new world deception', *Conservation Biology* 8, 4 (1994), 1146–48; Randall Kramer, Carel van Schaik and Julie Johnson, eds, *Last Stand: Protected Areas and the Defense of Tropical Biodiversity* (New York: Oxford University Press, 1997); John Oates, *Myth and Reality in the Rain Forest: How Conservation Strategies Are Failing in West Africa* (Berkeley: University of California Press, 1999);

18 Ben Minteer and Thaddeus Miller, 'The New Conservation Debate: Ethical Foundations, Strategic Trade-offs, and Policy Opportunities', *Biological Conservation* 144, 3 (2011), 945–47.

19 Peter Wilshusen et al., 'Reinventing a square wheel: Critique of a resurgent "protection paradigm" in international biodiversity conservation', *Society and Natural Resources* 15 (2002), 17–40.

various guises, modified and moulded by the study of rapidly changing empirical circumstances in many parts of the world.[20] At the same
time, it seems that this backbone has lost much of its earlier appeal,
especially in academic circles though perhaps less so in the policy
world. With a fundamental social science critique of CBC and the
end of much of its popular funding appeal in practice, the people
versus parks 'backbone' certainly can no longer represent an overall
conceptualization of mainstream conservation.[21] It is and will remain
a central element to this conceptualization, but one that has been
overtaken by other discussions and dynamics.

### MAINSTREAM CONSERVATION: AN UPDATE

With mainstream conservation, Brockington, Duffy and Igoe refer to
'a particular historical and institutional strain of western conservation', practised and promoted especially by large, powerful international conservation organizations and agencies.[22] They emphasize that
this strain has, almost from the start, centred on both the parks and
people debate *and* conservation's 'collaborative legacy' with prominent business interests.[23] From the time Brockington and colleagues
published their book until now, more than a decade later, the latter

---

20    Such as the effects of the South African rhino-poaching crisis on local communities around the Kruger National Park, which has dramatically altered the relations
between park and people yet again. See Elizabeth Lunstrum, 'Green Militarization: Anti-
Poaching Efforts and the Spatial Contours of Kruger National Park', *Annals of the American
Association of Geographers* 104, 4 (2014), 816–32; Rosaleen Duffy, 'Waging a war to save
biodiversity: The rise of militarized conservation', *International Affairs*, 90 (2014), 819–34;
Bram Büscher and Maano Ramutsindela, 'Green Violence: Rhino Poaching and the War to
Save Southern Africa's Peace Parks', *African Affairs* 115, 458 (2016), 1–22.

21    Blaikie, *Is Small*; Bram Büscher, 'Seeking Telos in the "Transfrontier":
Neoliberalism and the Transcending of Community Conservation in Southern Africa',
*Environment and Planning A* 42, 3 (2010), 644–60.

22    Brockington et al., *Nature Unbound*, 9.

23    Brockington et al., *Nature Unbound*; Also Mark Barringer, *Selling Yellowstone:
Capitalism and the Construction of Nature* (Lawrence: University Press of Kansas, 2002);
Kenneth MacDonald, 'Business, Biodiversity and New "Fields" of Conservation: The World
Conservation Congress and the Renegotiation of Organisational Order', *Conservation and
Society* 8, 4 (2010), 256–75.

dimension has further intensified and expanded. These are the 'other dynamics' that need to be emphasized: the ways that conservation has further embraced the practices, imaginaries and discourses of contemporary capitalism.[24] An update of contemporary mainstream conservation thus needs to account for this intensified integration.

While Western conservation has always been closely conjoined with capitalist development[25], the 'mainstreaming' of the relationship between capitalism and conservation arguably started in earnest in the early 1990s. Triggered by broader sustainable development discourses, the drive to merge conservation and development concerns was signified by revamping older and promoting new 'market-based instruments' (MBIs).[26] Examples of these include tourism and forms of ecotourism (which had accompanied protected area development from the start and includes wildlife hunting), bioprospecting, payments for environmental services (PES), and other mechanisms intended to combine forms of (neoliberal) economic development with environmental conservation. The aim of these interventions was to harness the economic value of in situ resources in order to incentivize their preservation. Kathleen McAfee presciently called this strategy 'selling nature to save it'.[27]

Drawing on a parallel trend of increasing privatization and marketization in conventional primary commodity markets discussed as 'neoliberal natures', this trend in conservation became

---

24    Bram Büscher and Robert Fletcher, 'Accumulation by Conservation', *New Political Economy* 20, 2 (2015), 273–98; Jessica Dempsey, *Enterprising Nature: Economics, Markets, and Finance in Global Biodiversity Politics* (London: Wiley, 2016).

25    In this book, we regularly speak of 'capitalist development', while also referring to capitalism and development separately. These two (capitalism and development), however, should not be conflated, as they are not the same thing.

26    The historical dynamics on which these policy ideas are based go far back, including how, from the time of the industrial revolution, 'nature's elements, along with the social conditions of human existence, have increasingly been brought within the sphere of the economy and subjected to the same measure, that of profitability' John Bellamy Foster, *The Vulnerable Planet: A Short Economic History of the Environment* (New York: Monthly Review Press, 1999), 35.

27    Kathleen McAfee, 'Selling nature to save it? Biodiversity and green developmentalism', *Society and Space* 17, 2 (1999), 133–54.

analysed as 'neoliberal conservation'.[28] Here the analysis shifts 'the focus from how nature is used in and through the expansion of capitalism, to how nature is conserved in and through the expansion of capitalism'.[29] Conservation, in other words, has moved beyond a Polanyian double-movement to accompany the march of capitalist progress by trying to selectively reign in or counterbalance its concomitant destruction of nature and biodiversity. It is becoming a potential – yet vital – force in fostering capitalist growth in its own right.

The neoliberal approach was rapidly and enthusiastically adopted by many of the most influential players in the global conservation movement. This includes the big non-governmental organizations (BINGOs) such as Conservation International (CI), The Nature Conservancy (TNC), World Wildlife Fund (WWF), Wildlife Conservation Society (WCS), and the International Union for Conservation of Nature (IUCN), but also intergovernmental financial institutions like The World Bank, IMF and the United Nations Environment Programme (UNEP) as well as prominent business 'partners', many of which coordinated within the World Business Council for Sustainable Development (WBCSD). These various actors are, in turn, conjoined within an increasingly dense and self-referential network, of which IUCN is a key component.[30]

---

28   Nik Heynen et al., *Neoliberal Environments: False Promises and Unnatural Consequences* (London: Routledge, 2007); Sian Sullivan, 'The Elephant in the Room? Problematising "New" (Neoliberal) Biodiversity Conservation', *Forum for Development Studies* 12, 1 (2006), 105–35; Jim Igoe and Daniel Brockington, 'Neoliberal Conservation: A Brief Introduction', *Conservation and Society* 5, 4 (2007), 432–49; Bram Büscher et al., 'Towards a Synthesized Critique of Neoliberal Biodiversity Conservation', *Capitalism Nature Socialism* 23, 2 (2012), 4–30; Bram Büscher, Wolfram Dressler and Robert Fletcher, eds, *Nature^TM Inc.: Environmental Conservation in the Neoliberal Age* (Tucson: University of Arizona Press, 2014).

29   Büscher et al., 'Towards a Synthesized Critique', 4.

30   MacDonald, 'Business Biodiversity'; Kenneth MacDonald and Catherine Corson, '"TEEB Begins Now": A Virtual Moment in the Production of Natural Capital', *Development and Change* 43, 1 (2012), 159–84; Catherine Corson, Kenneth MacDonald and Benjamin Neimark, special issue on 'Grabbing Green', *Human Geography* 6, 1 (2013); Peter Wilshusen and Kenneth MacDonald, 'Fields of green: Corporate sustainability and the production of economistic environmental governance', *Environment and Planning A* 49, 8 (2017), 1824–45.

The partner companies that the big non-governmental organizations currently collaborate with, depend upon and even share staff with is highly illustrative in this respect: they are the largest and many of the most environmentally destructive capitalist corporations in the world. It is for this reason that we highlight the centrality of neoliberalism to contemporary mainstream conservation in general.

Importantly, the link between conservation and capitalism becomes 'mainstream' in two ways. On the one hand, we see that the 'particular historical and institutional strain of western conservation' that Brockington and colleagues describe has become more intensely and overtly capitalist in its goals, expressions, imaginations and ways of operating. To provide but one illustrative example, in explaining his involvement in the United Nations Environment Programme's TEEB (The Economics of Ecosystems and Biodiversity) initiative intended to monetarily value and create markets for trade in 'ecosystem services', Pavan Sukhdev, a former executive of Deutsche Bank, relates: 'As an investment banker with another life built over fifteen years around my passion for the economics of nature . . . I am often asked how I reconcile my capitalist background with my commitments to nature and the environment . . . I give my stock reply "I don't reconcile them – I am a total capitalist".'[31]

On the other hand, we witness how conservation has become more central to global mainstream capitalist dynamics. Hence mainstream capitalism is quickly coming to grips with the importance of conservation to capitalist processes, even if this is mostly still discursive at present.[32] An important example in this regard is the 'Natural Capital Coalition', which brings together over 200 governmental, business and conservation organizations and whose central point of departure is that the future of capitalist business needs to

---

31    Pavan Sukhdev, 'Three-dimensional capitalism', *The Guardian*, theguardian.com, accessed 28 August 2018.

32    Büscher and Fletcher, 'Accumulation by Conservation'; Jessica Dempsey and Daniel Suarez, 'Arrested development? The promises and paradoxes of "selling nature to save it"', *Annals of the American Association of Geographers* 106, 3 (2016), 653–71.

take conservation of 'natural capital' into account.[33] The crucial point is that from both the side of conservation and from the side of capitalist industry, the link between the two has become more intense, accepted and mainstream.[34] This fundamental development – together with the point to be developed further in chapters two and three that capitalism is inherently environmentally unsustainable – is the reason why we argue that a critique of capitalism must be at the heart of any meaningful prospects for the future of conservation.

Claiming that capitalism and conservation are increasingly intertwined and mainstream is not to imply a straightforward, one-dimensional or clear process and result, nor that this is merely a recent phenomenon. To the contrary: this intertwining and main-streaming is highly uneven, complex, multidimensional, political, and deeply historical – just like capitalist uneven geographical development more generally.[35] Our thinking on this, therefore, stays far from any determinism. It instead embraces uncertainty, complexity and change as fundamental dynamics of contemporary capitalist political economy and its uneven geographical development. At the same time, we can discern broad yet specific historical trends and forms running through these uneven and complex developments.

In an earlier article building on world system perspectives, we argued that the global conservation movement can be seen to have moved through three broad, overlapping stages.[36] These stages represent different ways in which conservation functions as a component of the capitalist world economy facilitating the internalization of environmental conditions in order to safeguard or expand capital accumulation. They therefore also logically parallel historical shifts in the dominant regime of capitalist accumulation within the global

---

33    'Coalition Organizations', Natural Capital Coalition, naturalcapitalcoalition.org, accessed 28 August 2018.

34    This is not to say that there is no resistance against or discomfort with this trend, as there certainly is. We will come back to this in later chapters.

35    This will be the theoretical background to the development of a set of principles in chapter four.

36    Büscher and Fletcher, 'Accumulation by Conservation'.

economy as a whole. Analysts have suggested that these regimes have transitioned, firstly, from 'organized' or 'Fordist' to 'disorganized' or 'post-Fordist', 'flexible' forms.[37] Secondly, in the present period, scholars describe a further shift away from commodity production of any sort towards an emphasis on financialization – what David Harvey calls 'fictitious capitalism'.[38]

Building on this, we have suggested that the global conservation movement has broadly moved through three related stages that we call fortress, flexible, and fictitious conservation, corresponding with the historical movement from protected area creation through community-based conservation with its preferred integrated conservation and development projects (ICDPs) and attendant income-generation mechanisms to the increasing focus on financialization through neoliberal market engagement (table 2).

## Table 2. Accumulation by Conservation

| Period | Regime of Accumulation | Key Characteristics | Dominant Ideology | Conservation Approach | Key Mechanisms |
|---|---|---|---|---|---|
| 1860s-1960s | Colonial / Fordist / Organized Capitalism | Vertical integration; Statism; violence | Liberalism / Keynesianism | Fortress Conservation | Protected Areas; State funding; wildlife tourism |
| 1970-2000 | Post-Fordism / Disorganized Capitalism | Flexible accumulation; decentralization | Roll-back Neoliberalism | Flexible Conservation | CBC; ICDPs; Biosphere reserves; Ecotourism; Bioprospecting |
| 1990s | | | Roll-out Neoliberalism | | TFCAs; PES |
| 2000-Present | Financialization / Casino Capitalism | Spectacular accumulation, networks, crisis | | Fictitious Conservation | Carbon markets; species/wet-lands banking; financial derivatives; REDD |

Source: Büscher and Fletcher, *Accumulation*, 284.

---

37    Scott Lash and John Urry, *The End of Organized Capital* (Madison: University of Wisconsin Press, 1987); David Harvey, *The Condition of Postmodernity: An Inquiry into the Origins of Cultural Change.* (Oxford: Basil Blackwell, 1989); Giovanni Arrighi, *The Long Twentieth Century: Money, Power and the Origins of our Times* (London: Verso, 2009).

38    Harvey, *The Condition*.

When we therefore claim that mainstream conservation needs to be updated by emphasizing how it is now more intensely capitalist, this is in no way to imply a linear, ahistorical or all-encompassing trend. Rather, it is to suggest precisely that we are witnessing an *intensification* of longer-standing, uneven dynamics. All this makes 'mainstream conservation' an extremely complex and diverse proposition, rendering the generalizations necessary to make sense of things inevitably unfair and tenuous with respect to many actors, situations and positions.[39] Yet, in all this diversity and complexity, two key elements remain fundamental to mainstream conservation: that conservation is and has long been a capitalist undertaking (and hence not a bulwark against capitalism, as it has sometimes been portrayed), and that it is fundamentally steeped in human–nature dichotomies that have indeed haunted capitalism itself for centuries.

To this we must add that mainstream conservation is mainstream not only because the ideas expressed are dominant and globally hegemonic, but also because they are endorsed and advanced by globally dominant actors including those previously mentioned.[40] It is therefore crucial to note that radical challenges to mainstream conservation also mean radical challenges to these actors and hence to many entrenched power structures. Because of its import, this point will inform our ensuing discussions of the challenges to mainstream conservation presented by the Anthropocene.

### ANTHROPOCENE CHALLENGES TO MAINSTREAM CONSERVATION

In 2012, Peter Kareiva, then Chief Scientist at The Nature Conservancy, Michelle Marvier and Robert Lalasz published what quickly became a famously controversial article entitled 'Conservation in the Anthropocene'. They argued that mainstream conservation was failing to stop biodiversity loss and that even a growing global protected

---

39   As it has always been, as also stressed by Brockington et al., *Nature Unbound*, 9–10.
40   Again, the Natural Capital Coalition is an apt illustration here; see link in footnote 33 above.

area estate would not change this. For too long, they insisted, conservation had been working against people rather than through and with people, especially the poor in the Global South. The authors believed it was time, therefore, for conservationists to drop unrealistic myths of 'wilderness' and 'pristine nature', which the Anthropocene in any case renders obsolete. Instead, conservation should 'demonstrate how the fates of nature and of people are deeply intertwined – and then offer new strategies for promoting the health and prosperity of both'.[41] They also offered concrete suggestions on how to achieve this, worth quoting in full:

> Conservation should seek to support and inform the right kind of development – development by design, done with the importance of nature to thriving economies foremost in mind. And it will utilize the right kinds of technology to enhance the health and well-being of both human and nonhuman natures. Instead of scolding capitalism, conservationists should partner with corporations in a science-based effort to integrate the value of nature's benefits into their operations and cultures. Instead of pursuing the protection of biodiversity for biodiversity's sake, a new conservation should seek to enhance those natural systems that benefit the widest number of people, especially the poor. Instead of trying to restore remote iconic landscapes to pre-European conditions, conservation will measure its achievement in large part by its relevance to people, including city dwellers. Nature could be a garden – not a carefully manicured and rigid one, but a tangle of species and wildness amidst lands used for food production, mineral extraction, and urban life.[42]

This new conservation recycling of the idea of nature as a garden was also the central message of a book, entitled *Rambunctious Garden*, that came out the year before Kareiva and colleague's piece. In this book, science journalist Emma Marris asserted in similar terms as

41   Kareiva et al., 'Conservation'.
42   Kareiva et al., 'Conservation'.

Kareiva et al., 'if we fight to preserve only things that look like pristine wilderness, such as those places currently enclosed in national parks and similar refuges, our best efforts can only retard their destruction and delay the day we lose. If we fight to preserve and enhance nature as we have newly defined it, as the living background to human lives, we may be able to win.'[43]

Marris thus pleads passionately for the 'joyful' and experimental designing of a global rambunctious garden that contains 'nature that looks a little more lived-in than we are used to and working spaces that look a little more wild than we are used to'.[44]

An embrace of the Anthropocene is foundational to this perspective. In this bold new epoch, Kareiva et al. contend, 'it is impossible to find a place on Earth that is unmarked by human activity' and hence 'conservation's continuing focus upon preserving islands of Holocene ecosystems in the age of the Anthropocene is both anachronistic and counterproductive'.[45] While rarely mentioning the Anthropocene specifically, Marris speaks similarly:

Today, our increasing awareness of the long history, massive scope, and frequent irreversibility of human impacts on the rest of nature make the leave-it-alone ethic even more problematic than it was in 1995. Climate change, land-use change, global species movements, pollution: these global forces affect every place, even those protected as parks or wildernesses, and dealing with them requires increasingly intensive intervention.[46]

There are many other interesting elements in these and related interventions, such as by journalist Fred Pearce among quite a few others,

---

43   Marris, *Rambunctious*, 151.

44   Marris, *Rambunctious*, 171, 151. See also Michelle Marvier, 'New Conservation is True Conservation', *Conservation Biology* 28, 1 (2014), 1–3.

45   Kareiva et al., 'Conservation'.

46   Emma Marris, 'Handle With Care', *Orion Magazine*, orionmagazine.org, accessed 28 August 2018.

including many associated with The Breakthrough Institute.[47] Common in all of these interventions is a conceptualization of nature that aims to move beyond dichotomies, boundaries and limits. In Kareiva et al.'s words:

> We need to acknowledge that a conservation that is only about fences, limits, and faraway places only a few can actually experience is a losing proposition. Protecting biodiversity for its own sake has not worked. Protecting nature that is dynamic and resilient, that is in our midst rather than far away, and that sustains human communities – these are the ways forward now. Otherwise, conservation will fail, clinging to its old myths.

Marris, similarly, believes we must shed old-fashioned ideas about boundaries and 'baselines'. 'Rambunctious gardening', she writes, 'creates more and more nature as it goes, rather than just building walls around the nature we have left.'[48] Finally, with specific reference to the heated discussion on alien and invasive species, Pearce argues that:

> Conservationists need to take a hard look at themselves and their priorities. . . . Nature no longer congregates only where we expect to find it, in the countryside or in 'pristine' habitats. It is increasingly eschewing formally protected areas and heading for the badlands. Nature doesn't care about conservationists' artificial divide between urban and rural or between native and alien. If conservationists are going to make the most of the opportunities in the twenty-first century to help nature's recovery, they must put aside their old certainties and ditch their obsessions with lost causes, discredited theories, and mythical pristine ecosystems.[49]

---

47  The Breakthrough Institute is a think tank founded by Michael Shellenberger and Ted Nordhaus, authors of the controversial report *The Death of Environmentalism* (Michael Shellenberger and Ted Nordhaus, *The Death of Environmentalism: Global Warming Politics in a Post-Environmental World*, thebreakthrough.org). Their website first published Kareiva's et al.'s essay and subsequently awarded Marris its Breakthrough Paradigm Award.

48  Marris, *Rambunctious*, 3.

49  Pearce, *The New Wild*, 176.

What is striking about this perspective is how it has taken up aspects of social science critiques of the nature concept and redeployed these in particular ways to support its own positions – something we will analyse in more detail in the next chapter. All of this is couched in assertions that the realities of the Anthropocene reinforce these critiques and so necessitate a wholesale rethinking of the global conservation movement and the means and meaning of environmentalism in a 'post-wild' or 'post-nature' world. What is more, new conservationists have very explicitly taken up social scientists' critiques regarding the development impacts and possibilities of conservation. There are two sides to this issue. The first is that conservation must not hurt people – especially poor people living near or displaced by protected areas – and it should ideally benefit them. The second is that conservation will likely fail if it does not simultaneously address the social causes of biodiversity loss.

So, 'in order to save the orangutan', Kareiva and colleagues assert, 'conservationists will also have to address the problem of food and income deprivation in Indonesia. That means conservationists will have to embrace human development and the "exploitation" of nature for human uses, like agriculture, even while they seek to "protect" nature inside of parks'.[50] Development, however, is understood in a particular way, as *capitalist* development, a position that remains close to mainstream conservation and its infatuation with market-based solutions to conservation challenges. In calling for attention to the human side of conservation, many critical social scientists have also pointed to the problems of doing so through the market-based instruments increasingly advocated in the growing neoliberalization trend within the mainstream conservation movement.[51] In this, crit-

---

50   Kareiva et al., 'Conservation'.

51   James McCarthy, 'Devolution in the woods: Community forestry as hybrid neoliberalism', *Environment and Planning A* 37 (2005), 995–1014; Dressler et al., 'From hope'. See also George Holmes, Chris Sandbrook and Janet Fisher, 'Understanding conservationists' perspectives on the new-conservation debate', *Conservation Biology* 31, 2 (2017), 353–63, who identify a 'critical social science' position among conservationists in relation to the new conservation debate.

ics – ourselves included – have pointed to the paradox in this advocacy that capitalist mechanisms are promoted to address problems that are in large part caused by capitalist development itself.[52]

Yet this neoliberal approach is precisely what Kareiva and colleagues advocate in their call to integrate conservation and development.[53] Marris, to be sure, is more reticent, remaining relatively agnostic concerning questions of economics. About the ecosystem services perspective for instance, she writes that 'arguments come from the "what have you done for me lately" school of ecology'.[54] She does not, however, take a clear position on the question of economic valuation of ecosystems or other forms of development herself. As the essays collected by Ben Minteer and Stephen Pyne in *After Preservation: Saving American Nature in the Age of Humans* illustrate, this type of new conservation has become a broad church that includes many different positions.[55]

Generally, however, Minteer and Pyne assert that a 'traditional focus on the wilderness' and a 'knee-jerk hostility to corporate America and distaste for the market' are considered 'outdated preservationist beliefs' to be 'roundly rejected by the new Anthroprocene-ic environmentalists'.[56] For our purposes, we therefore distil the main contribution and challenge by new conservationists down to the argument that embracing capitalism-for-conservation does not require yielding to the human–nature dichotomies that capitalism normally thrives on. This, as it turned out, is a radical position, with respect to both mainstream conservation and another set of radical proposals

---

52  Bram Büscher, 'Payments for Ecosystem Services as Neoliberal Conservation: (reinterpreting) Evidence from the Maloti-Drakensberg, South Africa', *Conservation and Society* 10, 1 (2012), 29–41; Robert Fletcher, 'Using the Master's Tools? Neoliberal Conservation and the Evasion of Inequality', *Development and Change* 43, 1 (2012), 295–317.

53  Kareiva, along with his co-author Lalasz, were both working for The Nature Conservancy at the time of writing, one of the big non-governmental organizations most commonly identified as central to the neoliberal conservation approach.

54  Marris, *Rambunctious*, 163.

55  Ben Minteer and Stephen Pyne, eds, *After Preservation: Saving American Nature in the Age of Humans* (Chicago: Chicago University Press, 2015).

56  Ben Minteer and Stephen Pyne, 'Writing on Stone, Writing in the Wind'. In Minteer and Pyne, *After Preservation*, 5.

we will discuss next. Whether this central claim of new conservationists is a tenable position is a question we will come back to later.

THE NEW BACK-TO-THE-BARRIERS

Many were not charmed by the new conservation proposals. In fact, it quickly drew incensed reactions from several of the same prominent conservation biologists central to the original neoprotectionist position. Miller et al. retorted that 'the assumption that managing nature for human benefit will preserve ecological integrity' is an 'ideology' that 'rests more on delusion and faith than on evidence'.[57] Michael Soulé, in an editorial in *Conservation Biology*, concluded bluntly 'that the new conservation, if implemented, would hasten ecological collapse globally, eradicating thousands of kinds of plants and animals and causing inestimable harm to humankind in the long run'.[58] Celebrity biologist E. O. Wilson even criticizes 'Anthropocene conservationists' for holding 'the most dangerous worldview' and for being 'unconcerned with what the consequences will be if their beliefs are played out'.[59] Finally, Harvey Locke proclaims:

> the death of the wild in favor of the garden with *Homo Sapiens* triumphant is no vision for those who proclaim to love nature. It will also inevitably be disastrous for the human species. We do not know how to run the world. It is time for our species to become humble and wise and to stop being greedy and clever.[60]

As also becomes clear from this quote, in contrast to the new conservationists, many neoprotectionists subject to critique the very idea of the Anthropocene altogether. In this, they deride the concept as a

---

57    Brian Miller, Michael Soulé and John Terborgh, '"New conservation" or surrender to development?', *Animal Conservation* 17, 6 (2014), 512.

58    Michael Soulé, 'The new conservation', *Conservation Biology* 27, 5 (2013), 896.

59    Edward Wilson, *Half-Earth*, 74–5.

60    Harvey Locke, 'Nature Needs (at least) Half: A Necessary New Agenda for Protected Areas', *Protecting the Wild*, George Wuerthner et al., 15.

fiction of human hubris that vastly overestimates the extent to which humans actually control nonhuman processes. The following statement is typical:

> The Anthropocene notion ... seriously exaggerates human influence on nature but also ... draws inappropriate metaphysical, moral, and environmental policy conclusions about humanity's role on the planet. Despite our dramatic impact on Earth, significant naturalness remains, and the ever-increasing human influence makes valuing the natural more, not less, important in environmental thought and policy.[61]

Others accept the reality of the concept yet argue that the political lessons Anthropocenists draw from it are misguided:

> I do agree ... that Earth has entered a human-dominated era ... Where I begin to part company with cheerleaders like Kareiva, Marvier, and Marris is in their embrace of the Anthropocene ... Too often, proponents of the Anthropocene seem more interested in normalizing these losses than in stopping them.[62]

'Rather than embrace the Anthropocene era,' Cafaro continues, 'conservationists should act to rein in its excesses'.[63] Mackey similarly contends that 'it is foolish and dangerous to confuse force with control. The Anthropocene, while an empirical fact, does not mean that humans "run the show." Rather, it means only that we can be powerfully disruptive.'[64] Wuerthner adds that 'there's a critical differ-

---

61 Ned Hettinger, 'Valuing Naturalness in the "Anthropocene": Now More than Ever'. In *Keeping the Wild: Against the Domestication of the Earth*, George Wuerthner, Eileen Crist and Tom Butler, eds (New York: Island Press, 2014), 174.

62 Philip Cafaro, 'Expanding Parks, Reducing Human Numbers, and Preserving All the Wild Nature We Can: A Superior Alternative to Embracing the Anthropocene Era'. In *Keeping the Wild*, George Wuerthner et al., 139–40.

63 Cafaro, 'Expanding Parks'. In *Keeping the Wild*, George Wuerthner et al., 139.

64 Brendan Mackey, 'The Future of Conservation: An Australian Perspective'. In *Keeping the Wild*, George Wuerthner et al., 129.

ence between documenting and acknowledging human impact and accepting it as inevitable and even desirable.'[65] Cafaro thus concludes: 'It is just not true that our only path is ever further into the Anthropocene. We can instead work to ratchet back the current, excessive human footprint on Earth and make a place (hopefully, many places) for other species to also flourish on our common home planet.'[66]

As a result of this critique of the Anthropocene concept and its embrace by new conservationists, neoprotectionists offer quite different solutions for the global environmental crisis. Most centrally, they make a plea for better understanding and accepting limits and boundaries: to human population growth, to places where 'humanity' should be allowed to develop, and – intriguingly – to consumption and economic growth as well. This latter limit has more recently been added onto the former set of limits that characterized these authors' earlier defence of protected areas against integrated conservation and development projects.[67] This earlier neoprotectionist literature became known as advocating a 'back-to-the-barriers' position and we therefore label this revised version critical of new conservation as the 'new back-to-the-barriers' or, simply, neoprotectionism.

In the face of calls to embrace diverse forms of human-focused conservation, the new back-to-the-barriers proponents assert that 'only within parks and protected areas will many large animals critical to ecological processes persist'. For these neoprotectionists, today, as in their preceding proposals, 'the center of traditional conservation' is still 'the preservation of biodiversity for ecosystem function and evolutionary potential . . . Doing this requires networks of protected

---

65   George Wuerthner, 'Why the Working Landscape Isn't Working'. In *Keeping the Wild*, George Wuerthner et al., 168.

66   Cafaro, 'Expanding Parks', In *Keeping the Wild*, George Wuerthner et al., 142.

67   Wilshusen et al., 'Reinventing a square wheel'; Jon Hutton, William Adams and James Murombedzi, 'Back to the Barriers? Changing Narratives in Biodiversity Conservation', *Forum for Development Studies* 2 (2005), 341–70.

lands; connectivity is a critical tenet'.[68] The logical consequence is that neoprotectionists demand another resurgence and expansion of fortress-style protection, arguing that we must:

> Protect and reconnect habitat, exclude poachers, and combat invasion by nonnative species. This is exactly what national parks and other protected areas are intended to do. There is no alternative. Parks and other strictly protected areas are the answer.

The conclusion therefore remains straightforward: 'the global strategy must be to expand the number and size of protected areas, interconnect them, and rewild them.'[69]

Neoprotectionists are nothing but steadfast on this point. However, in this most recent campaign, they have upped the stakes dramatically. Many in their camp no longer believe that 'the number and size of protected areas' need simply be 'expanded'; they now self-confidently – almost belligerently – assert that the protected area estate must be increased so dramatically as to encompass half the entire planet or more. Locke, for example, argues that 'it is time for conservationists to reset the debate based on scientific findings and assert nature's needs fearlessly.' So far, he contends, it has been politics that has set conservation goals. This has resulted in 'arbitrary percentages that rest on an unarticulated hope that such nonscientific goals are a good first step toward some undefined, better, future outcome'. Conservationists, Locke asserts, must now move beyond a 'destructive form of self-censorship' and promote targets based on 'scientific assessment, review, and expert opinion'.[70]

Conservation biologist Reed Noss and colleagues, writing in an editorial in *Conservation Biology* state that, 'In contrast to policy-driven targets, scientific studies and reviews suggest that some

---

68    Miller et al., '"New conservation"', 4.
69    John Terborgh, Foreword, *Protecting the Wild*, George Wuerthner et al., xiv, xvii.
70    Locke, 'Nature Needs', 3, 9.

25–75% of a typical region must be managed with conservation of nature as a primary objective to meet goals for conserving biodiversity'. Based on this, the authors recommend that:

> When establishing global targets . . . it would be prudent to consider the range of evidence-based estimates of 'how much is enough' from many regions and set a target on the high side of the median as a buffer against uncertainty. From this precautionary perspective, 50 per cent – slightly above the mid-point of recent evidence-based estimates – is scientifically defensible as a global target.[71]

More explicit is Wilson, the revered biologist, in his book *Half Earth*. Stating bluntly that 'humanity' is 'the problem', he believes that 'only by setting aside half the planet in reserve, or more, can we save the living part of the environment and achieve the stabilization required for our own survival'.[72] Clearly, Wilson and other neoprotectionists are very worried about the fate of the planet, which they believe is doomed if we do not do something drastic as soon as possible. Setting aside at least half the earth for 'self-willed' nature, they argue, is the only solution commensurate with the scale of the problem. This radical, if not extreme, proposal has also been taken up by big non-governmental organizations such as Conservation International and many wilderness organizations united in the 'Nature Needs Half' campaign.[73] Clearly, the human–nature dichotomy seems to become extremely rigid in this proposal, as aptly illustrated by the Nature Needs Half logo in figure 1.

---

71 Reed Noss et al., 'Bolder Thinking for Conservation', *Conservation Biology* 26, 1 (2012), 1–2. See the excellent response to this piece by Wilhere and colleagues that argues that Noss et al. 'conflate science with values': Wilhere et al., 'Conflation of Values and Science: Response to Noss et al', *Conservation Biology* 26, 5 (2012), 943–4.

72 Wilson, *Half-Earth*, 3.

73 Eric Dinerstein et al., 'An Ecoregion-Based Approach to Protecting Half the Terrestrial Realm', *BioScience* 67, 6 (2017), 534–45. It must be noted here that there seems to be a difference between Wilson's 'half earth' proposal and the broader 'nature needs half' campaign. The latter includes a diversity of protected area categories whereas it is unclear whether this is also the case in Wilson's plan. At the same time, the nature needs half campaign continues to enthusiastically endorse and champion Wilson and his book.

Figure 1. Nature Needs Half logo.

Source: natureneedshalf.org.

While this radical new back-to-the-barriers position is increasingly supported by many neoprotectionists, this does not mean that they all think alike. Above and beyond the general acceptance of the importance of a dramatic increase in protected areas, there are many issues on which neoprotectionists diverge, sometimes sharply. But there is one other, somewhat surprising issue where it seems that more and more neoprotectionists are starting to converge, namely the issue of how to relate to the global political economy. Without necessarily referring to capitalism as such, many clearly feel uneasy about things like consumption and economic growth.[74] Daniel Doak and colleagues, for example, criticize new conservation's embrace of the green economy, simplistic ideas about partnering with business, and the notion that people are focused most on economic self-interest rather than intrinsic and moral goals.[75] McCauley is even more explicit. He asserts that 'market-based mechanisms for conservation are not, unfortunately, the panacea that they have been made out to be' and proposes that 'we must redirect much of the effort now being devoted to the commodification of nature back toward instilling in more people a love for nature.'[76]

---

74    Although Paul Kingsnorth, for example, does explicitly link new conservationists with earlier 'Friedmanite neoliberals'. Paul Kingsnorth, 'Rise of the Neo-greens'. In *Keeping the Wild*, George Wuerthner et al., 3–9.

75    Daniel Doak et al., 'What is the Future of Conservation?' In *Protecting the Wild*, George Wuerthner et al., 32–3.

76    D.J. McCauley, 'Fool's Gold in the Catskill Mountains: Thinking Critically about

More such examples abound, but dissenting voices are also present. Most prominently, Wilson has an almost evangelical faith in the power of the 'free market'. Despite being critical of rising per-capita consumption patterns, Wilson assuages these concerns by promoting a worryingly simplistic vision of 'intensified economic evolution'. According to him, the 'evolution of the free market, and the way it is increasingly shaped by high technology', means that 'products that win competition today . . . are those that cost less to manufacture and advertise, need less frequent repair and replacement, and give highest performance with a minimum amount of energy'. He further contends that 'almost all of the competition in a free market, other than in military technology, raises the average quality of life'.[77]

We will come back to these simplistic and demonstrably false claims in chapters to follow, as they help to build the case for our own alternative proposal. For now, it is interesting to note that through this move, Wilson paradoxically ends up endorsing a similar proposal to some of the very Anthropocene conservationists he, in other respects, so opposes. Surprisingly, he even ends up advocating a vision of 'decoupling economic activity from material and environmental throughputs' in order to create sustainable livelihoods for a population herded into urban areas to free space for self-willed nature.[78] This vision, while grounded in a quite different overarching conceptual perspective, is in many ways quite similar to that which the ecomodernist Breakthrough Institute has recently promoted in its own proposal for land sparing and decoupling to increase terrain for conservation.[79]

Yet Wilson seems quite iconoclastic in this respect. Many other neoprotectionists are increasingly veering towards a more critical stance on the embrace of capitalism-for-conservation and would want

---

the Ecosystem Services Paradigm'. In *Protecting the Wild*, George Wuerthner et al., 36.

77   Wilson, *Half-Earth*, 191. Again, this completely opposite view from many 'Nature needs Half' proponents does not mean that the latter stop to cite him approvingly.

78   Wilson, *Half-Earth*, 194.

79   Linus Blomqvist, Ted Nordhaus and Michael Shellenberger, *Nature Unbound: Decoupling for Conservation*, thebreakthrough.org (2015).

to reign this in, just like they want to reign in population growth, land-use change, and much else that has so far been quite central to the development of global capitalism. This is, clearly, a radical proposal in a context where global capitalism is still hegemonic – something acknowledged by several neoprotectionists. Yet whether it is tenable to be increasingly critical of capitalism while holding one of capitalism's greatest vices – the human–nature dichotomy – central to one's plan for the future is something that needs to be critically evaluated.

### A FIRST ATTEMPT AT EVALUATING THE ANTHROPOCENE CONSERVATION DEBATE

Given all of this, how should we understand the current status of the great conservation debate, especially the latest, radical responses to the erstwhile dominance of mainstream conservation?[80] There are several ways in which we could proceed, but in this chapter's penultimate section we want to do two things: first, to discuss how different actors in the discussion and the conservation community more broadly have themselves evaluated the debate and how they view the main issues; second, to provide a brief evaluation of the conceptual logic and coherence of the main positions and issues under debate. The point of the latter aim is to provide the basis upon which in the next chapters we will, in more depth, assess whether these positions are tenable or not, theoretically as well as politically, and whether they could lead to just, effective and, equally importantly, realistic conservation proposals for the future.

First, how did different actors in these debates, and within the broader conservation community, understand and evaluate the latest iterations of the great conservation debate? Unsurprisingly, the two main protagonist camps discussed above responded in ways that befit their general outlook on conservation. Neoprotectionists see their

---

80    To be clear, there is a longer history of radical responses to and critiques of mainstream or dominant forms of conservation; the ones we are discussing here do not emerge from a historical vacuum.

position just as they view nature and wilderness itself: as under siege from multiple fronts. Johns relates:

> In the mid-1990s conservationists responded to a wave of ideological attacks directed at wilderness and biodiversity. In the last few years concerted attacks have again emerged, and, although they are shopworn, riddled with factual errors, and marbled with hierarchical values, they also appear well-funded, receive lots of media attention, and are advanced with great energy, as if careers depended on them.[81]

Harvey Locke even implies a stealthy betrayal of trust:

> In the last twenty years a more subtle and perhaps equally dangerous group has snuck up on conservationists. They come in stealth, professing to be allies with a fresh approach. They come armed with altruism – concern for the poor and disenfranchised humans around the world. Sharing this moral value, we conservationists listen to them, strive to accommodate their concerns, and then learn to our dismay that they don't share our basic goal of conserving wild nature.[82]

Perhaps this helps to explain the impassioned force of neoprotectionists' critique of the new conservation perspective. Such strong reactions to their work have, in turn, provoked consternation on the part of new conservationists. Why, Marris asks of neoprotectionist critics, 'do they worry so much about *expanding* our set of approaches to work for these goals to include more than just protected areas?'[83] Similarly, Marvier, on behalf of Kareiva and co-authors, queries

---

81   David Johns, 'With Friends Like These, Wilderness and Biodiversity Do Not Need Enemies', *Keeping the Wild*, George Wuerthner et al., 31–2.

82   Harvey Locke, 'Green Postmodernism and the Attempted Highjacking of Conservation', *Keeping the Wild*, George Wuerthner et al., 147.

83   Emma Marris, '"New conservation" is an expansion of approaches, not an ethical orientation', *Animal Conservation* 17, 6 (2014), 517, emphasis in original.

not without irony, 'We do not get it: why are people who love the diversity of plants and animals and habitats so afraid of a diversity of approaches and motivations within the conservation community?'[84]

But, for neoprotectionists, this is not the point. As Soulé argues, 'because its goal is to supplant the biological diversity-based model of traditional conservation with something entirely different, namely an economic growth-based or humanitarian movement, *it does not deserve to be labelled conservation.*' This is a heavy charge. Soulé makes this point for various reasons, but especially because he feels that new conservationists do not understand the basic science that conservation should be built on: 'most shocking is the dismissal by the new conservationists of current ecological knowledge. The best current research is solidly supportive of the connection between species diversity and the stability of ecosystems.'[85] More generally, much of the new and old back-to-the-barriers literature holds a similarly one-dimensional view of science as uncontested and apolitical; science that espouses a basic truth that only they understand and hence need to defend.[86]

Again, Marvier is shocked by how her group's understanding of science can be so interpreted. In an editorial tellingly entitled 'new conservation is true conservation', she argues that 'even more troubling is that Soulé's stance has no basis in fact. As one of the authors of what Soulé calls "the manifesto of the new conservation movement", I hope to set the record straight and to help move this debate beyond unproductive infighting.' She denies that new conservation dismisses the science or the need for protected areas and connectivity in general. Rather, she believes that conservation must expand beyond 'traditional' science: 'We need rigorous testing of new approaches and innovative new

---

84    Michelle Marvier, 'A call for ecumenical conservation', *Animal Conservation* 17, 6 (2014), 518.

85    Soulé, 'The new conservation', 895, emphasis added, 896.

86    Which, ironically, is similar to how many Anthropocene scientists see themselves, namely as 'luminaries of science' that need to 'educate and enlighten the whole world'. Christophe Bonneuil and Jean-Baptiste Fressoz, *The Shock of the Anthropocene: The Earth, History and Us* (London: Verso, 2016), 83.

science.'[87] Pearce is even more forceful on this point. In his book *The New Wild* he regularly counter-accuses 'traditional', neoprotectionist conservationists of adhering to poor, outdated, orthodox science when it comes to the benefits and dangers of alien and invasive species and that, in some cases, conservationists have even resorted to 'Orwellian science' and 'ideology', rather than 'good science'.[88]

Science – like nature – is clearly more dynamic and amenable to multiple interpretations for new conservationists than it is to neoprotectionists. Yet, we believe that it is not just science itself that is at stake in the discussion, even though it is important that the two camps differ on what science is and should be about. What is also fundamentally at stake in this dispute is what science should lead to in practice. For neoprotectionists, this is a radical separation between humans and nonhuman nature in order to protect the latter from increased human influence. For new conservationists, this is a radical acceptance of the mixing of humans and nonhumans into potentially exciting new assemblages. In our terms, all this suggests that what is most fundamentally at stake here is the nature–culture dichotomy itself and how to relate scientific findings and endeavours to this binary – and vice versa. This is such a central issue that we will devote the next chapter to exploring it further.

Other significant issues of contention are the developmental aspirations of new conservation. Soulé again: 'The key assertion of the new conservation is that affection for nature will grow in step with income growth. The problem is that evidence for this theory is lacking. In fact, the evidence points in the opposite direction, in part because increasing incomes affect growth in per capita ecological footprint.'[89] Marvier disputes this. She argues that 'we advocate building a solid foundation from the bottom up and providing alternative livelihoods to the poor so that they are not forced to illegally harvest resources or otherwise work against protected areas.' Central to this conflict is the

---

87    Marvier, *New Conservation*, 1.

88    Pearce, *The New Wild*, 69–70.

89    Soulé, 'The new conservation', 895.

intrinsic value of nature, long an essential pillar of the neoprotection-ists' perspective. As Marvier contends:

> Soulé claims that 'new conservationists demand that nature not be protected for its own sake but that it be protected only if it materially benefits human beings.' To the contrary, I encourage the conservation community to continue working in this vein. However, at least in the United States, surveys demonstrate that messages about protecting biodiversity or nature for its intrinsic value are inspiring for relatively narrow segments of the population, particularly those who self-identify as conservationists or environmentalists.[90]

She goes on to suggest that moving beyond nature for nature's sake will allow more people to join the conservation cause, and, for that, poverty needs to be addressed. This is something about which neoprotectionists are rather sceptical. They are not necessarily afraid of reaching out to more people, but are certainly concerned, as noted above, that 'increasing incomes affect growth in per capita ecological footprint.'[91] More examples of this tension could be mentioned (and will be in the following chapter), but we argue that what is most fundamentally at stake here is not just the intrinsic value of nature itself, but how this value features or gets recognized. To be blunt, we argue that new conservationists generally see opportunities in 'modern' capitalist economies and the selling of ecosystem services, while neoprotectionists are critical of this (save for outliers like E.O. Wilson). What makes this more complicated still is that this fundamental debate is mostly waged under the rubric of 'development' rather than capitalism per se – though, we contend, it is a *capitalist mode of development* that is fundamentally at issue here.

Neoprotectionists diverge strongly from new conservationists in their perspective on the relationship between conservation and development and the obligation of conservation to the poor. In fact,

---

90    Marvier, *New Conservation*, 2.
91    Soulé, 'The new conservation', 895.

many neoprotectionists, as they have for quite some time, explicitly reject the conjoining of development and conservation aims altogether. Hence they decry 'justifying biodiversity protection based on narrowly conceived human well-being (essentially cost–benefit analysis)'; 'decision-making dominated by the desires to optimize for efficiency and maximize short-term gains'; and 'exploiting nature for the exclusive purpose of human gain'.[92] Importantly, they contend that 'the economy's dominion over us is all too often conceded and rationalized with garden metaphors and ideologies of balanced domestication'.[93] Mackey asserts that 'a utilitarian attitude toward nature is an insufficient foundation for conservation in the twenty-first century. Alone, this attitude inexorably results in ecosystems becoming depauperate and simplified to the point where they are no longer, among other things, self-organizing and resilient'.[94]

Yet others in the neoprotectionist camp, by contrast, do advocate bringing development into conservation policy. Often this is reluctant, produced by a sense of necessity or inevitability. Thus, Wuerthner concedes, 'Given our current global population and dependence on technology, humanity may have no choice but to "work the landscape"'.[95] Others appear more enthusiastic. Sounding quite similar to Kareiva and Marris, Curt Meine, the conservation biologist and historian, asserts:

> We need to think of conservation in terms of whole landscapes, from the wildest places to the most urban places . . . We need to do more and better conservation work outside protected areas and sacred spaces; on our 'working' farms, ranches, and forests; and in the suburbs and cities where people increasingly live.[96]

92   Johns, 'With Friends Like These', 33; Mackey, 'The Future', 132; Locke, 'Green Postmodernism', 147. All of these are from *Keeping the Wild*, George Wuerthner et al.

93   Lisi Krall, 'Resistance'. In *Keeping the Wild*, George Wuerthner et al., 209.

94   Mackey, 'The Future'. In *Keeping the Wild*, George Wuerthner et al., 135–6.

95   Wuerthner, 'Why the Working Landscape'. In *Keeping the Wild*, George Wuerthner et al., 166.

96   Curt Meine, 'What's So New about the "New Conservation"?' In *Keeping the Wild*, George Wuerthner et al., 54.

Some go so far as to themselves advocate economic valuation and market mechanisms for conservation. Conservationist Kathleen Fitzgerald states, 'Biodiversity offsets and credits, as well as carbon credits, offer potential market solutions to sustaining parks'. She explains: 'If the local community felt that they were benefiting from conservation – through wildlife-based tourism, for example – and if these benefits outweighed the losses resulting from human-wildlife conflict, the situation undoubtedly would be different'.[97] Celebrity primatologist Jane Goodall writes, 'Another way to show that protecting rather than destroying forests can be economically beneficial is by assigning a "monetary" value to living trees and compensating governments, landowners, and villagers for conserving'. She adds as an example that a key market-based instrument known as REDD+ (Reducing Emissions from Deforestation and Forest Degradation), 'assigns a value for the carbon stored in different kinds of forests and forest soils, so that appropriate compensation can be paid to those who protect their forests'.[98]

For some, promotion of development occurs in terms of strict spatial separation wherein pure conservation is to be practiced in some spaces and intensive development in others – a version of the more general approach often termed 'land sparing'.[99] In such a strategy, Crist describes, 'Barring people from sources of livelihood or income within biodiversity reserves (prohibiting settlements, agriculture, hunting, mining, and other high-impact activities) needs to be offset by coupling conservation efforts with the provision of benefits for local people'.[100] E. O. Wilson advocates an extreme version of this strategy as well.

---

97    Kathleen Fitzgerald, 'The Silent Killer: Habitat Loss and the Role of African Protected Areas to Conserve Biodiversity', *Protecting the Wild*, George Wuerthner et al., 183, 186.

98    Jane Goodall, 'Caring for people and Valuing Forests in Africa', *Protecting the Wild*, George Wuerthner et al., 25.

99    Ben Phalan et al., 'Reconciling Food Production and Biodiversity Conservation: Land Sharing and Land Sparing Compared', *Science* 333 (2011), 1289–91.

100    Eileen Crist, 'I Walk in the World to Love It', *Protecting the Wild*, George Wuerthner et al., 87.

It is clear, in sum, that two of the biggest issues that new conservationists and neoprotectionists debate are, first, how to relate to human–nature dichotomies and, second, the prospects of successfully combining conservation with contemporary capitalism (again mostly couched in the language of 'development'). This, then, forms a good bridge to deepen our own evaluation of the debate in the next two chapters, from the perspective of a political ecology critical of contemporary capitalism. In brief, through this frame, we will show that, underlying both radical challenges to mainstream conservation, as well as mainstream conservation itself, are theoretical and/or logical contradictions regarding key issues and concepts that first need to be sorted and explained. These include – amongst others – the intrinsic versus the exchange values of nature; the 'proper' relations between humans and nonhumans and how to mix or separate them; and how both of these fit within a broader development model that responds to the dynamics of the Anthropocene. On these issues, we find that, on both sides, several arguments and positions are untenable.[101]

Concerning new conservation, we believe it is conceptually incoherent and untenable to embrace capitalism-for-conservation while arguing that this necessitates abandoning the same human–nature dichotomies that capitalism constructs and normally thrives on. At the same time, we believe that neoprotectionists are highly contradictory in believing that we can simply separate our way out of environmental trouble through a massive increase of protected areas and connectivity and even reserving half of the earth for nature and the other half for people or 'development'. After all, it is this same capitalist development that is intent upon continually transgressing such boundaries in search of new spaces and sites for accumulation.

What we therefore need is a more consistent, coherent frame and set of principles to make sense of the issues that both neoprotectionists

---

101   We will leave E. O. Wilson out of this equation here, as we have already argued earlier that his position is so riddled with contradictions, simplistic and – frankly – dangerous, that it is difficult to take his intellectual position in the debate as a seriously tenable one. See Bram Büscher and Robert Fletcher, 'Why E. O. Wilson is wrong about how to save the Earth', *Aeon*, 1 March 2016, aeon.co, accessed 28 August 2018.

and new conservationists struggle with – issues that we will be tackling in chapter four.[102] And this is especially important since both have important critiques of mainstream conservation with which we do agree and that we will incorporate into our own proposal for the future of conservation. Yet, in order to get there, we must first delve deeper into the complex and often confusing fundamentals of the debate, which we will do in the next two chapters.

CONCLUSION

The great conservation debate and its recent radical additions are anything but mundane or boring. With the stakes as high as 'the future of life on the planet', as some neoprotectionists frame the problem, there is no shortage of emotion, sharpness and venom in the debates. This book is our attempt to make sense of and contribute to the debate. This chapter sought to lay the basis for this contribution by providing a first appraisal of the current discussion concerning how to save nature in the Anthropocene. In doing so, we must admit to a sense of unease while writing and debating. This is not because we have to admit that our perspective, like all others, is a partial one, steeped in our own biases and informed by our own experiences, our research and our political, scientific and related interests. It is also not because we are necessarily omitting, generalizing and simplifying important issues.

Rather, our sense of unease stems from anthropological inclinations. Delving deeply into debates – as when delving into ethnographic realities of particular places when doing anthropological research – makes one realize the numerous shades of grey that can never be understood fully nor represented adequately. This is again inevitable, but the difference that anthropological engagement makes is to try and appreciate the lived reality of particular 'communities'. In analysing the great conservation debate, it is clear that the lived

---

102   This point may go against the instinct of many conservationists and even academics that we need less debate and instead more action 'on the ground'. We disagree. Yes: we need action on the ground. But this is always accompanied by thinking through, about and around this same action. The one cannot be separated from the other.

reality of the conservation community is a tense and pressurized one, imbued with a great sense of crisis and responsibility. This lived reality is reflected in the numerous contributions to and reflections on the debate, more of which will be presented in ensuing chapters. While cutting corners in order to deal with complexities and nuances, we hope that this chapter has nevertheless been able to convey a sense of this lived reality. This is important, we believe, because it might help to find ways to move forward across differences. In chapter four, we will come back to this point.

Our more grounded goal was to distil the main issues at stake in these complex debates, which we argue revolve around two main axes: the human–nature dichotomy and the ecological merits or perils of contemporary capitalism. Both issues are not straightforward, and there can be no straightforward, black-and-white arguments for or against them. Indeed, there is a distinct danger in presenting them this way, as it does not correspond to empirical reality and the nuances of the debate. We therefore need to do justice to the potentially radical natures of these alternative proposals by discussing them in more depth to show in greater detail how and why they are radical and important, yet contain several untenable contradictions.

# 2

# Dichotomous Natures

In the current 'great conservation debate', it seems there is increasingly less common ground to stand on. Should we be mourning the 'End of the Wild', following Stephen Meyer? Or should we celebrate the 'New Wild', as Fred Pearce urges? Are we living through an age of 'biological annihilation' or is nature 'thriving in an age of extinction'?[1] Should we follow the call to now fully and responsibly accept human stewardship of an Anthropocene earth? Or is this typical of human hubris and should we be sceptical of any attempt to place humanity at the steering wheel of spaceship earth? Should we be radically mixing societies and biodiversity into new and potentially exciting 'socionatural' arrangements or should we radically separate people and much of the rest of biodiversity in order to enable more sustainable futures? Or are all these considerations unrealistic and ought we instead simply to focus on improving mainstream conservation 'business as usual'? These important questions, and others, are raised by the current debate. We add one more: are there ways to defuse their all-or-nothing, black-and-white connotations and find other ways to frame the Anthropocene conservation debate altogether?

Clearly, the arbiter in this discussion cannot be science. Or, at least, not science alone.[2] As we saw in the previous chapter, how to

---

1    Stephen Meyer, *The End of the Wild* (Cambridge, MA: MIT Press, 2006); Ceballos et al., 'Biological annihilation'; Thomas, *Inheritors*.

2    We want to be clear that we are not dismissing science or scientific findings nor are we being unappreciative of the natural sciences. To the contrary: following authors in the critical social sciences, and those in many other scientific fields, we should not and

interpret the role of science in conservation and act on its findings is precisely one of the major issues at stake. Science, no matter how much some neoprotectionists and other conservationists would like to believe otherwise, is always already political; its outcomes and their relevance and potential are always subject to broader political, economic, social, cultural, historical, environmental and other contexts. The same goes for nature, as Christian Marazzi explains:

> Nature, as Einstein noted, is not the univocal text theorized by the scientists belonging to the Newtonian tradition, who thought that the observation of Nature and the deduction of its internal laws was sufficient to find the scientific legality of the physical world. The experience of theoretical inquiry has actually shown that Nature is, rather, an *equivocal* text that can be read according to *alternative modalities*.[3]

Yet, to say that nature is an 'equivocal text' should not be interpreted as a statement of radical postmodern relativism, as Harvey Locke might claim.[4] He and other neoprotectionists have a point that several social scientific 'turns' into postmodern deconstructionism, new materialism and hybridism have become quite outlandish if not foolish.[5] But this does not invalidate the simple *fact* that different people hold different ideas about reality, science and nature. What is therefore badly needed in the debate, we concluded in the previous chapter, is a logical, coherent and convincing frame or set of principles to help assess the issues at stake, to place them within broader contexts and to enable forms of political action moving forward. The aim of this and

---

cannot 'build walls' between the sciences. Bonneil and Fressoz, *The Shock of the Anthropocene*, 21; See also Jeremy Davies, *The Birth of the Anthropocene* (Oakland: University of California Press, 2016); Ian Angus, *Facing the Anthropocene: Fossil Capitalism and the Crisis of the Earth System* (New York: Monthly Review Press, 2016).

   3  Christian Marazzi, *Capital and Affects: The Politics of the Language Economy* (Los Angeles: Semiotext(e), 2011), 43, *italics in original*.

   4  Locke, 'Green Postmodernism'.

   5  See Andreas Malm, *The Progress of this Storm: Nature and Society in a Warming World* (London: Verso, 2018). Hornborg, 'Dithering while the planet burns'.

the next chapter is to work towards such a frame by delving deeper into the main issues raised in chapter two.

In this way, we want to turn the usual order of things around: instead of presenting a theoretical frame through which to approach the Anthropocene conservation debate, we want to highlight several conceptual, theoretical and logical contradictions within the current debate as the basis for formulating a set of principles through which to assess the debate and move it forward. To do so, it is important to make our starting point and basic assumptions explicit. As previously stated, our analysis is grounded in a 'political ecology critical of contemporary capitalism'. In the next section, we briefly clarify what we mean by this and how this relates to our conception of theory. From there, we move deeper into the debate, exploring in more detail the two main issues we have identified as both characterizing and dividing different positions within it: the nature–culture dichotomy, in the current chapter; and the relation between conservation and capitalism in the next. Together, these explorations lead up to our evaluation of the debate as the basis for our own alternative proposal of convivial conservation.

## A POLITICAL ECOLOGY CRITICAL OF
## CONTEMPORARY CAPITALISM

Our contention is that a political ecology centred on a critique of contemporary capitalism can shift the Anthropocene conservation debate onto a more stable, coherent, and realistic basis.[6] This, to be sure, is not a 'closed' theoretical frame where all issues are settled. Just

---

6    For good overviews of, introductions into and edited volumes on the rich tradition of political ecology: Paul Robbins, *Political Ecology: A Critical Introduction* (Malden, MA: Wiley, 2012); Roderick Neumann, *Making Political Ecology* (London: Routledge, 2005); Richard Peet, Paul Robbins and Michael Watts, *Global Political Ecology* (London: Routledge, 2011); Wendy Harcourt and Ingrid Nelson, eds, *Practicing Feminist Political Ecologies: Moving Beyond the 'Green Economy'* (London: Zed Books, 2015); Raymond Bryant, ed., *The International Handbook of Political Ecology* (Cheltenham: Edward Elgar, 2015); Tom Perrault, Gavin Bridge and James McCarthy, eds, *The Routledge Handbook of Political Ecology* (London: Routledge, 2015).

as 'science' is political, so is theory, which means that it must always be open.[7] This is also not to assert that science or theory must be *driven* by one's politics; these should be driven primarily by sound empirical research based on credible methodology.[8] But, as these processes are themselves always infused by politics, and occur within larger political contexts, they can only be made sense of by (inherently political) theories of how the world works and can be understood.[9] Crucial, therefore, is to make one's guiding theoretical assumptions explicit, something that is often lacking within the current Anthropocene conservation debate, and perhaps one of the reasons why it is so antagonistic rather than *agonistic*.[10]

Our guiding theoretical assumptions are arguably two of the most basic assumptions informing political ecology, namely that ecology is political and that the most foundational and powerful contextual feature to take into account when making sense of ecological issues, including conservation, is (the capitalist) political economy. Yet, the point that these assumptions are broadly shared within the field of

---

7   Our understanding of theorizing is here inspired by David Harvey's theory of uneven geographical development. This, according to Harvey, is a loose conception of theory: 'one that acknowledges the power and importance of certain processes that are specifiable independently of each other but which can and must be brought together in a dynamic field of interaction'. Hence: 'theory should be understood . . . as an evolving structure of argument sensitive to encounters with the complex ways in which social processes are materially embedded in the web of life', with a commitment to 'bottom-up theorizing', which: 'entails viewing any particular event set as an internalization of fundamental underlying guiding forces. The task of enquiry is to identify these underlying forces by critical analysis and detailed inspection of the individual instance'. David Harvey, *Spaces of Global Capitalism: Towards a Theory of Uneven Geographical Development* (London: Verso, 2006), 76, 79, 86.

8   And hence our arguments are also deeply informed by our own empirical research.

9   We are thus explicitly not interested in providing an all-encompassing theoretical account of the Anthropocene and all its socio-ecological dimensions. Others have already made important inroads here, and we build on their groundbreaking work. See Bonneuil and Fressoz, *The Shock of the Anthropocene*; Angus, *Facing*; Davies, *The Birth*; Leslie Head, *Hope and Grief in the Anthropocene: Re-conceptualising Human–Nature Relations* (London: Routledge, 2016); John McNeill and Peter Engelke, *The Great Acceleration: An Environmental History of the Anthropocene since 1945* (Cambridge, MA: Belknap Press, 2016).

10   Chantal Mouffe, *On the Political* (London: Routledge, 2005), 20.

political ecology is not the only reason why we believe they provide a good foundation for our discussion. Two further reasons are worth emphasizing, and they also provide a glimpse of how we understand theory and science more generally. First, these two assumptions are not *just* political: the dominance of contemporary capitalism and the statement 'ecology = politics' are also straightforward empirical facts and hence need to be taken seriously in any scientific endeavour focused on conservation.

Second, these assumptions, and their fluid meanings, have been intensely discussed for a long time in political ecology, and there is no agreement on their interpretation. This is crucial, as it means that we can learn from and build on the many theoretical disagreements, contestations and explorations that have animated political ecology over the last decades. Thus, while we state that the assumptions themselves are *facts*, their interpretation and meaning are not, which is necessary to open up theoretical *and* political space to move forward and to deal with the assumptions. Specifically, this open and creative approach to theory pursues what McKenzie Wark calls 'alternative realism'. In her *Theory for the Anthropocene*, Wark makes the case to move beyond both 'capitalist realism' (there is no alternative to capitalism) and 'capitalist romance' (the 'mirror image' of capitalist realism, which advocates a future similar to a supposedly balanced pre-capitalist past). Instead, alternative realism 'opens towards plural narratives about how history can work out otherwise'. It is a 'realism formed by past experience, but not confined to it'. This requires a theorizing that is rooted in material historical experience and in imaginative prospects.[11] It must, in short, be *revolutionary*.[12]

As we saw, some neoprotectionists make a similar argument when it comes to why they believe their radical proposals should be

11   McKenzie Wark, *Molecular Red: Theory for the Anthropocene* (London: Verso, 2015), xxi.

12   See Fred Magdoff and John Bellamy Foster, *What Every Environmentalist Needs to Know About Capitalism: A Citizen's Guide to Capitalism and the Environment* (New York: Monthly Review Press, 2011), 122; Neil Smith, 'The Revolutionary Imperative', *Antipode* 41, 1 (2010), 50–65.

taken seriously. New conservationists, likewise, are also fully aware of the radical implications of some of their arguments. This awareness on both sides, however, has not hindered their willingness to step into the debate in order to try and effect change in conservation practice. It might have even spurred them on more. This is, we believe, important testimony to the 'lived realities' of the debate, and the people behind it. They realize, as do many others, that we live in a time of radical choices and that choices currently being made have far-reaching ramifications. This is why it is crucial to delve deeper into the key issues at stake in the Anthropocene conservation debate.

### RADICAL CHOICES AND RAMIFICATIONS

While still in its early stages, the potentially massive ramifications, as well as the foundational nature of the Anthropocene conservation debate, have already been recognized widely. As we intimated in the introduction, these included a range of actors trying to understand the parameters, origins and effects of the debate. This has led to a range of different responses. Some seem rather taken aback by the heated debate, even calling it 'vitriolic'. Conservation scientists Heather Tallis and Jane Lubchenco, supported by 238 signatories, spearheaded a comment in *Nature* calling 'for an end to the infighting' that, they claim, 'is stalling progress in protecting the planet'.[13] Others welcome the heated debate. Political ecologists Brett Matulis and Jessica Moyer, commenting on this *Nature* piece, contend that calls for consensus are futile given that there are in fact fundamental incompatibilities between the positions advanced by the two camps in the debate. They also highlight just how narrow a range of participants in the global conservation movement this debate includes and how many other perspectives on appropriate forms of conservation would be excluded even if the two extremes could be somehow unified. They call instead for an 'agonistic' conservation politics in

---

13   Heather Tallis and Jane Lubchenco et al., 'A call for inclusive conservation', *Nature* 515 (2014), 27–8.

which debate is not suppressed but, on the contrary, opened further to include a wider range of perspectives.[14]

Other commentators have tried to engage more directly with issues in the debate itself. Geographer Paul Robbins, for example, lauded the new conservationist attempts to stop blaming people, especially those who are marginalized, for bad conservation results, which, in his words:

> Portends a real shift not just in doing conservation, but in rethinking the basis for all of what would best be termed the 'Edenic sciences', including conservation biology as well as the fields of invasion biology and restoration ecology. Channelling their research into the explanation, analysis, and encouragement of diversity where people live and work, the authors herald a fundamental shift in hypotheses and methods in these sciences, as we move forward into the Anthropocene.[15]

But at the same time as they applaud new conservation for moving beyond old nature–culture dichotomies, Robbins and others worry about the optimism with which Kareiva et al. and many major conservation organizations put their faith in partnering with capitalist corporations. Robbins warns that 'corporations can be bad news' and chides Kareiva and colleagues for being naïve in too easily embracing capitalist models of development and corporate funding. Lisa Hayward and Barbara Martinez, similarly, caution that without appropriate risk management and strategies for measuring success '"Conservation in the Anthropocene" will diminish conservation's reputation and its capacity to spur positive change, and, at worst, may justify the distortions of those who seek to profit at the expense of both people and nature'.[16]

---

14    Brett Matulis and Jessica Moyer, 'Beyond Inclusive Conservation: The Value of Pluralism, the Need for Agonism, and the Case for Social Instrumentalism', *Conservation Letters* 10, 3 (2016), 279–87. This same point has been made by Castree and colleagues in relation to discussions in the broader environmental humanities. Noel Castree et al., 'Challenging the Intellectual Climate', *Nature Climate Change* 4, 9 (2014), 763–68.

15    Paul Robbins, 'Corporate partners can be bad news', *Breakthrough Journal*, April 2012.

16    Lisa Hayward and Barbara Martinez, 'The wrong Conservation Message', *Breakthrough Journal* April 2012.

The latter positions resonate strongly with our own. Hence, we will spend some time discussing this issue in more depth later. First, however, we need to do more justice to the nuances in the debate, while also providing more evidence for what we believe are ultimately the two main, interrelated axes of contention: the nature–culture dichotomy and the relationship between conservation and capitalism. We start with the issue at the heart of it all: the nature of 'nature' itself.

### THE NATURE OF NATURE

First and foremost among the issues of contention within the great conservation debate has always been the meaning of the term 'nature'. It would, perhaps, not be an exaggeration to say that this is the key foundational issue around which the whole discussion pivots. One of the central components of common critiques of mainstream conservation is that it has, historically, rested on a conceptual distinction between opposing realms of nature and culture that conservation practice has, in a sense, sought to render material through the creation of protected areas from which human inhabitants were often forcibly removed.[17] This dichotomy, and the particular understanding of (nonhuman) nature to which it gives rise, has been problematized as a culturally specific construction largely limited to 'Western societies' in the modern era. Such a strict separation between opposing conceptual realms, it is argued, does not reflect the different ways in which other peoples throughout the world understand relationships between humans and other living beings.[18] So why, precisely, is this dichotomy such a big issue, and how do different actors in the debate deal with it?

---

17   Igoe, *Conservation*; Chris Sandbrook, 'What is conservation?', *Oryx* 49 (2015), 565–66.

18   Cronon, 'The trouble with wilderness'; Braun and Castree, *Remaking Reality*; Philippe Descola, *Beyond Nature and Culture* (Chicago: Chicago University Press, 2013). Important to add is that few within this literature go so far as to endorse a purely idealist position that there exists no biophysical substance to reality, as critics have frequently misinterpreted this position, for instance, David Kidner, 'Fabricating nature: A critique of the social construction of nature', *Environmental Ethics* 22, 4 (2000), 339–57.

To start with the last part of this question, mainstream conservationists have generally been ambivalent about the concept of nature.
On the one hand, many claim that a nature–culture separation is an
impediment to conservation: it enforces a sense of distance and alienation from nonhumans, and conservationists therefore often call for
greater 'connection with nature' through direct experience in outdoor
landscapes.[19] In their rhetoric and actual practice, on the other
hand, conservationists commonly continue to reinforce separations
between people and the very nature we are all supposed to be part
of. This is most visible in the continued enforcement of conventional
protected areas, but also in newer market-based mechanisms such as
ecotourism, payments for environmental services, and species banking in which conservation and development are supposed to become
one and the same.[20]

More contradictory still, even as they advocate greater connection with nature, conservationists often *simultaneously* reinforce a
sense of separation from nature. This, then, provides a first glimpse
of what is so problematic about the nature–culture dichotomy:
humans are supposed to be part of nature, but are at the same time
often seen as separate from it. Conservation International's 'Nature
Is Speaking' campaign epitomizes this problematic ambivalence
(see figure 2). This campaign features a series of short films in which
high-profile celebrities like Harrison Ford and Julia Roberts assume
the voices of natural forces (such as water and Mother Nature) and
decry humans' rampant assault upon them. One of these short films,
narrated by Robert Redford as a redwood tree, insists that the solution to this destruction is for humans to recognize that they are 'part
of nature, rather than just using nature'.[21] Yet the campaign's own

---

19    Matthew Zylstra et al., 'Connectedness as a core conservation concern: An interdisciplinary review of theory and a call for practice', *Springer Science Reviews* 2 (2014),
119–43.

20    Robert Fletcher, 'Connection with nature is an oxymoron: A political ecology of
"nature-deficit disorder"', *The Journal of Environmental Education* 48 (2017), 226–33.

21    'Robert Redford is the Redwood', Nature is Speaking, conservation.org, accessed
27 November 2017.

motto ('Nature Doesn't Need People, People Need Nature') emphasizes this same separation between people and nature that is seen as
the problem, a separation further reinforced by many of these short
films in which narrators explicitly speak, as elements of nature, to
their distinction from a generic humanity. Julia Roberts, as Mother
Earth, for instance, proclaims, 'I am nature. I am prepared to evolve.
Are you?'[22]

Figure 2. CI signs at the World Parks Congress, Sydney, November 2014.

Photos by Bram Büscher.

Anthropocene conservationists, as we have seen in the previous chapter, embrace the mounting critique of the nature–culture dichotomy.
Kareiva and colleagues assert, 'One need not be a postmodernist
to understand that the concept of Nature, as opposed to the physical and chemical workings of natural systems, has always been a
human construction, shaped and designed for human ends.' On this
basis they advocate greater integration of human and nonhuman
processes within a variety of different strategies, including integrated-
conservation-and-development programmes, biosphere reserves,
biological corridors, assisted migration routes, and even the creation of 'novel ecosystems'. Central to all these is a 'new vision of a
planet in which nature – forests, wetlands, diverse species, and other

---

22   'Julia Roberts is Mother Nature', Nature is Speaking, conservation.org, accessed
27 November 2017.

ancient ecosystems – exists amid a wide variety of modern, human landscapes'.[23]

Since at least the 1990s, neoprotectionists have strongly contested this view. They argue that nature is not a social construction but a real entity that stands to some extent independent, 'self-willed' and 'autonomous' with respect to human perception and action. From this perspective, those who critically reflect on the concept of nature are themselves often criticized for endorsing an extreme position that denies the existence of physical reality altogether.[24] Yet, as with mainstream conservation, this perspective is ambivalent. Some neoprotectionists, like David Johns and Roderick Nash, accept the assertion that humans are part of nature:

> How can human behavior be anything but part of Nature? We are the products of evolution; we breathe air, eat, and are otherwise dependent upon the Earth. Unless one invokes the supernatural then, by definition, everything we do is natural, and that doesn't get us very far.[25]

Of course humans remain 'natural.' But somewhere along the evolutionary way from spears to spaceships, humanity dropped off the biotic team and, as author and naturalist Henry Beston recognized, became a 'cosmic outlaw.' The point is that we are no longer thinking and acting like a part of nature. Or, if we are a part, it is a cancerous one, growing so rapidly as to endanger the larger environmental organism.[26]

At the same time, such statements conflict with a common desire amongst neoprotectionists to preserve nature as a 'self-willed' force independent of human intervention and cordoned off within depopulated protected areas. Assertions of the 'need to share the world with

---

23   Kareiva et al., 'Conservation'.
24   Kidner, 'Fabricating nature'.
25   Johns, 'With Friends Like These', 37.
26   Roderick Nash, 'Wild World'. In *Keeping the Wild*, George Wuerthner et al., 184–5.

nature', 'the will to create a new humanity that respects nature's freedom and desires', or that 'it is wrong for humanity to displace and dominate nature', again imply a separation between humans and the nature we are supposedly part of.[27] This, clearly, is problematic. But another central concern of the global conservation movement illustrates this contradiction – and hence of the role of the dichotomy in the broader Anthropocene conservation debate – even more sharply: the desire not just to protect nature, but to preserve *wilderness*.

## THE REALITIES OF WILDERNESS

For many conservationists, the nature they defend is often directly equated with wilderness.[28] Wilderness was paradigmatically defined by the 1964 US National Wilderness Preservation Act as 'an area where the earth and its community of life are untrammeled by man, where man himself is a visitor who does not remain.' As noted in chapter one, the aim to preserve wilderness within protected areas has always only been one model of conservation that has coexisted with other competing approaches from the outset. Yet the North American wilderness park has long stood as the main model for the global expansion of protected areas in the nineteenth and twentieth centuries. In this way, and further reinforced after the paradigmatic definition by the US Wilderness Act, the very act of preserving wilderness has ensured and even deepened the centrality of the nature–culture binary in global conservation.[29]

Following Paul Wapner, there are two main reasons why a focus on 'wilderness' deepens the dichotomy, one material and one discursive.[30] Materially, it is well documented that many areas that are

---

27    Locke, 'Nature Needs', 11; Crist, 'I Walk', 95; Cafaro, 'Expanding Parks', 145.

28    Michael Derby et al., for instance, focus their analysis on '"nature," or what we will call "wilderness"'. Michael Derby, Laura Piersol and Sean Blenkinsop, 'Refusing to settle for pigeons and parks: Urban environmental education in the age of neoliberalism', *Environmental Education Research* 21, 3 (2015), 379.

29    Taylor, *The Rise*.

30    Wapner, *Living*.

considered wildernesses to be preserved within protected areas were made so by forcibly evicting the former inhabitants of these areas. It is therefore only through violent acts of displacement that they were given the *appearance* of unpopulated pristineness. What is painfully contradictory here is that the same indigenous people who in many places long managed landscapes that became attractive to conservation were subsequently removed (or even exterminated) in order to preserve what then became 'wilderness'.[31] Rod Neumann astutely labelled this material dynamic 'imposing wilderness'.[32]

At the same time, the contradictory material production of wilderness needed also to be discursively produced, in order to be (seen as) legitimate and 'real'. In Igoe's perceptive words, this 'process of erasure had to erase itself'.[33] Only by writing people out of landscapes could protected areas also discursively take on the semblance of 'untrammeled' wilderness. Needless to say, these contradictory dynamics, which were also often racist, colonialist and imperialist, have been heavily criticized. The foundational text here is William Cronon's essay 'The Trouble with Wilderness', where he stated that wilderness 'far from being the one place on earth that stands apart from humanity, is quite profoundly a human creation'.[34] Cronon and others challenged the very idea that wilderness can or ever has existed, which de facto renders it 'an impossible geography'.[35]

This critique of the ontology of the wilderness conventionally prized by conservation is one of the main issues that new

---

31    William Denevan, 'The pristine myth: The landscape of the Americas in 1492', *Annals of the Association of American Geographers* 82, 3 (1992), 369–85; Kat Anderson, *Tending the Wild: Native American Knowledge and the Management of California's Natural Resources* (Berkeley: University of California Press, 2005); Clark Erickson, 'Amazonia: The historical ecology of a domesticated landscape, *Handbook of South American Archaeology*, Helaine Silverman and William H. Isbell, eds (New York: Springer, 2008), 157–83.

32    Neumann, *Imposing Wilderness*.

33    Igoe, *Conservation*, 85.

34    Cronon, 'The trouble with wilderness', 69.

35    Jamie Lorimer and Clemens Driessen, 'Wild experiments at the Oostvaardersplassen: Rethinking environmentalism in the Anthropocene', *Transactions of the Institute of British Geographers* 39 (2013), 169–81; cf. Robert Fletcher, 'Against Wilderness: Green Theory and Praxis', *The Journal of Ecopedagogy* 5 (2009), 169–79.

conservationists have embraced in support of their position. As Kareiva et al. assert,

> The wilderness ideal presupposes that there are parts of the world untouched by humankind ... The truth is humans have been impacting their natural environment for centuries. The wilderness so beloved by conservationists – places 'untrammeled by man' – never existed, at least not in the last thousand years, and arguably even longer.

On this basis they contend that:

> Conservation cannot promise a return to pristine, prehuman landscapes. Humankind has already profoundly transformed the planet and will continue to do so ... conservationists will have to jettison their idealized notions of nature, parks, and wilderness – ideas that have never been supported by good conservation science – and forge a more optimistic, human-friendly vision.[36]

Marris, similarly, describes a 'post-wild' world in which we 'must temper our romantic notion of untrammeled wilderness and find room next to it for the more nuanced notion of a global, half-wild rambunctious garden'. This, she suggests, is

> a much more optimistic and a much more fruitful way of looking at things ... If you only care about pristine wilderness ... you're fighting a defensive action that you can never ultimately win, and every year there's less of it than there was the year before ... But if you're focused on the other values of nature and goals of nature, then you can go around creating more nature, and our kids can have a world with more nature on it than there is now.[37]

---

36   Kareiva et al., 'Conservation'.
37   Marris, *Rambunctious*, 2.

This, clearly, is one of the contentions most disputed by neoprotectionists. Wilson insists that 'areas of wilderness . . . are real entities'.[38] In a section entitled 'wilderness is real', Locke even argues that 'to those of us who have experienced such primeval places, claims of the non-existence of wilderness are absurd and offensive'.[39]

A number of interrelated arguments are mobilized to support these assertions. First, neoprotectionists dispute research concluding that indigenous inhabitants have long tended many 'wilderness' areas. Instead, they contend that in reality there were far fewer such inhabitants than researchers claim and that these inhabitants altered the landscape far less than is suggested. Foreman points out that 'the combined population of Canada and the United States today is over 330 million' while 'the pre-Columbian population was little more than 1 percent of that'. Moreover, 'There were large regions rarely visited by humans – much less hosting permanent settlements – because of the inhospitality of the environment, the small total population of people at the time, uneven distribution, limited technology, lack of horses, and constant warfare and raiding' and hence human 'impact until very recently was scattered and light'. As a result, environmental campaigner and Earth First! co-founder Dave Foreman asserts, 'The issue is not whether natives touched the land, but to what degree and where. Even if certain settled and cropped places were not self-willed land due to native burning, agriculture, and other uses, it does not follow that this was the case everywhere'.[40] He favourably quotes geographer Thomas Vale who argues that:

The general point . . . is that the pre-European landscape of the United States was not monolithically humanized . . . Rather, it was a patchwork, at varying scales, of pristine and humanized conditions.

38   Wilson, *Half-Earth*, 78.
39   Locke, 'Green Postmodernism', 157.
40   Dave Foreman, 'Humanized Pre-Columbian Landscape'. In *Keeping the Wild*, George Wuerthner et al., 115–17.

A natural American wilderness – an environment fundamentally molded by nature – did exist.[41]

Second, neoprotectionists contest claims concerning the number of people displaced to create wilderness protected areas and the extent to which this occurred. Environmental historian Emily Wakild asserts that 'history in many cases shows that people were not kicked out; national parks were designed with them in mind'.[42] Environmental sociologist Eileen Crist adds that 'recent research has revealed that systematic data about the impact protected areas have had on local communities worldwide (and under what conditions that impact has been beneficial or detrimental) is "seriously lacking." What's more, the overwhelming majority of the world's rural and urban poor do not live near wilderness areas'.[43]

Third, in a different yet related vein, neoprotectionists hold that an area need not be entirely 'pristine' to be considered wilderness. Wilson points out that 'Nowhere in the U.S. Wilderness Act do words like "pristine" appear'. Foreman agrees: 'Places do not have to be pristine to be designated as wilderness; the Wilderness Act never required pristine conditions'. Wuerthner goes further than this insisting that 'no serious supporters of parks believe these places are "pristine" in the sense of being totally untouched or unaffected by humans'. And in responding directly to Kareiva et al., Kierán Suckling, the Executive Director of the Center for Biological Diversity retorts:

Do Kareiva et al. expect readers to believe that conservation groups are unaware that American Indians and native Alaskans lived in huge swaths of what are now designated wilderness areas? Or that

---

41   Thomas Vale, 'The Myth of the Humanized Landscape: An example from Yosemite National Park', *Natural Areas Journal* 18, 3 (1998), 234. Another example comes from Peter Alagona, *After the Grizzly: Endangered Species and the Politics of Place in California* (Berkeley: University of California Press, 2013).

42   Emily Wakild, 'Parks, People, and Perspectives: Historicizing Conservation in Latin America'. In *Protecting the Wild*, George Wuerthner et al., 44.

43   Crist, 'I Walk', 93.

they mysteriously failed to see the cows, sheep, bridges, fences, fire towers, fire suppression and/or mining claims within the majority of the proposed wilderness areas they have so painstakingly walked, mapped, camped in, photographed, and advocated for? It is not environmentalists who are naïve about wilderness; it is Kareiva et al. who are naïve about environmentalists. Environmental groups have little interest in the 'wilderness ideal' because it has no legal, political or biological relevance when it comes to creating or managing wilderness areas. They simply want to bring the greatest protections possible to the lands which have been the least degraded.[44]

Some even contend that places inhabited by low numbers of indigenous peoples can in fact still be considered wilderness. Wilson insists that 'wildernesses have often contained sparse populations of people, especially those indigenous for centuries or millennia, without losing their essential character'.[45] Environmentalists Harvey Locke and Philip Dearden assert that 'low intensity indigenous occupation of an area through low impact subsistence activity is consistent with the wilderness concept'. The author and environmentalist Paul Kingsnorth elaborates:

> The Amazon is not important because it is untouched; it's important because it is wild, in the sense that it is self-willed. Humans live in and from it, but it is not created or controlled by them. It teems with a great, shifting, complex diversity of both human and nonhuman life, and no species dominates the mix.[46]

Neoprotectionists, in short, have tried hard to re-operationalize and reconceptualize the concept of wilderness in order to respond to, and

---

44   Wilson, *Half-Earth*, 77; Dave Foreman, *Rewilding North America: A Vision for Conservation in the Twenty-first Century* (New York: Island Press, 2004), 123; Wuerthner, 'Why the Working Landscape'. In *Keeping the Wild*, George Wuerthner et al., 169; Kierán Suckling, 'Conservation in the Real World', *Breakthrough Journal* (2012).

45   Wilson, *Half-Earth*, 77–8.

46   Locke and Dearden, 'Rethinking protected area categories', 6; Kingsnorth, 'Rise of the Neo-greens', 7.

even accommodate, some of its material and discursive histories. In this they keep coming back to one main point, captured poignantly by Wolke: 'Absolute pristine nature may be history, but there remains plenty of wildness on this beleaguered planet.'[47] This perspective allows for the reintroduction of the wilderness as a *relative* rather than absolute concept. Thus, Locke and Dearden,

> acknowledge that there are few areas on Earth that at some time have not sustained human impacts. We know that every drop of rain that falls anywhere on this planet bears the imprint of industrial society. But we also know that there are great variations in the degree of humanity's impacts on the rest of nature. The difference in human impact on nature from the practice of intensive cultivation in a humanized landscape compared to the impacts of deposition of minute traces of industrial chemicals in a wild, uncultivated and unpopulated area is not just a difference in degree, it is a difference in kind. The term wilderness captures this difference.[48]

Bringing these different lineages in the concept's development together, we again see the same problematic and ambiguous binary: wilderness should be able to contain and has always contained people, but, at the same time, should ideally not contain people. What, arguably, makes this discussion sharper than, or simply different from, the 'nature' discussion above is that it is harder to erase or deny the dichotomy. At the very least, it shows important nuances in the debate to which we could not yet do justice in chapter one, namely that we have seen that neoprotectionists are not as rigid on this point as it might sometimes appear. In fact, we need to go one step further still.

---

47   Howie Wolke, 'Wilderness: What and Why?' In *Keeping the Wild*, George Wuerthner et al., 199.

48   Locke and Dearden, 'Rethinking protected area categories', 6.

## FROM WILDERNESS TO WILDNESS, VIA 'REWILDING'?

In response to these debates concerning the nature of nature and realities of wilderness, many advocate a conceptual shift from *wilder*ness' to *'wild*ness'.[49] Legal anthropologist Irus Braverman even sees this shift as one of the central dynamics of contemporary conservation more generally. The shift from wilderness to wildness, has, in fact, been endorsed by neoprotectionists, Anthropocenists and critical social scientists alike, albeit in quite different forms. Briefly outlining these will help to further clarify the importance of and nuances in the role of the nature–culture dichotomy within the debate.

Already before they suffered a full-frontal attack for their dismissal of the concept of wilderness, new conservationists had started emphasizing how their proposal retains elements of 'wildness' within a human-dominated landscape. Marris, for instance, envisions 'a global, half-wild rambunctious garden', while Kareiva et al. advocate a 'tangle of species and wildness amidst lands used for food production, mineral extraction, and urban life'.[50] This, obviously, comes quite close to how critical social scientists have advanced their own vision of 'feral' landscapes incorporating elements of 'wildness'.[51] As Cronon stated some time ago, 'If wildness can stop being (just) out there and start being (also) in here, if it can start being as humane as it is natural, then perhaps we can get on with the unending task of struggling to live rightly in the world – not just in the garden, not just in the wilderness, but in the

---

49    Often thereby invoking Thoreau's famous maxim 'In wildness lies the preservation of the world' and pointing out that this has frequently been misread as 'wilderness'. See Braverman, *Wild Life*.

50    Marris, *Rambunctious*, 2; Kareiva et al., 'Conservation'.

51    Cronon, 'The trouble with wilderness'; Sarah Whatmore and Lorraine Thorne, 'Wild(er)ness: Reconfiguring the geographies of wildlife', *Transactions of the Institute of British Geographers* 23, 4 (1998), 435–54; Steve Hinchliffe et al., 'Urban wild things: A cosmopolitical experiment', *Environment and Planning D: Society and Space* 23 (2005), 643–58; Steve Hinchliffe, 'Reconstituting nature conservation: Towards a careful political ecology', *Geoforum* 39 (2008), 88–97. Braverman, *Wild Life*; Lorimer, *Wildlife*.

home that encompasses them both.'[52] Jamie Lorimer more recently elaborated:

> There is a common assumption that the end of Nature equates to an end to wildness, a domestication of the planet. This is the case only if we accept the mapping of wildlife to wilderness, to places defined by human absence. Instead, wildlife lives among us. It includes the intimate microbial constituents that make up our gut flora and the feral plants and animals that inhabit urban ecologies. Risky, endearing, charismatic, and unknown, wildlife persists in our post-Natural world.[53]

Yet some in the neoprotectionist camp insist that this is a slippery slope in that all wildness should not be considered equal. Seeking to recapture a notion of wilderness in the face of such slippage, Michael Derby and colleagues contend 'that the "wilderness" we encounter in cities is qualitatively different from what is encountered in predominantly undomesticated areas. Despite the procession of birds that might flock overhead, the coyotes that roam urban alleyways, or the families of raccoons that rummage through garbage bins, cities are not wilderness on its own terms.' As a result, these authors assert:

> The wilderness that we know of the backcountry is predominantly wild beyond our wanting and doing, it is self-arising and unpredictable; we have not tamed it or turned it into a delightful display of aesthetics. It is messy and complex beyond our control and beyond easy understanding. It forces us to be humble and attentive in ways that seem more rare within an urban setting. As educators, we need to acknowledge such radical differences in the knowing and being that take place across locales, from the urban park to the arctic tundra and everything in-between.[54]

---

52   Cronon, 'The trouble with wilderness', 90.
53   Lorimer, *Wildlife*, 7.
54   Derby et al., 'Refusing to settle', 379, 385.

Wildness, for both neoprotectionists and new conservationists, is thus understood as a spectrum, with fully human-dominated landscapes on the one end and (almost) fully nature-dominated landscapes on the other. A key objective is to 'rewild' areas to a state of wildness approximating to an acceptable degree a pre-human – or at least pre-modern – landscape. For new conservationists, this is merely one strategy among many intended to create a variety of landscapes combining humans and nonhumans in myriad combinations.[55] For neoprotectionists, however, rewilding towards a pre-human baseline becomes the core strategy of the new back-to-the-barriers programme. The very concept, indeed, was developed by neoprotectionists. As Lorimer and colleagues describe, 'The term rewilding first emerged from a collaboration between the conservation biologist Michael Soulé and the environmental activist David Foreman in the late 1980s that led to the creation of The Wildlands Project.'[56] The idea was expanded by Dave Foreman as a novel paradigm for conservation throughout North America, via his Rewilding Institute, a project he, Soulé and others subsequently promoted in the flagship scientific journal *Nature*.[57] A similar proposal to rewild Europe has been advanced, coordinated by the group Wild Europe.[58] Rewilding plans have been discussed and/or developed for various other areas as well.

Although many variations of the concept exist, the basic idea of rewilding is to cordon off spaces that have been previously subject to human alteration so that 'natural' processes can take over and evolve of their own accord.[59] Rewilded spaces can range from small isolated plots like the well-known Oostvaardersplassen in the Netherlands, to the ambitious vision of rewilding whole continents, like North

---

55    See esp. Marris, *Rambunctious*.

56    Jamie Lorimer et al., 'Rewilding: Science, Practice, and Politics', *Annual Review of Environment and Resources* 40 (2015), 41.

57    Foreman, *Rewilding North America*; Josh Donlan et al., 'Re-wilding North America', *Nature* 436 (2015), 913–14.

58    George Monbiot, *Feral: Rewilding the Land, Sea and Human Life* (New York: Penguin, 2013).

59    Dolly Jørgensen, 'Rethinking rewilding', *Geoforum* 65 (2015), 482–88; Lorimer et al., 'Rewilding'.

America, by creating vast ranges inhabited by introduced species bearing resemblance to animals that were endemic to the continent before humans' arrival. As this proposal makes clear, a common but not universal ground for different rewilding projects is 'a desire to shift the reference baseline for conservation towards the ecological conditions that existed at the end of the Pleistocene'.[60]

As George Monbiot describes, as opposed to conventional conservation, which 'seeks to manage nature as if tending a garden', rewilding aims 'to permit ecological processes to resume'. It is about 'resisting the urge to control nature, and allowing it to find its own way'. Monbiot claims, 'the ecosystems that result are best described not as wilderness but as self-willed: governed not by human management but by their own processes'.[61] Rewilded spaces, however, do not solve the contradiction of the human–culture dichotomy; they are 'man-made to be wild, created from nothing to look as if [they] had never changed'. To achieve this, they must therefore be intensely managed to appear as if unmanaged, left to their own devices. In the process, consequently, the rewilding 'concept tends to reinforce the line between humans and nature'.[62]

What is ironic – and very interesting in relation to this book's discussion – is that rewilding is a strategy promoted by *both* the new conservationists and some of their neoprotectionist critics as 'a model for conservation in the Anthropocene'.[63] Marris includes rewilding as a central element of her rambunctious garden, while Soulé was among the group to first propose the plan to rewild North America (even if he and compatriots, as we have seen, dispute the Anthropocene idea per se). A common rewilding strategy, then, is approached from two opposite viewpoints: a recuperation of a semblance of wilderness, on the one hand; a 'post-wild' plan to consciously make and manage

---

60   Lorimer and Driessen, 'Wild Experiments', 172. See also Jamie Lorimer and Clemens Driessen, 'Bovine biopolitics and the promise of monsters in the rewilding of Heck cattle', *Geoforum* 48 (2013), 249–59.

61   Monbiot, *Feral*, 8–10.

62   Marris, *Rambunctious*, 70, 63.

63   Lorimer and Driessen, 'Wild Experiments', 174.

nature, on the other. In this and other ways, the distance between new conservation and neoprotectionist positions seems to diminish substantially. But they remain far from convergent, and neither camp resolves or deals satisfactorily with the nature–culture dichotomy.

## DISSECTING THE DICHOTOMY

So where do we stand on the question of the nature–culture dichotomy? What is clear from the preceding discussion is that new conservationists have put their finger on this sore spot in the history, theory and practice of conservation in a way that many critical social scientists using similar or related arguments have rarely been able to do. Anthropocenists have even been able to push many hardcore neoprotectionists to not only think about the issue in a profound way but also to acknowledge, to varying degrees, its importance and to respond to the challenges posed. Yet, how new conservationists have further developed this point deserves closer scrutiny and will lead us necessarily to the other main issue in the debate: the relationship between conservation and capitalism.

Central for new conservationists is the fact that conservation is not any longer something that is done behind symbolic and material fences or through the separation of 'humans' from 'nature'. Instead, they stress that conservation must be done throughout all human activity, and especially *economic* activity. That is, the conservation of nature should become valued throughout the economy in such a way that contradictory dichotomies between humans and nature are no longer necessary to 'protect' nature 'from' people. For this to occur, the material economy must be reconfigured so as to create value for ecology and economy alike. It is in this way that they connect a critique of the nature–culture dichotomy to the promotion of capitalist conservation.

This position, however, is logically and historically untenable. We argue that the strides made towards moving beyond the dichotomies new conservationists decry are deeply hindered by their endorsement of capitalist conservation. There are several important reasons for this. First and most fundamentally, *it is under capitalism itself that this stark distinction between human and nonhuman natures has been reinvented and reinforced.*[64] The key dynamic through which this happened is what Marx called the 'metabolic rift'. This concept describes 'the process whereby the agronomic methods of agro-industrialisation abandon agriculture's natural biological base, reducing the possibility of recycling nutrients in and through the soil and water'.[65] Simultaneously, it signals how social life in urban areas has been progressively separated from the productive capacity of rural spaces during the development of capitalism from the sixteenth and seventeenth centuries onwards.[66] All this meant not only that capitalist agriculture had to sustain productivity on a 'deteriorating ecological base'[67] but that *the development of capitalism increasingly succeeded in fundamentally changing how many humans relate to and think about (the rest of) nature.*[68]

This latter point is worth dwelling on a bit more, as it goes to the roots of why so many philosophers as well as social *and* natural scientists have argued, and continue to argue, that the nature–culture

---

64   Jason Moore, *Capitalism in the Web of Life: Ecology and the Accumulation of Capital* (London: Verso, 2015).

65   Philip McMichael, 'Feeding the World: Agriculture, Development and Ecology', *Socialist Register 2007: Coming to Terms with Nature*, Leo Panitch and Colin Leys, eds, (London: The Merlin Press, 2006), 177. Jason Moore considers this early manifestation of the nature–culture dichotomy so foundational that he argues that the 'history of capitalism can be conceptualized as a series of successive, historical breaks in nutrient cycling'. Jason Moore, 'Environmental Crises and the Metabolic Rift in World-Historical Perspective', *Organization and Environment* 13, 2 (2000), 127.

66   It must be noted, however, that 'while Marx's clearest articulation of metabolic rift was in the context of the rifts in capitalist agriculture and industrialization, the concept does not posit either of these as its "historical origins"'; Brian M. Napoletano et al., 'Has (even Marxist) political ecology really transcended the metabolic rift?' *Geoforum* 92 (2018), 93; Foster, *The Vulnerable Planet*.

67   McMichael, 'Feeding', 177. Mustafa Koc and Kenneth Dahlberg, in this regard, argue: 'When all the impacts of globalization are considered, a wide variety of analysts have concluded that the so-called success of the current food system – its great productive capacity – is also its biggest liability for long-term economic and ecological sustainability'. Mustafa Koc and Kenneth Dahlberg, 'The Restructuring of Food Systems: Trends, Research and Policy Issues', *Agriculture and Human Values* 16 (1999), 113.

68   Whereby the idea of the metabolic rift needs to stay in tune with insights into soil and nutrient dynamics, as Mindi Schneider and Philip McMichael argue; Mindi Schneider and Philip McMichael, 'Deepening, and Repairing, the Metabolic Rift', *Journal of Peasant Studies* 37, 3 (2010), 461–84.

dichotomy is deeply problematic. World systems sociologist Jason Moore even argues that this 'dualism drips with blood and dirt, from its sixteenth century origins to capitalism in its twilight'.[69] The reason for making such a strong statement is that the specific nature–culture dichotomy inaugurated by the onset and development of capitalism allowed for new forms of rational, technocratic, mechanistic and profit-driven manipulation of nature – including humans and, especially, women. This manipulation could only be morally, ethically or socially permissible – even *thinkable* – if humans saw themselves as different – or rather, became *alienated* – from 'the rest of nature'.[70] Carolyn Merchant's exposition of what she calls 'the death of nature' is still seen as the classic statement of what this perspective leads to. Through this term, she wanted to draw attention to the reduction of nature to an inanimate, technocratically manipulable object:

> The removal of animistic, organic assumptions about the cosmos constituted the death of nature – the most far-reaching effect of the scientific revolution. Because nature was now viewed as a system of dead, inert particles moved by external, rather than inherent forces, the mechanical framework itself could legitimate the manipulation of nature. Moreover, as a conceptual framework, the mechanical order had associated with it a framework of values based on power, fully compatible with the directions taken by commercial capitalism.[71]

This portrayal of nature would be totally unacceptable to most neoprotectionists, who are generally keen to emphasize the deep spiritual, ethical or otherwise 'inherent' values and 'forces' of a 'self-willed' nature.[72] Indeed, this is precisely why wilderness is so important to

69    Moore, *Capitalism in the Web of Life*, 4.

70    Two classic statements regarding the gender aspects of the nature–culture divide are: Sherry Ortner, 'Is Female to Male as Nature Is to Culture?' *Feminist Studies* 1, 2 (1972), 5–31; Silvia Federici, *Caliban and the Witch: Women, the Body and Primitive Accumulation* (New York: Autonomedia, 2004).

71    Carolyn Merchant, *The Death of Nature: Women, Ecology and the Scientific Revolution* (New York: HarperOne, 1983), 193.

72    A point that, although in different ways, continues to be made in relation to

them, namely as a counter to the mechanical, rational, technocratic (and often literal) 'death of nature' in so many places 'developed' by a globalizing capitalist economy.[73] The history of conservation, more generally, is analogous to this argument, in that it served as a counter to the rapid destruction (and subjugation) of nonhuman nature brought about by emergent forms of uneven capitalist development. The irony here – and this brings us to a second fundamental point – is that the very effects of the nature–culture dichotomy leading to the death of nature were increasingly countered by a deepening of this *same dichotomy*, in materially and discursively separating people from nature, through conservation generally and, especially, through the development of protected areas.

## CONSERVATION, CAPITALISM AND THE NATURE–CULTURE DICHOTOMY

In other words – and this is a crucial argument in the book – *conservation and capitalism have intrinsically co-produced each other, and hence the nature–culture dichotomy is foundational to both.* This point can, again, quite easily be illustrated by looking at historical evidence, in particular the earliest foundations of modern conservation that were laid in a swiftly industrializing Great Britain in the seventeenth and eighteenth centuries. As has been highlighted many times by different authors, it was during this time that the infamous enclosure movement not only established elite tracts of 'wild' lands mostly used for preservation and hunting but at the same time forced people out of rural subsistence and so aided in the formation of the labour reserves that industrial capitalism needed.[74]

---

'lively commodities' such as the animal trade, under capitalism. Rosemary Collard and Jessica Dempsey, 'Life for Sale? The Politics of Lively Commodities', *Environment and Planning A* 45, 11 (2013), 2682–99; Maan Barua, 'Lively Commodities and Encounter Value', *Society and Space* 34, 4 (2016), 725–44.

73  Though, ironically, many still rely heavily on – indeed enjoy working with – hypermodern models and technical tools for monitoring, managing and planning wilderness areas.

74  Igoe, *Conservation*; William Adams, *Against Extinction: The Story of Conservation*

Political Economist Michael Perelman, in particular, shows how the English Game Laws that prohibited rural dwellers and peasants from hunting and collecting wood from 1671 onwards 'became part of the larger movement to cut off large masses of the rural people from their traditional means of production'. This combined dynamic of rural dispossession and emerging elite appreciation for 'wild' lands increasingly led, later in the eighteenth century, to what Perelman refers to as a 'new vision of nature'. According to him, 'polite society no longer admired highly artificial landscapes. Nature was to be managed in such a way that it would look natural.'[75] In other words, early bourgeois ideas about conservation were directly linked to processes of capitalist accumulation and the separation of people from land and 'biodiversity'.[76] This separation, as Environmental historian Dorceta Taylor shows, was further reinforced through the development of country estates, green 'urban enclaves' and urban parks in England and, later, the north-eastern US, allowing elite industrialists to distinguish themselves, and help spur 'early conservation efforts'.[77]

These dynamics intensified unevenly along with capitalism itself and spread, through subjugation and colonization, among other processes, to different parts of the world. According to Igoe, the spread of this dichotomous, western form of (what was to become 'mainstream') conservation moved principally from England to the United States and through colonization to other parts of the world but had several other forms and origins as well, including from France, Germany and elsewhere.[78] This process of the intensification

---

(Earthscan, London, 2004). Though it should be added that the formation of hunting reserves was much older still.

75    Michael Perelman, *The Invention of Capitalism: Classical Political Economy and the Secret History of Primitive Accumulation* (Durham: Duke University Press, 2000), 39, 56.

76    This history, to be sure, and risking overemphasizing the point, is incredibly complex and deserves much more explication. For our argument, however, just mentioning the historical fact suffices. For background reading, see for example, Eric Hobsbawm's chapter on land in *The Age of Revolution* (London: Penguin, 1962).

77    Taylor, *The Rise*, 43–8.

78    Igoe, *Conservation*.

and concomitant spread of conservation and capitalism, clearly, is enormously complex and multidimensional, and cannot here be treated in the depth it deserves.[79] Yet the historical fact remains that conservation, and in particular the creation of nature reserves and fortress protected areas, played a crucial role in what Marx called 'primitive accumulation': the original capitalist process of wresting people from the land through acts of often violent enclosure, forcing them to move across the metabolic rift from country to town in search of urban wage employment.

In her insightful article connecting conservation and primitive accumulation, political ecologist Alice Kelly argues that 'protected area creation, like primitive accumulation, is a violent, ongoing process that alters social relations and practices which can be defined by the enclosure of land or other property, the dispossession of the holders of this property and the creation of the conditions for capitalist production that allow a select few to accumulate wealth'.[80] Importantly, she shows that the people displaced by protected area creation are not necessarily moved in order to create a workforce for capital; they often become simply 'surplus populations'.[81] Instead, capital accumulation through protected area creation can also be

---

79   See John MacKenzie, *The Empire of Nature: Hunting, Conservation and British Imperialism* (Manchester: Manchester University Press, 1988); Richard Grove, *Green Imperialism: Colonial Expansion, Tropical Island Edens and the Origins of Environmentalism, 1600-1860* (Cambridge, UK: Cambridge University Press, 1995); Brockington et al., *Nature Unbound*; Taylor, *The Rise*.

80   Alice Kelly, 'Conservation practice as primitive accumulation', *Journal of Peasant Studies* 38, 4 (2011), 687.

81   Tanya Li shows that this process is arguably most dramatic in Asia. According to her, 'there are three main vectors of rural dispossession in Asia today, none of which has any intrinsic link to the prospect of labour absorption. One is the seizure of land by the state, or state-supported corporations, a practice that is widespread in China, India, and Southeast Asia. The second is the piecemeal dispossession of small-scale farmers, unable to survive when exposed to competition from agricultural systems backed by subsidies and preferential tariffs. The third is the closing of the forest frontier for conservation.' She concludes that in Southeast Asia, 'all three vectors are operating in a kind of pincer movement, dispossessing rural people to a degree that is unprecedented in this region'. Tania Li, 'To Make Live or Let Die? Rural Dispossession and the Protection of Surplus Populations', *Antipode* 41, 1 (2009), 71-2.

'direct' through the commodification of nature wrought by (eco) tourism and other market mechanisms.[82]

These forms of conservation commodification, in turn, come with their own ways of reinforcing the nature–culture dichotomy: in trying to connect people to nature, ironically, they often have the opposite effect of further separating them.[83] Mechanisms like payment for environmental services, biodiversity offsets, and wetlands banking, for instance, all entail efforts to deliver revenue to resource-dependent populations to support conservation as an offset for the impacts of intensified development elsewhere.[84] As Melissa Leach and Ian Scoones point out in relation to carbon offset schemes, 'almost by default, and often against the wishes of project designers, "fortress" forms of conservation forestry in reserves, or uniform plantations, under clear state or private control, become the only way that carbon value can be appropriated through these mechanisms'.[85]

Moreover, the transfer of funds in these mechanisms is almost always from North to South, grounded in the rationale that offsets are most efficient when directed to where opportunity costs are lowest.[86] In the process, these neoliberal conservation mechanisms reinforce a separation between those living in industrialized societies and the

---

82 This is certainly not to claim that protected areas (PAs) were always and everywhere created only to facilitate capitalist accumulation. Clearly many are not, having been developed through state regulation and financing and never generating revenue to cover even their operating cost. The point is that, regardless of their *raison d'être*, even in such cases PAs can work to further overall capitalist development by enclosing rural areas and hence expanding an industrial proletariat. And increasingly, within the neoliberal era, many PAs are pressured to demonstrate their capacity to generate profit.

83 Robert Fletcher, *Romancing the Wild: Cultural Dimensions of Ecotourism* (Durham: Duke University Press, 2009); Fletcher, 'Connection with nature'.

84 Büscher et al., *Nature™ Inc.*

85 Melissa Leach and Ian Scoones, 'Carbon forestry in West Africa: The politics of models, measures and verification processes', *Global Environmental Change* 23, 5 (2013), 965. Also Esther Turnhout, Katja Neves and Elisa de Lijster, 'Measurementality in biodiversity governance: Knowledge, transparency, and the Intergovernmental Science–Policy Platform on Biodiversity and Ecosystem Services (IPBES)', *Environment and Planning A* 46, 3 (2014), 581–97.

86 Molly Doane, *Stealing Shining Rivers: Agrarian Conflict, Market Logic, and Conservation in a Mexican Forest* (Tuscon: University of Arizona Press, 2012).

'natural' spaces these people are invited to visit or conserve elsewhere. Ecotourism, probably the most common form of support for community-based conservation, is then promoted as a means to overcome this division by transporting participants 'back to nature' where their payments can incentivize local conservation efforts.[87] As a result of such practices, the nature–society division is effectively globalized as a component of uneven development.

## CONCLUSION

Much more could be said about these historical dynamics and indeed the importance of extensive historical analysis for understanding contemporary conservation more generally. But the key point that this chapter aimed to make is that the nature–culture dichotomy has long been and continues to be deeply implicated in the continuing co-production of capitalism and conservation. This often occurs, as we have shown, even under approaches that self-consciously seek to collapse the dichotomy by integrating economic and ecological aims in particular spaces. Hence, even if newer market-based conservation mechanisms, such as payments for ecosystems services or natural capital accounting, intentionally seek to overcome the separation between nature and people imposed by the fortress conservation model, they commonly risk reinforcing this same divide through the boundary-making promotion of capitalist logics.[88] Consequently, even when actors deliberately try to move away from the nature–culture dichotomy, as the new conservationists do, they still risk reproducing it in practice if they rely on capitalist mechanisms to achieve conservation.[89]

---

87   Fletcher, *Romancing the Wild.*

88   To be sure, we are not arguing that this logic always works out like this in practice. In fact, it more-than-often does not, as we have shown in previous research: Büscher, 'Payments for Ecosystem Services'; Robert Fletcher and Jan Breitling, 'Market Mechanism or Subsidy in Disguise? Governing Payment for Environmental Services in Costa Rica', *Geoforum* 43 (2012), 402–11.

89   Theoretically, this point can be taken quite a bit further. One could for example argue that an intriguing contradiction between dichotomies/limits and overflow emerges with the new conservation position: Capitalist conservation is built and depends on (the idea

Phrased differently, while new conservation aims to do away with *certain* nature–culture dichotomies, particularly that between the 'wild' and the 'domesticated', they do not discuss or even acknowledge other, subtler yet fundamental dichotomies that they establish or strengthen through their support for capitalist conservation. While new conservation's commitment to moving beyond the nature–culture dichotomy goes deeper than mainstream conservation, it is still not very deep.[90] After all, mainstream conservation, while adhering mostly to 'established' western boundaries around nature for conservation, also commonly acknowledges that this alone is not enough and that a more all-encompassing 'sustainable' or 'green' socio-ecological system needs to be built as well.

In essence, then, new conservation may seem to be a radical alternative to mainstream conservation, but in practice it is decidedly less so. The focus of the new conservation on (overcoming) dichotomies differs from mainstream conservation in degree, not in kind. Both mainstream and new conservation commonly place their faith in capitalist conservation to save nature, which, as we have shown in this section, paradoxically reinforces the very dichotomy that new conservation wants to overcome. This, however, is only one aspect of the troubles with capitalism and its relation to conservation.

---

of) dichotomies and limits, while the socionatures that it mobilizes are increasingly recognized by many conservationists to overflow or exceed these limits and dichotomies. This, in turn, takes on special connotations under capitalism, as the latter has a special relation to limits and boundaries as both impediments to and sources of the creation of new value. Joel Kovel, *The Enemy of Nature: The End of Capitalism or the End of the World?* (London: Zed Books, 2002); Bram Büscher, *Transforming the Frontier: Peace Parks and the Politics of Neoliberal Conservation in Southern Africa* (Durham: Duke University Press, 2013).

90  Braverman, *Wild Life*, 46.

# 3

# The Change Capitalism Makes

In their critique of new conservation, neoprotectionists commonly point to problems of 'growth', 'development', and 'consumption' as key threats to conservation. What they often fail to make explicit – with important exceptions – is that the (socially and environmentally) unsustainable forms of growth, development, and consumption they decry are essential to the sustenance of the capitalist economy itself. A substantial body of research has demonstrated that capitalism is an inherently expansionary system driven by a demand for continual growth in order to overcome the cyclical stagnation that afflicts it. Hence, the last five centuries during which the world has been increasingly – though extremely unevenly – integrated within a single global economy and its resources progressively exploited should be understood, in large part, as a function of the demands of capital. One of the main means of sustaining this growth is through stimulating ever-increasing consumption of an expanded range of products that are often quickly rendered obsolete in order to spur still further consumption. Seriously addressing development, growth, and consumption must therefore lead to a critical focus on the capitalist economy itself.

This, however, is more easily said than done. The 'capitalist economy' is a tremendously complex and contested set of dynamics, ideas and practices that far exceeds those around commodity production, consumption and circulation. Capitalism is decidedly not one-dimensional, in other words, and we must be careful not to 'dichotomize' reality into capitalist versus non-capitalist forms.[1] Alongside these real-world dynamics, complex and extensive debates have developed that are beyond the scope of this book. What matters here is the broader point that capitalist economic development has proven to be profoundly destructive and unsustainable – socially and environmentally. This chapter seeks to explain why this is so, how different actors within the Anthropocene conservation debate have engaged with this important issue and why a shift to a postcapitalist form of conservation is necessary.

Building on the discussions of the metabolic rift in the previous chapter, we start by explicating why this leads to a fundamental contradiction between capitalism and sustainability. Based on recent literature, we emphasize two points. First, that the central problem in the relation between capitalism and sustainability cannot be attributed to the metabolic rift in isolation but must equally emphasize the problem of alienation. Second, that both of these deeply relate to the question of the dichotomy between humans and nature,[2] but that we cannot resort to 'hybridist' monism (seeing the world essentially as one) to move beyond this issue, despite current theory suggesting precisely this. Following recent critiques, we assert that making meaningful distinctions between otherwise integrated parts ('nature' and 'society') is critical for an effective ecological politics to address the unsustainability of capitalism.

At the same time, we show that the role of conservation in global capitalism that these recent critiques neglect is critical to bolster this argument. As we already pointed out in the last chapter, conservation often posits itself directly as a solution to the problem of alienation

---

1 We hereby refer to, lean on and critically engage with traditions in the literature that argue that there are, and that there have always been, spaces not fully captured by or even 'autonomous' from, capital and capitalism. J.K. Gibson-Graham, *A Postcapitalist Politics* (Minneapolis: University of Minnesota Press, 2006). J.K. Gibson-Graham, 'Diverse economies: Performative practices for "other worlds"', *Progress in Human Geography* 32, 5 (2008), 613–32. Paolo Virno and Michael Hardt, eds, *Radical Thought in Italy: A Potential Politics* (Minneapolis, University of Minnesota Press, 1996); Sylvère Lotringer and Christian Marazzi, eds, *Autonomia: Post-Political Politics* (New York: Semiotext(e), 2007).

2 Napoletano et al., 'Has (even Marxist)'.

by allowing humans to experience a connection with a wild, 'auton-omous' nature, seemingly unchanged by capitalism or 'humanity'. Neoprotectionists, especially, come back to this point time and again, arguing that this type of nature is critical both for human sanity and for the survival of our planet. Yet, while they seem to suggest that this implies taking political economy seriously, their bold, new proposal to turn half the planet into protected areas actually achieves the oppo-site, or so we will argue. Through a critical discussion of the 'half earth' idea, we will show that neoprotectionists contradict their own scepti-cism regarding capitalist growth and consumerism by drawing atten-tion (and serious discussion) away from these issues to, once again, focus exclusively on some idealized form of autonomous nature.

This has serious consequences. Not only would 'half earth' dramatically widen the rift between humans and the rest of nature, it also does little to solve historical deprivations caused by both conser-vation and development, including mass poverty. This idea demands that we refocus attention on the close links between conservation and development. Not only is this crucial in order to do justice to the – very real – poverty caused by conservation, but also to demystify development's history and potential. After all, capitalist growth and consumerism are often referred to as – or even replaced with – the more general and positive-sounding 'development'.

By building an understanding of the relationship between conser-vation and development, we show that the latter, especially the way it is currently promoted by new conservationists, is not the answer to conservation's poor social record either. In fact, we show that conservation and *capitalist* development have increasingly become one and the same in the eyes of many conservationists via the idea of 'natural capital'. To truly drive the point about capitalism's unsus-tainability home, therefore, we end the chapter by summarizing our earlier arguments on this latest stage, what we call 'Accumulation by Conservation'.

## THE UNSUSTAINABILITY OF CAPITALISM

The argument that capitalism is ecologically unsustainable is not straightforward and has been discussed at length in various quarters over the last decades. Unsurprisingly, a great chunk of this has centred on understanding 'the significance of Marx's analysis to the contemporary ecological movement'.[3] These are not the only discussions on capitalism's ecological consequences by far, but two of their key contributions are worth highlighting for our purposes. The first refers to what the late sociologist James O'Connor called capitalism's 'second contradiction'.[4] O'Connor argued that, in addition to the first contradiction of capitalism where capital over-accumulates beyond demand, capitalism harbours a second contradiction revolving around a tension between the need for continual growth to stave off overproduction crisis and the inherently finite nature of the material resources upon which this growth depends. As resources become increasingly taxed by the quest for continual growth they become scarcer, causing costs to rise and profits to fall. In this way, O'Connor argued, efforts to resolve capitalism's first contradiction end up exacerbating its second, and vice versa, *ad infinitum*. In the process, natural resources are depleted and both waste and pollution accumulate while economic crisis forever looms on the horizon. The combination of first and second contradictions, according to O'Connor, render capitalism essentially unsustainable in both economic and environmental dimensions.

While this was seen as a breakthrough, O'Connor's second contradiction was also criticized, as 'it tended to subsume environmental contradictions within economic crisis, while failing to see *ecological crises* as serious problems in their own right'. In short, economic crisis

---

3    John Bellamy Foster and Paul Burkett, *Marx and the Earth: An Anti-Critique* (Leiden: Brill, 2017), 2–11.

4    James O'Connor, 'Capitalism, nature, and socialism: A theoretical introduction,' *Capitalism Nature Socialism* 1 (1988); 11–38; James O'Connor, 'Is sustainable capitalism possible?' In *Food for the Future: Conditions and Contradictions of Sustainability*, P. Allen, ed. (New York: Wiley-Interscience, 1994).

could lead to ecological damage, but not vice versa. It is this point in particular that subsequent analyses sought to remedy, especially by revisiting the ideas of Marx, along with other nineteenth-century thinkers, around the metabolic rift. As noted by sociologist John Bellamy Foster and economist Paul Burkett: 'the intensifying ecological problem of capitalist society could be traced therefore mainly to the rift in the metabolism between human beings and nature (that is, the alienation of nature) that formed the very basis of capitalism's existence as a system, made worse by accumulation, i.e. capitalism's own expansion.'[5] In other words, economy and ecology are always dialectically integrated, parts of a metabolic unity, that capitalism ruptures by turning human and nonhuman nature into commodities to stimulate growth *ad infinitum*. This is the ultimate reason why capitalism is unsustainable and why revolution is imperative.

Yet this conclusion, while important, does not answer anything or provide a way forward. It also does not mean that capitalism will 'automatically' be toppled as ecological crises reach boiling point. According to David Harvey, Naomi Klein and others, evidence suggests that capitalism might be able to not only deal with but, more dangerously, profit from ecological disaster.[6] The imperative for revolution therefore also comes from another reason for capitalism's unsustainability, namely its tendency to lead to extreme alienation from nature, understood as the 'estrangement of the necessary organic relation between human beings and nature'[7] In a sense, this argument provides another, deeper understanding of the problem of the nature–culture dichotomy: Not only are human and nonhuman natures often seen as separate, they have also become deeply estranged from each other.[8] Interestingly,

---

5   Foster and Burkett, *Marx and the Earth*, 5–6.

6   David Harvey, *Seventeen Contradictions and the End of Capitalism* (London: Profile Books, 2014), 260; Naomi Klein, *The Shock Doctrine. The Rise of Disaster Capitalism* (New York: Picador, 2007).

7   Harvey, *Seventeen*, 261; Foster and Burkett, *Marx and the Earth*, 37, 235.

8   Napoletano et al., 'Has (even Marxist)'. This is not to imply that humans can *ontologically* become estranged from the larger nature of which they are part, only that they can develop an illusory, yet material sense of such alienation (see Fletcher, 'Connection with nature').

from a theoretical point of view, this has, perhaps indirectly, led to various 'turns' in contemporary theory under labels such as 'more-than-human' and 'animal' geographies and 'new materialism'. While diverse, these perspectives all stress a need to bring ecosystems, nature and animals back into the analysis and focus on what unites human and nonhuman natures rather than what differentiates them. Yet, in doing so, they have swung the pendulum much too far: They seemingly aim to erase many if not most meaningful and essential distinctions between humans and the rest of nature that remain essential for ecological politics.[9]

This, then, is where we need to become more precise about the dichotomy. The fact that human natures and nonhuman natures are always inherently co-constituted does not mean, in our view, succumbing to monism and seeing everything in the world as simply 'hybrids' or 'assemblages'. Following other scholars, we argue that moving beyond the dichotomy – and hence acknowledging the fundamental and organic co-constitution of human and nonhuman natures – requires at the same time careful analytical and empirical acknowledgement of the 'relative autonomy of parts' across and between the different categories, especially in relation to the role of humans.[10] As Kate Soper asserts, a meaningful ecological politics can only occur based on a critical realist 'acknowledgement of human exceptionality'.[11] Only this stance can acknowledge human alienation from nature as a possibility, and thus open up potential for different and *better* relationships between humans and the rest of nature. The next chapter will explicate these issues more fully.

## A REVOLUTION OF CAPITALISM?

In all of this, the question concerning the necessity for revolution remains. After all, the basic unsustainability of (contemporary)

---

9   Malm, *The Progress.*

10   Richard Lewontin and Richard Levins, in Malm, *The Progress*, 182.

11   Kate Soper, *What is Nature? Culture, Politics and the Non-Human* (Cambridge, MA: Blackwell, 1995), 40.

capitalism has also been endorsed by many capitalist actors, who see a better capitalism as the logical answer. Increasingly influential initiatives such as *Breakthrough Capitalism* and *Plan B* make this explicit; they plainly state that the way capitalism currently operates is 'failing economically, socially and environmentally' and that, following Peter Bakker, the president of the World Business Council on Sustainable Development, 'we need a revolution of capitalism'.[12] Crucially, however, these actors believe that capitalism can be *made* sustainable. Through market-based instruments (MBIs) and other forms of economic valuation, but also broader 'varieties of green capitalism' such as the 'green economy', global capitalist actors are currently trying to imagine and – to a degree – build a new, more environmentally sensitive accumulation model in response to the global ecological crisis.

In doing so, many draw on the influential 'manifesto for sustainable capitalism' by Al Gore and David Blood, which argues that we must move away from 'short-termism' and build 'a more long-term and responsible form of capitalism'.[13] This includes negation of the alienation from nature through the commodification of conservation. In other words, this is a form of accumulation that takes conservation not as a Polanyian double-movement in response to environmental destruction, but aims to render it equal to – and so balance out – extraction and destruction while ensuring that humans can continue to be connected to and derive meaning from the rest of nature. Indeed, through ecotourism, nature documentaries, adventure sports and so forth, connection to nature to deal with modern-day alienation has become extremely profitable. The model of conservation that follows from this we have previously labelled 'accumulation by conservation'.

This, then, is the one element that many critical scholars of the relation between capitalism and the environment often forget or minimize: the essential role that conservation has long played in the

---

12    See breakthroughcapitalism.com and bteam.org.

13    Al Gore and David Blood, 'We Need Sustainable Capitalism', 5 November 2008, algore.com, accessed 6 October 2017.

development of global capitalism. According to David Harvey, alienation comes from 'the kind of ecological system that capital constructs',
namely as 'functionalist, engineered and technocratic'.[14] Andreas
Malm holds that 'the curse of capital is that it can emancipate itself
from nature in all its sparkling autonomy only by colonising it, lining
it up in rows and marching it off to the chimneys of accumulation'.[15]
But while this is often true, nature's autonomy is explicitly promoted
in much conservation policy and posited as a direct response and as
a way to mediate and even 'offset' the other forms of alienated natures
that 'capital constructs'. Later in this chapter, we will show that this
form of capitalist displacement of the alienation problem does not
actually solve capitalism's fundamental unsustainability. But, for now,
it is important to acknowledge that conservation has long seen its role
as putting boundaries around certain natures in order to 'save' them
from the chimneys of capital (or from 'humans' more generally) and to
allow them to remain as 'autonomous' as possible. Neoprotectionists,
especially, worry about this though we need to clarify precisely what
they mean when they refer to autonomy or 'self-willed'. This is, we
argue, the change that capitalism makes.

## CAPITALIST CHANGE AND CONSERVATION

In our reading of both recent and older neoprotectionist literatures,
a core element that comes back time and again is the question of
change. The global capitalist economy is a major change-machine
and has dramatically transformed social and ecological environments
worldwide.[16] Many neoprotectionists – and, indeed, many mainstream
conservationists – dislike and/or resist these types of human-induced

---

14  Harvey, *Seventeen*, 261.

15  Malm, *The Progress*, 211.

16  To be sure, even though we will argue that capitalism is logically unsustainable,
we are emphatically not arguing that all of capitalist change has been for the worse. The
question of how to evaluate capitalist change on a general level depends on the extremely
complex and situated positionalities of different actors, whereby the distribution of fortune
and misfortune depends on numerous factors, including but not only the worldviews of
these actors. Cf. Harvey, *Seventeen*.

change, especially when these render natural environments 'engineered, functionalist and technocratic'. Soulé, for example, expresses
a common concern when he writes that 'the global speedup affects
everything, from the pace of elections to how fast we walk, to happiness metrics, stock trades, and the rate of species extinction – which is
expected to grow by a factor of 10,000 compared to its preagricultural
baseline rate'.[17]

Consequently, neoprotectionists have long advocated for establishing boundaries and limits to human-induced change, including
the growth and spread of humans themselves. This basic element of
the neoprotectionist perspective, it seems, has now evolved (again
with some important exceptions) to increasingly include more radical
critiques of growth, consumerism and development more generally.
This stance is most clearly evident in growing rewilding campaigns
advocating a return to a 'prehuman baseline' from which *all* (directly)
human-induced change is eliminated, but it is apparent in less extreme
(neo)protectionist positions as well.

As noted above, the history of conservation is often depicted as a
Polanyian 'double-movement' to counter the most devastating effects
of global capitalism (both socially and ecologically, although neoprotectionists focus almost exclusively on the latter). This double-movement perspective is deeply engrained within the fabric of conservation
and its science. Much of conservation biology, after all, is about trying
to understand the effects of human-induced change on biodiversity
and what species and ecosystems need in order to survive despite these
changes.[18] Hence, in addition to the particulars of ecological function
and behaviour, a key question for contemporary conservation biology is: how do human-induced land-use or ecosystemic changes and
other broader economic, social and related dynamics affect nonhuman nature and how can this be mitigated so that the latter remains as
autonomous as possible and ecosystems, species and their functions
remain viable for the long term?

---

17    Soulé, 'The new conservation', 67.
18    Pearce, *The New Wild*, 70.

In answering this question, the issue of 'baselines' or thresholds is, again, central; it is not for nothing that Marris starts her book by criticizing conservation's obsession with baselines. The idea of baselines is essentially to establish a certain desired 'natural' state of plant and animal species and an ecosystemic balance which can be retained or, if necessary, recreated through activities such as rewilding.[19] As Tim Caro and colleagues describe, 'planning and setting goals for conservation action usually require relatively intact areas that serve as baselines for comparisons and to set targets'.[20] As previously noted, this baseline is commonly – implicitly or explicitly – a 'prehuman' one. In this way, Marris asserts,

> For many conservationists, restoration to a prehuman or pre-European baseline is seen as healing a wounded or sick nature. For others, it is an ethical duty. We broke it; therefore we must fix it. Baselines thus typically don't just act as a scientific before to compare with an after. They become the good, the goal, the one correct state.

But, Marris continues, the 'most vexing issue with prehuman baselines is that they are increasingly impossible to achieve – either through restoration or management of wild areas. Every ecosystem, from the deepest heart of the largest national park to the weeds growing behind the local big-box store, has been touched by humans.'[21]

In attacking the nature–culture dichotomy from the perspective of the Anthropocene, new conservationists thus also question and aim to rethink a foundational element of conservation policy and science: how to understand and deal with human-induced ecological

---

19    The idea of thresholds and broader, related ideas around 'planetary boundaries' and 'tipping points' come from the same basic worry, but focus on the opposite side, namely the question of to what degree certain natural or ecosystems, dynamics, processes or spaces can be changed without drastically changing shape, function or (ecological) 'service'. Will Steffen et al., 'Planetary Boundaries: Guiding human development on a changing planet', *Science* 347, 6223 (2015), 736–47.

20    Tim Caro et al., 'Conservation in the Anthropocene'. In *Keeping the Wild*, George Wuerthner et al., 112.

21    Marris, *Rambunctious*, 3, 5.

change.[22] In fact, they go one step further still. Some argue that we need to embrace and move along with the 'great change machine' itself. As Kareiva et al. paradigmatically pointed out, 'instead of scolding capitalism, conservationists should partner with corporations in a science-based effort to integrate the value of nature's benefits into their operations and cultures'.[23] This is nothing short of a complete transformation of the historical framing of conservation within broader processes of capitalist change; instead of a countermovement to ameliorate its worst ecological impacts, conservation is now urged to become part and parcel of this specific form of change and its 'operations and cultures'. In other words, while capitalism and conservation have always been intimately related, the nature of this relation, according to new conservationists, needs to be drastically transformed.

Hence, what new conservation is effectively advocating – and what further differentiates it from mainstream capitalist conservation – is not just a paradigm shift, but also a cultural and institutional shift in relation to the very *spirit* of conservation practice and science. All of this, as we saw, is clearly much too drastic a change for those who see themselves as 'real' or hardcore conservationists. In fact, it is precisely this proposed shift that according to Soulé is so drastic that it 'does not deserve to be labelled conservation' at all.[24] Conservation, according to most neoprotectionists, is not about moving along with forms of capitalist change; it is, ultimately, about placing boundaries around this change; about drawing 'lines in the sand' – both geographically

---

22   Thomas, *Inheritors of the Earth*, 8, *emphasis added*, is paradigmatic here: 'The biological world is in constant flux. Dynamic change means that we face an indefinite future of biological gains as well as losses – often with humans the underlying cause. What are we to make of this human-altered world? The default stance of conservation is to keep things as *unchanged* as possible or, alternatively, to return conditions to what they used to be, or somehow to make the Earth "more natural" (*which can only be interpreted as meaning 'with reduced human impact'*). Not only are these untenable aspirations while the world's human population continues to grow and each of us consumes more resources, but hold-the-line strategies implicitly dismiss as undesirable the continuing biological gains of the human epoch. Where is the logic in this?'

23   Kareiva et al., 'Conservation'.

24   Soulé, 'The new conservation', 895.

through protected areas and in the social, economic, political and reproductive realms via regulation and other policy measures.

We have already given some examples, but several key statements from neoprotectionists drive the point home: Paul Kingsnorth describes conservation as 'trying to protect large functioning ecosystems from human development'; Tom Butler as 'promoting a reasoned discussion of retrenchment' in the face of a 'modern, techno-industrial society where the civil religion of progress means ever-more commodification of nature to serve economic growth'; and, in response to new conservationists' assertion that nature is constantly changing, Curt Meine pithily asserts,

> that not all change is created equal; that the causes, rates, spatial scales, types, and impacts of ecological disturbance and environmental change vary; that natural and anthropogenic change are interwoven in complex ways; and that our challenge is to calibrate more finely our understanding of historic change, and to explore more carefully our ethical response to the human role amid such change.[25]

While both radical camps seek to ameliorate the negative effects of capitalist change, in short, they fundamentally differ concerning *how* to deal with this change. So, what if we approach the Anthropocene conservation problem from the other end, from the perspective of neoprotectionists? How do their proposed solutions hold up to the 'great change machine' they so desperately want to curtail?

### RESISTING (CAPITALIST) CHANGE?

In chapter three, we already outlined the untenable contradictions in the new conservation strategy in terms of moving along with capitalist forms of change. But the neoprotectionist response to the new conservation agenda and the subsequent intensification of their earlier ideas

---

25   Kingsnorth, 'Rise of the Neo-greens', 5; Tom Butler, 'Lives not our Own'. In *Keeping the Wild*, George Wuerthner et al., xii; Meine, 'What's So New', 50.

and proposals also contain several untenable contradictions. What the current neoprotectionist response in effect seems to boil down to is a retreat into – or a harkening back to – more classical or traditional understandings of conservation, conservation science and how these have regarded, conceptualized and institutionalized nature, wilderness and development. Several neoprotectionists, as we have shown, literally feel they are 'under attack' for this position. In response, they strike back by retrenching into their favoured fortress position. This counter-attack has several important dimensions.

A rather quixotic dimension is that many neoprotectionists seem to want to go back in time, in two ways. First, by quite literally taking nature to a time before it was changed by humans and their economic and various modes of operation and production. Here, the obsession with baselines is again crucial: the idea that nature, in earlier times, before capitalist development, when humans were less dominant or even absent altogether, was somehow purer, more pristine, even 'Edenic' and 'untouched'. These oft-used terms indicate that any form of human-induced change renders nature to some degree 'impure', modified, spoiled. If we were to take this logic too seriously, it would mean that conservation becomes logically impossible in the Anthropocene, where there is a broad consensus – even among neoprotectionists – that no nature on planet earth is *actually* 'untouched'. The only thing then to do, paradoxically, is to use an often-heavy human hand to create and/or maintain wilderness spaces that reduce 'unwanted' human influence to a minimum.

Second, and more figuratively, neoprotectionists seek to go back to an institutional time when they could focus mostly on nature, and not so much on people. The sea change that has taken place with the rise of the community-based conservation and people-and-parks paradigms in the 1990s and early 2000s – opposed by many of these same neoprotectionists at the time[26] – was not only the start of broader efforts to neoliberalize nature and conservation, but also a major change in how conservation had to operate institutionally. Instead of

---

26   Oates, *Myth and Realities*; Terborgh, *Requiem*.

a predominant focus on nature and the protected areas where 'pristine' nature was found, conservationists and conservation organizations now had to take diverse social surroundings, especially around protected areas, seriously. This had major organizational, institutional and discursive implications. As a large literature has shown, organizations set up 'people-and-parks' or 'community' departments and started emphasizing the many benefits that communities can or should derive from conservation.[27] As a South African protected area manager told one of us in 2007, 'in the last years, South African National Parks [the national parks authority] has had to change as an organization to take into account the surroundings of protected areas and not regard them as pure islands. There was a realization that we do not live in isolation'.[28]

This process was, and still is, difficult or uncomfortable for many conservationists. As John Terborgh and Carel van Schaik, two well-known neoprotectionists, asserted:

No apology should be required for adhering to the accepted definition of a (national) park as a haven for nature where people, *except for visitors, staff, and concessionaires,* are excluded. To advocate anything else for developing countries, simply because they are poor (one hopes, a temporary condition) is to advocate a double standard, something we find deplorable.[29]

These authors and others essentially seek to detach conservation from specific political, economic and social contexts and to advocate a universal blueprint of a classical protected area to ground conservation efforts throughout the world. This, however, does not mean that

---

27    Borgerhoff Mulder and Coppolillo, *Conservation*; Sibongile Masuku van Damme and Lynn Meskell, 'Producing Conservation and Community in South Africa', *Ethics, Place & Environment* 12, 1 (2009), 69–89.

28    Interview with a South African National Parks park manager, 31 May 2007.

29    John Terborgh and Carel van Schaik, 'Why the World Needs Parks'. In *Making Parks Work: Strategies for Preserving Tropical Nature*, John Terborgh et al., eds (Washington, DC: Island Press, 2002), 6.

neoprotectionists are against addressing poverty per se, as they are sometimes accused of. Rather, many of them believe that development interventions should take place independently from conservation, since attempting to merge the two aims is seen to undermine both.[30] For them, the traditional institutional strategy for saving nature behind fences and the 'hard certainties it offers' is seen as the most realistic and effective way to operate in a growing state of 'siege'.[31] Neoprotectionists' emphasis is therefore on 'saving nature' rather than addressing social issues. It is this emphasis that is meant to ensure that the ecological base upon which humanity depends stays intact. The problematic contradiction is therefore not necessarily that neoprotectionists are 'against people'.[32] It is, rather, that they think they can resolve the ecological contradictions of capitalism by fortifying and amplifying the nature–culture dichotomy, that is, by putting (more) boundaries between people and nature.

There is some logic in this position. After all, these tactics seem to have saved important tracts of nature from previous waves of capitalist development.[33] At the same time, neoprotectionists – like all of us – cannot actually go back in time (even though they do at times seem to try, particularly through attempts at rewilding). The desire to turn back the clock thus leads to some strange contradictions. One especially interesting example in the context of this book concerns the relation between notions of self-willed nature and neoprotectionists' worries about capitalist consumerism and development. As Lorimer and Driessen note of the neoprotectionists' rewilding programme: 'fungible, laissez-faire neoliberal natures and fluid, self-willed ecologies are ontologically not that different'. Ecologist Curtis Freese, from a neoprotectionist perspective, similarly describes potential

---

30    John Terborgh et al., eds, *Making Parks Work*.

31    Daniel Brockington, *Fortress Conservation: The Preservation of the Mkomazi Game Reserve, Tanzania*, (Oxford: James Currey, 2002), 127.

32    Bram Büscher, and Wolfram Dressler, 'Linking Neoprotectionism and Environmental Governance: On the Rapidly Increasing Tensions Between Actors in the Environment-Development Nexus', *Conservation and Society* 5, 4 (2007), 586–611.

33    George Wuerthner et al., eds, *Protecting the Wild*.

synergies between 'the growing ecological movement for rewilding and emerging methods of payment for ecosystem services of range-lands'.[34] The question of how to tackle capitalist imperatives of growth and consumerism therefore remains rather vague, and certainly not answered by a focus on protected areas or rewilding.[35]

Another important dimension in this discussion, noted by Braverman, is that, while neoprotectionists hold on to dualism in theory, they are often forced to be 'holistic in their practice'.[36] Hence, even while neoprotectionists passionately argue for separating humans and nature in very dichotomous ways, they themselves also realize that, in practice, they do need to deal with people, politics and real-world contradictions. Irus Braverman supports her statement by citing a conservation biologist who argues that conservation practice is often a 'sophisticated bricolage approach to the world'. While this may be true, whether it counts as a 'holistic' approach is questionable. Holism in practice may be what transpires *despite* dualist theory. But the latter does not provide a good guide for proactive holistic prac-tice, nor does it provide a convincing answer to the broader problems of capitalist change about which neoprotectionists feel increasingly uneasy. Arguably, the most illustrative example of this is the recent 'half earth' or 'nature needs half' proposal advanced by Wilson and many others.

### HALF EARTH TO THE RESCUE?

According to neoprotectionists, science indicates that the only way to tackle the ecological crisis, and so avoid the collapse of human

---

34 Lorimer and Driessen, 'Wild Experiments', 179. Curtis Freese, 'A New Era of Protected Areas for the Great Plains'. In *Protecting the Wild*, George Wuerthner et al., 211.

35 To add to this point: attempting to cordon off portions of the planet does nothing to address economic growth *in general*. It may reduce the spread of the capitalist economy to some degree in some places, but this only means that the growth imperative must contin-ually intensify exploitation of the remaining available space, which would be an unsustain-able situation for both this space and conservation areas that will be inevitably impacted by the spill-over effects of this overdevelopment.

36 Braverman, *Wild Life*, 47.

civilization, is to turn half the planet into a protected area. But it is not just science that led them to this radical proposal. It is also a newfound assertiveness to be bold about what is needed in the face of overwhelming odds and the urgency of the 'sixth extinction' crisis. And this newfound assertiveness means defending what they 'know' to be right and proven effective: protected areas. Hence it should be no surprise that, in the face of an extreme problem, they propose an equally extreme solution. As the slogan 'nature needs half' indicates, the focus is again fully back on nature and what 'it' needs. Essentially: more space to be autonomous, away from humans or human-induced change.[37]

There are many problematic aspects to this proposal. Together with a group of scholars, we highlighted some of these.[38] For one, much research has shown that protected areas often do not work very well in many biodiverse areas and in many countries with weak governance regimes.[39] So how will the half-earth plan be implemented in practice? How will these protected areas remain socially, politically and culturally legitimate? How will forms of corruption, and the fact that many protected areas are either paper parks in practice or simply have porous borders that do little to stop resource extraction, impact the plan? And how will neoprotectionists halt the increasing intrusion of extractive industry into protected areas?[40] These are just a few illustrative issues where this dualistic solution cannot provide a good guide to actual conservation practice in its local and broader social,

---

37   Humans, according to E.O. Wilson, behave as the 'most destructive species' and a 'hostile race of aliens'. Wilson, *Half-Earth*, 54, 72.

38   Bram Büscher et al., 'Half-Earth or Whole Earth? Radical ideas for conservation and their implications', *Oryx* 51, 3 (2017), 407–10.

39   Prakash Kashwan, 'What explains the demand for collective forest rights amidst land use conflicts?' *Journal of Environmental Management* 183 (2016), 657–66.

40   Roldan Muradian, Mariana Walter and Joan Martinez-Alier, 'Hegemonic Transitions and Global Shifts in Social Metabolism: Implications for Resource-rich Countries: Introduction to the Special Section', *Global Environmental Change* 22, 3 (2012), 559–67; Nathalie Butt et al., 'Biodiversity Risks from Fossil Fuel Extraction', *Science* 342 (2013), 425–26; Esteban Suárez et al., 'Oil Industry, Wild Meat Trade and Roads: Indirect Effects of Oil Extraction Activities in a Protected Area in North-Eastern Ecuador', *Animal Conservation*, 12 (2014), 364–73.

political economic, cultural and other contexts. This is in large part, we contend, because the effort to deal with these issues does not address their foundation in the capitalist processes of expansion and accumulation outlined earlier.

Hence, despite their impassioned critique of the effects of both capitalist development and capitalist conservation and the need to defend against these, neoprotectionists offer few concrete suggestions for how this can be done, beyond vague calls for stronger states to intervene to protect threatened resources in revived fortress fashion. Or, in Wilson's case, a confused, ungrounded faith in the free market's invisible hand. In making such calls, they do not address the initial critiques of fortress conservation either. These showed that, in reality, the approach did not work very well in many circumstances, particularly in societies with weak impoverished states under the influence of powerful multinational conglomerates eyeing their valuable natural resources. Hence, community-based conservation and other mechanisms intended to link conservation and development sought precisely to introduce other means whereby states and citizens could be induced to support conservation in place of a faltering fortress model. It is unclear how an even stronger insistence on imposing a model that was often ineffective in the first place is intended to stand as a realistic, workable model for the future.[41]

Another set of problematic issues regarding 'half-earth' relate to the issue of 'development' and its negative impacts on conservation. The major contradiction here is that while the 'half-earth' solution is proposed to address these effects, it almost completely ignores what humans are supposed to do in 'their' side of earth. How will neoprotectionists ensure that the activities of the human-half of earth, arguably still fully integrated into (intensifying?) capitalist development, will not affect the 'nature-half'? One only has to think here about climate change or many other effects of contemporary industrial production, transport and consumption that easily cross borders to show how gratuitous and contradiction-riddled this plan really is. Simplistically

---

41   Wilshusen et al., 'Reinventing a square wheel'.

shutting half the earth away behind park boundaries, in short, cannot solve or contain the negative effects of a capitalist development model that does not respect (and in fact thrives on transcending) boundaries in the first place.[42] While half of nature on earth is supposed to be left unchanged by humans, the ways in which human-oriented activities and processes affect nature on a global scale are almost completely ignored.

This leads to a related point. The half-earth proposal, and indeed the broader neoprotectionist perspective, fails to explain how poverty can be addressed alongside conservation. After all, dramatic poverty continues to persist alongside many conservation areas, and – important social justice implications notwithstanding – this continues to diminish conservation's effectiveness due to the increased pressure it places on protected resources by people with often few other options.[43] More generally, it is apparent that socio-economic inequality is, on the whole, inversely proportionate to effective conservation, and facilitates (increasingly violent) conflicts around protected areas.[44] Turning half-earth into a reality under present socio-political arrangements would likely make all this worse, as it would require massive dispossession and relocation of poor and marginalized communities, making the enlarged protected area estate overall more socially unsustainable.

The importance of addressing poverty for conservation is something that new conservationists have usefully brought back to the

---

42   Kovel, *The Enemy*.

43   Rosaleen Duffy et al., 'Towards a new understanding of the links between poverty and illegal wildlife hunting', *Conservation Biology* 30, 1 (2016), 14–22.

44   Gregory Mikkelson, Andrew Gonzalez and Garry Peterson, 'Economic Inequality Predicts Biodiversity Loss', *PLOS One* 2, 5 (16 May 2007), plos.org; Tim Holland, Garry Peterson and Andrew Gonzalez, 'A cross-national analysis of how economic inequality predicts biodiversity loss', *Conservation Biology* 23, 5 (2009), 1304–13; Chistina Hicks et al., 'Engage key social concepts for sustainability', *Science* 352 (2016), 38–40; Rosaleen Duffy, *Nature Crime: How We're Getting Conservation Wrong* (New Haven, CT: Yale University Press, 2010); Duffy, 'Waging a war'; Justin Brashares et al., 'Wildlife Decline and Social Conflict', *Science*, 345 (2014), 376–78; Büscher and Ramutsindela, 'Green Violence'; Francis Massé and Elizabeth Lunstrum, 'Accumulation by securitization: Commercial poaching, neoliberal conservation, and the creation of new wildlife frontiers', *Geoforum* 69 (2016), 227–37.

centre of attention. Yet, the way they have mainly done so is by using the language and promise of 'development'. As Kareiva and colleagues paradigmatically noted, 'Conservation should seek to support and inform the *right kind of development* – development by design, done with the importance of nature to thriving economies foremost in mind. And it will utilize the right kinds of technology to enhance the health and well-being of both human and nonhuman natures.'[45] This may sound good at a superficial level. But it is illusory when the 'development' they are talking about is specifically *capitalist* development, which tends to exacerbate the very inequality – and hence often also the poverty – that new conservationists seek to redress.[46] This is yet another element of the unsustainability of capitalism that must be rendered explicit.

## THE CONTRADICTIONS OF *CAPITALIST* DEVELOPMENT

The starting point for most contemporary mainstream discourses about capitalism and policies on development is that the latter is needed to address poverty. Famous development pundits like Jeffrey Sachs, for example, have repeatedly stated that focused development assistance can solve extreme poverty in a generation. His understanding of development, however, is rather blunt and linear:

> As a global society, we should ensure that the *international rules of the game in economic management* do not advertently or inadvertently set snares along the lower rungs of the ladder in the form of inadequate development assistance, protectionist trade barriers, destabilizing global financial practices, poorly designed rules for intellectual property, and the like, that prevent the low-income world from *climbing up the rungs* of development.[47]

---

45 Kareiva et al., 'Conservation', emphasis added.

46 Thomas Piketty, *Capital in the Twenty-First Century* (Cambridge, MA: Harvard University Press, 2014).

47 Jeffrey Sachs, *The End of Poverty: Economic Possibilities for Our Time* (New York: Penguin, 2005), 24–5, emphasis added. One of the outcomes of this type of thinking was the

This discourse remains pervasive among international development planners. Capitalist development in this discourse is analogous to 'improvement', with its connotations of progress, betterment and positive change.[48] Importantly, however, capitalist development and 'improvement' share a long and closely intertwined history. Meiksins Wood argues that the concept of improvement 'tells us a great deal about . . . the development of capitalism', particularly in the context of seventeenth-century English agriculture:

> The word 'improve' itself, in its original meaning, did not mean just 'make better' in a general sense but literally meant to do something for monetary profit, especially to cultivate land for profit . . . By the seventeenth century, the word 'improver' was firmly fixed in the language to refer to someone who rendered land productive and profitable, especially by enclosing it or reclaiming waste.

Pushing this argument further, Meiksins Wood emphasizes that '"improvement" meant, even more fundamentally, new forms and conceptions of property'. With this, she refers to 'capitalist conceptions of property – not only as "private" but as *exclusive*'. This exclusion necessarily entails *enclosure*, which in turn means 'not simply a physical fencing of land but the extinction of common and customary use rights on which many people depended for their livelihood'.[49] Enclosure with its links to the history of protected areas and conservation more generally, then becomes a form of dispossession, as previously described. This process, as Perelman, Harvey and others emphasize, is a

---

millennium village development project, which assumed that poverty would be eradicated by establishing the enabling conditions of (biopolitical) capitalist society around property rights, investments, healthcare, schooling, and so forth. Critical analysis of these same villages has showed that this approach failed miserably in solving poverty and that in fact many people were dispossessed in the process. Japhy Wilson, 'The Village that Turned to Gold: A Parable of Philanthrocapitalism', *Development and Change* 47, 1 (2015), 3–28.

48   Tania Murray Li, *The Will to Improve: Governmentality, Development, and the Practice of Politics* (Durham: Duke University Press, 2007).

49   Ellen Meiksins Wood, *The Origin of Capitalism: A Longer View* (London: Verso, 2002), 106–8.

continuous and ongoing rather than an exclusively historical process (hence, Harvey's reworking of 'primitive accumulation' as 'accumulation by dispossession').[50] All this together risks becoming *cyclical* if we follow Li's argument that one of the several 'deeply embedded contradictions' in improvement and development discourses is 'the contradiction between the promotion of capitalist processes and concern to improve the condition of the dispossessed'.[51] *Development as capitalist improvement, ironically, is both the cause of and is often presented as the answer to dispossession, poverty and inequality.*

The conventional depiction of development as the antidote rather than cause of poverty and inequality presents an interesting and important parallel to the history of conservation, namely its common depiction as a Polanyian countermovement to capitalist 'progress'. Similarly, following Li, Meiksins Wood and others, development-as-improvement is historically and still often seen as a countermovement to the inevitable dispossession that follows capitalist development. Yet a substantial body of research in political ecology, post-development and other literatures demonstrates that instead of solving poverty, capitalist development has in fact long *produced*, and continues to produce, poverty, exclusion, marginalization and inequality.[52]

For us, this conclusion is grounded in theories of 'uneven geographical development'. While there are various theories to explain this, including problematic 'environmentalist' theories that attribute developmental (mis)fortunes to differential environmental conditions,[53] we here build again on David Harvey's perspective.

---

50    Perelman, *The Invention*; David Harvey, *The New Imperialism* (Oxford: Oxford University Press 2003).

51    Li, *The Will*, 31.

52    Arturo Escobar, *Encountering Development: The Making and Unmaking of the Third World* (Princeton: Princeton University Press, 1995); Ivan Illich, 'Development as Planned Poverty'. In *The Post-Development Reader*, Majid Rahnema and Victoria Bawtree, eds (London: Zed Books, 1997), 94–102. Rahnema and Bawtree, *The Post-Development*.

53    For example, Jared Diamond, *Guns, Germs, and Steel: The Fates of Human Societies* (New York: WW Norton & Company, 1997); Paul Collier, *The Bottom Billion: Why the Poorest Countries are Failing and What Can Be Done about It* (Oxford: Oxford University Press, 2008).

Harvey proposes four conditionalities as foundations for his theory of uneven geographical development: the material embedding of capital accumulation processes in the web of socio-ecological life; accumulation by dispossession; the institutional legitimation ('law-like character') of capital accumulation in space and time; and political and social struggles at various geographic scales.[54] One could say that these conditions generate a specific 'formative context' that ritualizes and naturalizes what Harvey calls capitalism's 'abstractions and fictions'.[55] It would take too much to fully explain these conditions in detail, and in any case this is not our objective here. The key elements we take from Harvey's theory are that capitalist accumulation is non-dichotomous but dialectical (embedded in the 'web of life'); that it creates systemic inequalities (by dispossessing some to allow others and the system to accumulate); and that all this is institutionalized and subject to struggle in myriad ways.

Harvey's theory of uneven geographical development, in short, demonstrates that people around the world are not poor because of their innate incapability to produce meaningful lives. They are poor because they are the losers in a broader political economic struggle based on accumulation by dispossession.[56] Capitalist development, therefore, entails an inherent and perennial set of contradictions, which is why it is crucial to move beyond it.[57] In failing to directly confront these contradictions, neither neoprotectionism nor new conservation actually resolve the critical issues of poverty and

----

54    Harvey, *Spaces of Global Capitalism*, 71, 75.

55    Harvey warns against construing these products of capitalism's logic as 'the property of some mystical external force – outside the "web of life" and immune to materialist influences' and locates agency with 'a disparate group of people called capitalists'. Capitalists, Harvey points out, adapt to new conditions, harnessing what Marx called the 'elastic' powers of capital in search of its surplus; capitalist historical geography is both flexible and adaptable.

56    Harvey, *The New Imperialism*; This also implies that we do not think that people stop being poor when they start earning more than a dollar and a half a day, as the World Bank would argue. Poverty is a much more complicated positionality that always relates to individual needs, possibilities and options within a more structural framework of constraints and opportunities that changes constantly and rapidly.

57    Harvey, *Seventeen*.

inequality in relation to conservation. And this is because neither adequately address the issue of *capitalist* development nor do they confront the urgent need to move beyond this if we are to achieve either conservation or poverty alleviation – let alone both in concert.[58]

Yet – and we want to be unequivocal here – this is not because contradictions are necessarily negative. As Harvey points out, 'the contradictions of capital have often spawned innovations, many of which have improved the qualities of daily life'. At the same time, however, he forcefully argues that capitalist development harbours various types of contradictions that make the system as a whole crisis-prone and inherently socially, economically, culturally and environmentally unstable and unsustainable. Several of these, according to Harvey, are 'disparities of income and wealth', 'capital's relation to nature' and 'universal alienation'.[59] In the remainder of this chapter, we will explore how these first two contradictions of capitalist development historically relate to, enable and ultimately undermine conservation. In further chapters, we will come back to the question of alienation.

## CONSERVATION AND CAPITALIST DEVELOPMENT

The historical relations between conservation and capitalist development are complex. One argument that we have been making in this book is that the close and inherent relations between these processes have

---

58    At their extremes, strangely, the two positions seem to converge to some degree in their efforts – equally confused from both sides – to address conservation and development together. As noted, Wilson advocates a process of 'decoupling' whereby intensive free-market based development grounded in accelerated technological innovation in one half of the earth would be offset by fortress conservation in the other. From the new conservation camp, the Breakthrough Institute has advanced its own proposal of decoupling for conservation in which, similarly, intensified forms of technology-dependent economic development in certain areas would supposedly free space for relatively hands-off conservation to flourish elsewhere (see the Ecomodernist Manifesto at ecomodernism.org). Yet neither proposal explains how poverty and inequality would be addressed in these visions or how the environmental impacts of this intensified development would be reconciled with the conservation they advocate.

59    Harvey, *Seventeen*, 4.

changed quite dramatically across time and space. If we would essentialize and simplify what in reality is a much more complex and nonlinear story it could roughly follow the trajectory of the 'great conservation debate' we outlined in chapter two. This means that conservation in the late nineteenth and early twentieth centuries acted principally – but certainly not exclusively – as a *bulwark* against the negative environmental and social consequences of capitalist development. In this way, conservation served in part to *safeguard* capitalism in helping the upper classes that dominated both industrial and conservation realms to cope with the rapid changes and concomitant social, environmental and political upheaval caused by capitalist development.[60] At the same time, conservation became a colonial movement, part of broader colonial state-building exercises in the service of empires.[61]

From the 1960s and 1970s, it became clear that conservation had to account for the social costs that accompanied this countermovement position. Hence, increasingly, conservation became framed *as a force of development* in its own right. At first, this mostly happened through tourism or as an outreach activity from behind the walls of the fortress. But this swiftly broadened to render conservation part and parcel of broader developmental processes and imaginaries. The emphasis changed to promoting conservation as a form of capitalist development itself.[62] As Paige West and many others have argued, since the 1980s, it was increasingly assumed that '*environmental conservation could be economic development* for rural peoples; that development needs, wants and desires, on the part of rural peoples,

---

60    David Bunn, 'An unnatural state: Tourism, water and wildlife photography in the early Kruger National Park'. In William Beinart and Joan McGregor, eds, *Social History and African Environments* (Oxford: James Currey, 2003), 199–220; Myles Powell, *Vanishing America: Species Extinction, Racial Peril, and the Origins of Conservation* (Cambridge, MA: Harvard University Press, 2016), 126.

61    Adams, *Against Extinction*; Grove, *Green Imperialism*.

62    We do not want to depict this as a process by which capitalism has progressively sought to internalize a previously external nature, however. As Moore, (*Capitalism in the Web of Life*, 57) insists, we must view 'capitalism as, at once, producer and product of the web of life', something he refers to as 'world-ecology'. Capitalism is therefore never *only* a system that stimulates capital as parasitic on life, but *also* as 'a way of organizing nature' itself (Moore, *Capitalism in the Web of Life*, 2).

could be met by the protection of "biodiversity" on their lands'.[63] Many neoprotectionists lamented this move, with John Oates complaining that 'conservation fell in love with economic development'.[64] Yet this was only the beginning. As West summarizes the argument made by Wolfgang Sachs, 'nature became valuable because it was the raw material for growth, and growth came to be articulated as "development"'. Development – or again more precisely *capitalist* development – thus had to start conserving this raw material from (extractive) development itself![65]

Then, even more recently, conservation became increasingly seen not merely as a development *opportunity* (or *necessity*), but as the basis for a new (sustainable) model of capitalist development entirely – one that we call 'accumulation by conservation'. This is, for instance, how we should read the statement by CEOs Rob Walton of Walmart (the retail corporation) and Wes Bush of Northrop Grumman (a security and military defence technology company) in support of Conservation International. Both contend that 'there is a direct connection between international conservation and America's economic and national security interests'.[66] This point recalls our assertion in chapter two that capitalist conservation has truly become *mainstream*. The acknowledgement that corporate elites are taking conservation seriously is but one illustration of this.[67]

---

63   Paige West, *Conservation is our Government Now: The Politics of Ecology in Papua New Guinea* (Durham: Duke University Press, 2006), xii, emphasis in original.

64   Oates, *Myth and Reality*, 43.

65   West, *Conservation*, 33. See also Büscher, *Transforming*.

66   See conservation.org. See also Rob Walton's discussions with Conservation International CEO Peter Seligmann, 'How We Came to Embrace Sustainability', 17 April 2012, walmart.com. Last viewed 20 March 2013.

67   MacDonald and Igoe et al. go one step further still, arguing that conservation has become a key concern of the 'transnational capitalist class' in erecting what Leslie Sklair calls a 'sustainable development historic bloc' globally (Leslie Sklair, *The Transnational Capitalist Class* (Oxford: Blackwell, 2001). See Kenneth MacDonald, 'The Devil is in the (Bio)diversity: Private Sector "Engagement" and the Restructuring of Biodiversity Conservation', *Antipode* 42, 3 (2010), 531; Jim Igoe, Katja Neves and Daniel Brockington, 'A Spectacular Eco-tour around the Historic Bloc: Theorising the Convergence of Biodiversity Conservation and Capitalist Expansion', *Antipode* 42, 3 (2010), 490.

The problem with this 'story line', however, is that the linearity it exudes renders it problematic. At best we can say that there might have been dominant tendencies in the historical relation between conservation and capitalist development, four of which, we argue, could be distinguished for analytical purposes: (1) conservation *as a bulwark against* development; (2) conservation *to safeguard* development; (3) conservation *as* development; and (4) conservation *is* development. These various iterations have emerged and withered in different times and spaces but also often functioned side-by-side or simply overlapped in the same time-space.

Regardless of the precise nature of the relation between conservation and capitalist development at any particular point of time, it is important to emphasize that the two processes have historically always been closely related. Moreover, *seldom, if ever, has conservation functioned to question capitalist development tout court.* Hence, even in those instances when conservation seemed to function as a bulwark against capitalist development did it rarely if ever lead conservationists to question the overarching model of capitalist progress, 'civilization' and development as a whole.[68] More commonly, 'an amalgam of utilitarianism, preservationism, conservationism, and capitalist interests' came together in what Dorceta Taylor calls 'business environmentalism', which she argues has historically infused the development of the conservation movement, in the US and elsewhere.[69]

All this makes the fundamental critique of capitalist dictums such as growth, consumerism and accumulation by neoprotectionists important and urgent. Yet their 'half earth' proposal, as we argued, does not provide any pointers for how to evaluate the currently dominant stage of the relation between conservation and capitalist

---

68   An interesting case study in this regard is the conservation of the California Redwood trees in the 1920s, where Madison Grant, the arch-racist of the US in those days, managed to keep lumber and mineral industries at bay, while skilfully using and abusing his elitist networks to get the Redwoods protected in public parks. See Jonathan Spiro, *Defending the Master Race: Conservation, Eugenics, and the Legacy of Madison Grant* (Burlington: University of Vermont Press, 2009), chapter 11, for details.

69   Taylor, *The Rise*, 27; also MacDonald, 'The Devil'; Igoe et al., 'A Spectacular Eco-tour'.

development, which we refer to as 'accumulation by conservation'. In the next section, we therefore summarize the assessment of accumulation by conservation we published earlier as it demonstrates what will result when conservation tries to align itself more fully with contemporary forms of capitalist change.

## ACCUMULATION BY CONSERVATION

Central to accumulation by conservation is the conviction that conservation must become a form of capitalist production, aiming to make the wider environment, and its 'ecosystematic embedding', conducive to the 'frantic economic urgency' of contemporary capitalism.[70] This works in several ways. First, conservation provides spaces for rest and recovery from this urgency. For instance it can mediate what Karl Polanyi refers to as the market's tendency to 'destroy society' and accommodate the countermovement we have mentioned several times.[71] Second, it facilitates the infusion of a deeper capitalistic logic within nature; the capitalization of nature 'all the way down', including to molecular and genetic levels.[72] Third, conservation addresses the metabolic rift, and hence the nature–culture dichotomy, by ostensibly offering an experience of 'nature–culture unity' to counter the sense of alienation produced by capitalist social and labour relations.[73] And fourth, accumulation by conservation claims to be able to resolve the fundamental contradictions of capitalist production by transforming capitalism into an ostensibly 'sustainable' form in which economic growth can be maintained without taxing environmental limits.

---

70   Fredric Jameson, *Postmodernism, or the Cultural Logic of Late Capitalism* (Durham: Duke University Press, 1991), 5.

71   Ecotourism is the quintessential expression of this dynamic; see Robert Fletcher and Katja Neves, 'Contradictions in Tourism: The Promise and Pitfalls of Ecotourism as a Manifold Capitalist Fix', *Environment and Society: Advances in Research* 3, 1 (2012), 60–77.

72   Kaushik Sunder Rajan, *Biocapital: The Constitution of Postgenomic Life* (Durham: Duke University Press, 2006); Neil Smith, 'Nature as Accumulation Strategy', *Socialist Register 2007: Coming to Terms with Nature*, Leo Panitch, Colin Leys, eds (London: Merlin Press, 2007), 16–36.

73   Fletcher and Neves, 'Contradictions in Tourism'.

Yet all of this leads to even more contradictions. One especially curious contradiction is that, via accumulation by conservation, mainstream conservation is at present fundamentally concerned with harnessing increased economic growth itself as the basis for the substantial revenue generation it views as necessary for the maintenance of a global protected area estate and related activities. The United Nations Environment Programme estimates, for instance, that global conservation will require an additional 200–300 billion USD in financing over the next decade to achieve its goals.[74] One of the main avenues for the pursuit of this funding advocated by both mainstream and new conservationists is, as we have noted, the harnessing of global financial markets to establish conservation as a new 'asset class'.[75] Achieving this would require continued growth in these financial markets and hence in the material economy underlying them.[76] Yet the vast majority of such growth depends on extractive and other environmentally destructive industries that increase pressure on those same protected resources that they are now expected to finance within this vision.[77] This approach is thus deeply and dangerously contradictory.

As with any form of accumulation, such contradictions can be overcome for a time through various forms of spatial or temporal displacement, but eventually this capacity for expansion will be

74    Diego Juffe-Bignoli et al., *Protected Planet Report 2014* (Cambridge, UK: UNEP–World Conservation Monitoring Centre, 2014).

75    Credit Suisse, WWF and McKinsey and Company, *Conservation Finance: Moving Beyond Donor Funding Toward an Investor-Driven Approach* (Zurich: Credit Suisse, WWF and McKinsey, 2014); Credit Suisse and McKinsey and Company, *Conservation Finance from Niche to Mainstream: The Building of an Institutional Asset Class* (Zurich: Credit Suisse and McKinsey, 2016); Clarmondial and WWF, *Capitalising Conservation: How Conservation Organisations Can Engage with Investors to Mobilise Capital* (Männedorf: Clarmondial).

76    Sarah Bracking, *The Financialization of Power: How Financiers Rule Africa* (London: Routledge, 2016).

77    Robert Fletcher, Wolfram Dressler, Bram Büscher and Zach Anderson, 'Questioning REDD+ and the Future of Market-Based Conservation', *Conservation Biology* 30, 3 (2016), 673–75. See also the Fortune 500 list of global companies, for example, to further back up this statement.

exhausted and the contradictions rendered unavoidable.[78] Hence, while, in the recent past, mainstream environmentalists pursued continued expansion of the global conservation 'estate' grounded in an unerring faith that concerns for conservation and development could be reconciled through market mechanisms, these trends have reversed themselves with the renewal of neoprotectionism, which calls for the consolidation and prioritization of the fortress conservation estate.[79] Although conservationists do not often explicitly acknowledge this themselves, what these neoprotectionist calls also point to is the more fundamental inability of accumulation by conservation to successfully capitalize on conserved nature despite decades of determined effort.[80]

This failure can be seen as the main drive behind some of the radical proposals now on the table, provoking a profound rethinking of the mainstream strategies pursued over the last century and a retraction in conservation's erstwhile globalization. After all, various world system theorists would contend that the move to financialization characterizing the current wave of 'fictitious' conservation increasingly promoted by mainstream conservationists, is usually something of a last-ditch effort to recover profit when concrete commodity markets have exhausted their potential within a given global cycle of accumulation.[81] As Giovanni Arrighi explains, the push towards financialization indicates that 'growth along the established path has attained or is attaining its limits, and the capitalist world-economy "shifts" through radical restructurings and reorganizations onto another path'.[82]

In these terms, the rise of financialized conservation can be seen as something of a desperate hope to finally successfully harness the

---

78  Harvey, *The Condition*.

79  Richard A. Fuller et al., 'Replacing underperforming protected areas achieves better conservation outcomes', *Nature* 466 (2010), 365–67.

80  Fletcher, 'Using the Master's Tools?'; Büscher and Fletcher, 'Accumulation by Conservation'.

81  Arrighi, *The Long*; Jason Moore, 'The End of the Road? Agricultural Revolutions in the Capitalist World-Ecology', 1450–2010, *Journal of Agrarian Change*, 10 (2010), 389–413.

82  Arrighi, *The Long*, 9.

long-promised capacity of conserved nature to pay for itself and deliver a profit that it heretofore failed to exhibit on a significant scale. Until now, global conservation has functioned mostly as a global subsidy system, redistributing resources to support conservation under the recurring assurance that this is merely a short-term support for the effort to generate self-sustaining markets for trade in environmental services, to eventually be withdrawn once such markets finally materialize. When these global markets fail to develop – as they have until now – the system turns to financialization instead to try to capture the promised potential that conservation has thus far proven unable to deliver.

This dynamic, importantly, is much broader than conservation. Focusing more on environmental dynamics around food production, extraction and general development patterns, Jason Moore comes to a similar conclusion. He states that 'neoliberalism has reached the limits of developmental possibilities, the financial crises and inflationary crescendo of 2008 marking the "signal" crisis of the neoliberal ordering of relations between humans and the rest of nature'.[83] Yet this intensification of crisis does not necessarily mean that capitalism will therefore collapse in the foreseeable future under the weight of its inherent contradictions, as Jason Moore, like James O'Connor, at times implies. Rather, as Arrighi, Foster and others point out, the capitalist system may simply reorganize on a new foundation for renewed accumulation, again pushing systemic crisis further into the future. In this way, capitalist development can continue alongside and even profit from ecological devastation in the short term even if it fails in its quest to offset this destruction through effective conservation.

Nor does this crisis imply that many things are not changing in the meantime and that serious attempts to develop accumulation by conservation – despite their own inherent contradictions – are not happening. And, as these attempts continue – even if they do not actually succeed in commodifying the resources they target or

---

83   Moore, 'The End', 391.

render capitalism sustainable – they change how we think about nature, wilderness and ecology more generally, namely as a nature in capital's own image; a nature that does what capital wants, and that 'needs' what capital needs. The nature that capital conserves, in short, is *natural capital*. It is therefore not coincidental that this has become the discursive label around which mainstream capitalist and both mainstream and new conservation interests have been integrating through initiatives like the Natural Capital Coalition. Natural capital, according to its proponents, is the ultimate form of 'conservation-*is*-development', the quintessential form of accumulation by conservation. Natural capital is capital conserving itself – the ultimate contradiction that makes revolution the only option left.

FULL CIRCLE?

One important question regarding the unsustainability of capitalism remains: in the face of the widespread failure of accumulation by conservation to achieve effective conservation, what other strategies are transpiring in practice to counter urgent threats to species and ecosystems? The answer seems to provide the final nail in the coffin of capitalist conservation, namely that we are currently witnessing a dramatic escalation of violence in relation to environmental protection in many parts of the world. This takes several forms. In parts of Africa, recent years have witnessed a dramatic surge in 'green militarization' or 'green violence' whereby increased poaching of endangered megafauna such as elephants and rhinos has been met with a resurgence of state-sponsored – often lethal – violence to police protected areas.[84] In Latin America, we have seen an exponential increase in violence directed against those opposing development projects, particularly extractive enterprises, on environmental grounds.[85]

---

84  See Duffy, 'Waging a war'; Lunstrum, 'Green Militarization'; Büscher and Ramutsindela, 'Green Violence'.

85  See Global Witness, *Deadly Environments: The Rise in Killings of Environmental and Land Defenders* (London: Global Witness, 2014); Murat Arsel, Barbara Hogenboom

While seemingly opposed to the financialization prescribed by accumulation by conservation, these 'green wars' may, in fact, be more intimately connected to the former than presumed. [86] Alexander Dunlap and James Fairhead, for instance, contend that the 'militarisation and marketisation of nature' are actually two sides of the same coin, in that 'new global "green" markets ... remain dependent on resource intensive structures and a military-industrial complex to police them.'[87] Foreshadowing this argument, the political philosopher John Gray observed some time ago:

> The connection between free markets and 'law and order' policies has never been inadvertent. As intermediary social institutions and the informal social controls of community life are weakened by market-driven economic change the disciplinary functions of the state are strengthened. The endpoint of this development comes when the sanctions of the criminal law become the principle remaining support of social order.[88]

Or, as the anthropologist and activist David Graeber warns more bluntly, 'Whenever someone starts talking about the "free market," it's a good idea to look around for the man with the gun.'[89] Sociologist Razmig Keucheyan goes further to argue more generally that

and Lorenzo Pellegrini, 'The extractive imperative and the boom in environmental conflicts at the end of the progressive cycle in Latin America', *The Extractive Industries and Society* 3 (2016), 877–79. While seemingly quite different, both forms of violence may be driven by similar forces. A common failure of neoliberal policies to achieve both conservation and development appears to have forced recourse to intensified forms of fortress protection, in the case of southern Africa, and aggressive suppression of resistance to expansion of the raw material extraction that was intended to be replaced by global market integration, in the case of Latin America. Arsel et al., *The Extractive*.

86    Bram Büscher and Robert Fletcher, 'Under pressure: Conceptualising political ecologies of Green Wars', *Conservation and Society* 16, 2 (2018), 105–13.

87    Alexander Dunlap and James Fairhead, 'The Militarisation and Marketisation of Nature: An Alternative Lens to "Climate-Conflict"', *Geopolitics* 19 (2014), 938.

88    John Gray, *False Dawn: The Delusions of Global Capitalism* (London: Granta, 1998), 32.

89    David Graeber, *The Utopia of Rules: On Technology, Stupidity, and the Secret Joys of Bureaucracy* (London: Melville House, 2015), 31.

'financialization and militarization are the system's two reactions to' periodic crisis. He explains:

> Throughout capitalism's existence, faced with crisis situations and the aggravated inequalities that they engender, it has resorted to the two solutions of financialization and war. In generating 'fictitious' capital, finance allows for the deferral and thus the temporary attenuation of the contradictions inherent to capitalist production (as its subprime lending mechanism recently once again demonstrated). War is the fruit of the inevitable conflicts that these contradictions periodically generate. The shrinking of profit opportunities and the need to guarantee control over the extraction and circulation of resources – but also the growing opposition to the system – tend to make political conflictuality increasingly acute.[90]

From this perspective, then, the failure of fictitious conservation via financialization may be seen to be largely responsible for the rise of green militarization and its attendant violence. Consequently, the main strategies prescribed by our two radical positions in the Anthropocene conservation debate – natural capital valuation for new conservation, expanded protected area enforcement for neoprotectionism – might be seen not as diametrically opposed but rather as two sides of the capitalist conservation coin.

## CONCLUSION

Several times in this chapter, we have argued that conservation and capitalism have become increasingly conjoined over time. It is important to be clear about what we mean with this. In no way are we implying that capitalist conservation is a done deal, or the teleological end-point of a long historical process. What we are arguing is that mainstream and 'new' conservation discourses (and to a much

---

90   Razmig Keucheyan, *Nature is a Battlefield: Towards a Political Ecology* (New York: Wiley, 2016).

lesser degree, their practices) have enabled a new understanding of
the links between capitalism and conservation whereby they have
become, for all intents and purposes, one and the same. The idea is,
simply put, 'to establish conservation as an asset class' within global
financial markets, whereby the difference with other credit classes is
no longer of interest or even visible for capitalist investors.[91] To put it
in the language of the Natural Capital Protocol:

> The Natural Capital Protocol is a framework designed to help gener-
> ate trusted, credible, and actionable information for business manag-
> ers to inform decisions. The Protocol aims to support better deci-
> sions by including how we interact with nature, or more specifically
> natural capital . . . Until now, natural capital has for the most part
> been excluded from decisions and when it is included it has been
> largely inconsistent, open to interpretation or limited to moral argu-
> ments. The Protocol responds by *offering a standardized framework
> to identify, measure and value impacts and dependencies on natural
> capital.*[92]

Through statements like these, what these actors basically seek to do
is to foreclose the debate concerning the appropriate relationship (or
lack thereof) between conservation and capitalism. As Mark Gough,
Executive Director of the Natural Capital Coalition that published the
Protocol cited above, asserts of his organization's effort to promote
natural capital valuation, 'The wave is coming. Either drown, or pick up
your surf board.'[93] For Gough and colleagues, capitalism and conservation really have become identical: conservation is finally taking up
its rightful place in dominant and 'standardized' capitalist frameworks
and ways of seeing, understanding, measuring and valuing the world.

---

91   Credit Suisse, WWF and McKinsey and Company, *Conservation Finance*, 6.

92   *Protocol Application Program*, Natural Capital Coalition, naturalcapitalcoalition.
org, accessed 28 August 2018, emphasis added.

93   'When it Comes to Natural Capital, it's Easy to Forget that We're on the Same
Team', Natural Capital Coalition for *Huffpost*, 16 September 2016, huffpost.com, accessed
12 December 2017.

We have argued in this chapter that this type of discourse is *fundamentally* wrong since capitalism is *fundamentally* unsustainable. At the same time, we have sought to highlight that broader debates making this argument often neglect or minimize conservation and its historical and changing role in relation to capitalist development. This role has not been straightforward: the long road to natural capital has come with many changes in conservation, capitalism, development and the relationships among them, all of which are complex, manifold and contested. This latter aspect is something that we have highlighted through neoprotectionists' concerns about consumption, growth and development. Yet capitalist conservation is contested in many other ways as well. Researchers, for example, worry that efforts to economically value natural resources as the basis for their conservation risk reducing their intrinsic, aesthetic and cultural values. In short: that they trigger further alienation. As environmental anthropologist Sian Sullivan contends,

> We are critically impoverished as human beings if the best we can come up with is money as the mediator of our relationships with the non-human world. Allocating financial value to the environment does not mean that we will embody practices of appreciation, attention, or even of love in our interrelationships with a sentient, moral and agential non-human world.[94]

Author and environmental activist George Monbiot, similarly, worries that the 'attempt to reconcile the protection of the living planet with commerce simply turns the biosphere into another corporate asset'.[95] This is a concern that most neoprotectionists share. A central element of the neoprotectionist position is in fact its questioning of how nature is valued within the capitalist vision that new conservationists promote. And, while many capitalist and conservation actors believe

---

94    Sian Sullivan, 'Green Capitalism, and the Cultural Poverty of Constructing Nature as Service Provider', *Radical Anthropology* 3 (2009), 26.

95    Monbiot, 'The faith in markets is misplaced'.

that this debate has now been closed with the advent of natural capital – an idea that, according to the Natural Capital Coalition, presents 'great opportunities to finally work together across the system, with the goal of conserving and enhancing our natural world'[96] – it means the debate is far from over.

Quite the opposite: the change that capitalism makes increasingly demonstrates that it is the political economic system that needs to change; that more people need to become (even more) serious about moving beyond capitalism, the nature it conserves and the types of development it embodies altogether.[97] The two radical challenges to mainstream conservation highlighted in this book allow us to see this more clearly, yet in and of themselves they cannot provide the way forward. For a more realistic and optimistic forward path, we need to reconfigure and redirect the radical potential of these proposals away from their inherent and crippling contradictions. That is the purpose of the next chapters.

---

96   'When it Comes to Natural Capital, it's Easy to Forget that We're on the Same Team', Natural Capital Coalition for *Huffpost*, 16 September 2016, huffpost.com, accessed 3 December 2016.

97   Interestingly, some analysts are no longer speaking about *whether* but about *how* capitalism will end: Wolfgang Streeck, *How Will Capitalism End?* (London: Verso, 2016).

# 4

# Radical Possibilities

The discussion in the preceding chapters shows that the three major conservation perspectives we have outlined and discussed – mainstream conservation, new conservation, and neoprotectionism – present contradictory and ultimately self-defeating positions. Yet, in highlighting the deficiencies of mainstream conservation, both of the new, more radical perspectives call our attention to important issues that must be addressed in their full complexity to lay the groundwork for developing a more tenable conservation strategy. Part of this entails looking beyond the complexity of the arguments themselves and to place the debate in relevant broader contexts. Accordingly, this chapter argues that, while there is a need to point out where the radical conservation alternatives are erroneous or contradictory, we must, at the same time, appreciate and harness their radical potential. In other words, coming to terms with the Anthropocene conservation debate and understanding its real significance means acknowledging the space it has opened up and the radical political potential it offers. This is crucial before we can present our own alternative conservation proposal in chapter five.

We have structured the chapter as follows. We start by summarizing our overall evaluation of the debate based on the preceding discussions. This is the foundation that will allow us, next, to look more closely at the radical potential of the alternatives currently on the table. We do so in two ways. First, by emphasizing what we call the 'lived reality' of the debate, in paying explicit attention to the exigencies of living through the Anthropocene and what this might mean for those who dedicate their lives to conservation. Key here is the idea of the 'great acceleration'. This concept aims to show how various socio-economic and 'earth system' trends all point to the utter unsustainability of the current development trajectory, and so imbue a great sense of urgency and threat. Subsequently, we argue that we need to bring this sense of the overwhelming lived reality of the Anthropocene back 'down to earth' by following those authors who are replacing the term Anthropocene by the more apt 'Capitalocene'. Simply put: humans cannot overcome the 'age of humans'; we can – indeed we *must* – overcome the 'age of capital'.

This leads us to the second way to understand the radical potential of the alternatives, namely how they open up space for and analysis of the political economy of conservation. Phrased differently, the two alternatives have opened a radical potential far beyond their own immediate arguments or domains of intervention. This allows them to be connected and reconnected to other debates – in political ecology, amongst others – that have long sought to understand and realize this same radical potential. We believe and hope that this also offers further impetus to existing and emerging alliances between and beyond the sciences, both to advance our understanding of contemporary conservation and to influence conservation praxis.[1] In order to start acting on this potential, this leads us, in the chapter's penultimate section, to outline several key principles derived from debates in political ecology that provide the theoretical basis for the convivial conservation proposal to follow in chapter five.

## EVALUATING THE ANTHROPOCENE CONSERVATION DEBATE

In chapter two, we offered a first attempt to evaluate the Anthropocene conservation debate. After discussing the outcomes of that first attempt in detail, we are now in a position to provide a more comprehensive – even blunt – overall evaluation of the debate.

---

1   This is a theme that has consistently garnered attention and analysis from both social and conservation sciences; see, amongst others, Chris Sandbrook et al., 'Social Research and Biodiversity Conservation', *Conservation Biology* 27, 6 (2013), 1487–90; Nathan Bennett et al., 'Conservation social science: Understanding and integrating human dimensions to improve conservation', *Biological Conservation* 205 (2017), 93–108.

First, we reject mainstream conservation. By 'reject' we do not mean that there is nothing good in mainstream conservation or that all people working on and in mainstream conservation are somehow 'bad'. Quite the opposite: we are both personally familiar with many dedicated conservationists who firmly believe that their organizations' approaches are in the interest of the common good as well as others who perhaps believe less in their organizations' approaches but nonetheless pursue conservation actions within complex contexts in a way they believe is just. We do not question their intentions or deny that their work often yields important results. But from the discussion above, as well as our own and many colleagues' research and analyses over the last decades, it has become clear that mainstream conservation is increasingly part of the problem rather than the solution.

In stating this, we are not dismissing the fact that mainstream conservation – in many places and different times – has been effective in conserving nonhuman nature. Rather, by emphasizing the historical and contemporary role of conservation in the context of global capitalism, we showed how it has been crucial to, and always part of, a broader political economy that is ultimately unsustainable. And, as mainstream conservation has continued to deepen its relations with capitalism, we cannot but conclude that it is – increasingly brazenly and self-consciously – part of the very problem it addresses – 'the problem' here being that many conservation biologists themselves continue to show that the state of biodiversity and ecosystems, in general, is not getting better but getting worse.[2]

Second, we have a lot of sympathy for the new conservation project to try to break through nature–culture dichotomies, to make conservation work for the poor and to advocate that conservation

---

2   Convention on Biological Diversity, *Global Biodiversity Outlook 4* (Montreal: CBD Secretariat, 2014); Tim Newbold et al., 'Has land use pushed terrestrial biodiversity beyond the planetary boundary? A global assessment', *Science* 353, 6296 (2016), 288–91; James Watson et al., 'Catastrophic Declines in Wilderness Areas Undermine Global Environment Targets', *Current Biology* 26, 21 (2016), 2929–34; Intergovernmental Science-Policy Platform on Biodiversity and Ecosystem Services, *Global assessment report on biodiversity and ecosystem services* (Bonn: IPBES, 2019).

science be more openly approached and interpreted. Yet, what is inconsistent in this approach is that efforts to resolve these issues would be undermined by new conservation's embrace of capitalist conservation. As we have shown, it is all well and good to say that one wants to move beyond rigid boundaries and dichotomies, but, as long as capitalist conservation requires these – which, as we have shown, it inevitably must – the whole project becomes dangerously contradictory and untenable. We therefore reject new conservationists' support for capitalist conservation but seek to retain some of the imaginative energy they bring in striving to move beyond problematic dichotomies and to centralize the need to integrate nature and people by directly addressing inequality and poverty.

Third, we are quite sympathetic to neoprotectionists' sense of urgency to reverse dramatic decline in global biodiversity and ecosystems and to allow nonhuman nature space to develop free from adverse human influence. Yet we are sceptical of the overall neoprotectionist project because of its extremely problematic proposals of separating people and nature, the blame for biodiversity loss it often attributes to population growth, especially that of the poor, and the other issues highlighted in previous chapters. This, however, is not to say that we reject this position altogether. The arguments that many neoprotectionists make regarding capitalist growth and our consumerist economy are ones with which we largely agree, while their strategies for demanding radical change in times of political lethargy are also inspiring and important. These more empowering directions in their thinking, however, come accompanied or become nullified by their negative and unrealistic proposals to separate people and nature, especially the nature-needs-half proposal, which takes this into extreme territory with potentially massive negative consequences.[3]

Pertinent for this chapter, therefore, is that there are some elements in both radical alternatives that we agree with and are inspired by and some that we strongly oppose. But, while this conclusion is important, it is not the end of our attempt to come to terms

---

3   Büscher et al., 'Half-Earth or Whole Earth?'

with the Anthropocene conservation debate. It is the transition to necessary next steps.

## THE MOMENT OF RADICAL POTENTIAL

To transition from an evaluation of the content of the Anthropocene conservation debate to its radical potential it is important to first pinpoint – and partly rehearse – exactly whence this radical potential emanates. As mentioned, both the nature–culture dichotomy and the links between capitalist development and conservation have been foundational throughout the history of conservation. In calling attention to these issues the radical proposals point to the core of what contemporary mainstream conservation is all about. Yet, one could argue, there are many other discussions, including in political ecology, geography, anthropology, sociology, philosophy and those beyond the academy, that have long addressed these root issues. These have rarely, however, sparked such a massive and consequential debate in conservation circles, nor have they done so within the current context of the Anthropocene discussion. Hence, the radical potential derives from the fact that a specific group of actors have pointed to these issues within a specific overarching context.

Regarding the former, the crucial point is that the core participants in both radical alternatives come from the 'inside' and are still tightly connected to mainstream conservation. The main proponents of both new conservation and the neoprotectionist position have earned their stripes in conservation theory and practice and occupy, or have occupied, key strategic positions in central institutions and in academic or professional networks. The pressing question, then, is why these insiders have *now* concluded that mainstream conservation is no longer sufficient and needs to be radically challenged. While we cannot be certain, there is one key element that we believe goes a long way to explaining this: the current empirical realities that conservationists confront on a daily basis. Both new conservationists and neoprotectionists believe that science tells them that certain core ideas and ideals of mainstream conservation *need* to be challenged, particularly due to the fact that the alarm indicators for biodiversity and ecosystems do not seem to be improving despite tremendous, longstanding and increasing mainstream efforts.[4] And, clearly, it can only take so long before certain actors can no longer deal with the increasing gap between vision and execution and start questioning not just the latter but also the former.[5]

This brings us to the specific context within which the Anthropocene conservation debate has erupted. The fact that the debate has triggered such a massive, consequential dispute demonstrates a deep unease with several core principles of mainstream conservation and how these are translated into conservation action. But, then again: critique of mainstream conservation has been around for a long time. And the gap between vision and execution in conservation is also longstanding. Why then, has the debate exploded, from the inside, *at this particular juncture*? In order to appreciate this, and at the same time to come to terms with the Anthropocene conservation debate on a deeper level, we argue that we must acknowledge not just the fact of the debate in and of itself, but the elements that combine to allow for this moment of radical potential. These elements are the 'lived reality' and the political economic context of the Anthropocene. It is the combination of these two elements that will allow us to appreciate the broader spaces and potential currently opening up within and beyond the debate. We therefore discuss these two elements in turn.

## LIVED REALITIES OF THE ANTHROPOCENE

In the introduction, we briefly discussed the radical challenges raised by the concept of the Anthropocene, especially the way it has rendered nature (even more) inherently social or 'human' and how it forces conservationists to rethink and contextualize science. But there is another crucial element to the Anthropocene debate, one that not only touches on political economic questions on an abstract level, but on a

---

4    Gerardo Ceballos et al., 'Accelerated modern human–induced species losses: Entering the sixth mass extinction', *Science Advances* 1, 5 (2015), e1400253; Ceballos et al., 'Biological annihilation'.

5    For more on this 'gap', see James Carrier and Paige West, eds, *Virtualisms, Governance and Practice: Vision and Execution in Environmental Conservation* (New York: Berghahn, 2009).

very personal, experiential level. This can best be explained by reference to 'the great acceleration'. The great acceleration, briefly summarized, refers to a series of indicators or trends across the socio-economic and earth system realms that all show a very similar 'hockey stick' pattern, strongly upward, or accelerating, as shown in figure four. In the words of Will Steffen and his colleagues, 'the term "Great Acceleration" aims to capture the holistic, comprehensive and interlinked nature of the post-1950 changes simultaneously sweeping across the socio-economic and biophysical spheres of the Earth System, encompassing far more than climate change'.[6] What the figures convey is a sense of overwhelming drama and scale: all the important indicators across the entire globe point in the same direction, one that is clearly unsustainable.[7]

Now, what this portrays is something radical; something so truly massive and staggering that we have a hard time grasping what exactly is going on here. Indeed, much of the Anthropocene conservation debate is geared precisely towards answering and illustrating this very question: what is going on that we now live in the age of 'the great acceleration', which is of such dramatic scale that it even transforms the geological structure of the earth itself? Spatially, temporally and in terms of sheer depth and impact, the Anthropocene thesis and the 'great acceleration' narrative it is increasingly constructed around are of a scale and magnitude that is virtually incomprehensible. So, imagine having to live through it! The lived reality of the Anthropocene, therefore, is one of sheer overwhelming magnitude; one that only few people claim to fully comprehend.[8] The rest of us, in the meantime,

---

6   Will Steffen et al., 'The Trajectory of the Anthropocene: The Great Acceleration', *The Anthropocene Review* 2, 1 (2015), 82.

7   See Bonneuil and Fressoz, *The Shock of the Anthropocene*, chapters three and four, where they criticize this idea of a linear 'great acceleration' by the 'anthropocenologists'. Indeed, they even argue that 'exaggerating a little, we could say that history for the anthropocenologists comes down in the end to a set of exponential graphs. The specificity of historical reasoning, the effort to construct an explanatory account, is eclipsed in favour of a descriptive and quantitative view'. Bonneuil and Fressoz, *The Shock of the Anthropocene*, 69–70.

8   Bonneuil and Fressoz go even one important step further to show how the scientists who 'illuminate' the public about the dangers of this new era, also position themselves as saviours of the planet: 'this then is a prophetic narrative that places the scientists of the earth system, with their new supporters in the human sciences, at the command post of a

have to sit back and ensure that we 'adapt' and become as 'resilient' as possible in the face of the threats looming over us.

Figure 3. The great acceleration.

Source: Steffen et al., 2015a.

If most of us ordinary citizens need to brace ourselves in the face of the 'great acceleration' and the grand yet highly uncertain changes and impacts it will inevitably bring, how must conservationists and conservation scientists feel about all this? Rightly so, it seems, with no small measure of anxiety and angst.[9] Indeed, both new conservationists and neoprotectionists agree that the current state of biodiversity in the Anthropocene presents an overwhelming picture, and an overwhelmingly negative one at that. Kareiva and colleagues, for instance, started their influential article as follows:

---

dishevelled planet and its errant humanity. A geo-government of scientists!' Bonneuil and Fressoz, *The Shock of the Anthropocene*, 80.

9   Paul Robbins and Sarah Moore argue that this context leads to a condition they label 'ecological anxiety disorder'. Paul Robbins and Sarah Moore, 'Ecological Anxiety Disorder: Diagnosing the Politics of the Anthropocene', *Cultural Geographies* 20, 1 (2012), 3–19.

By its own measures, conservation is failing. Biodiversity on Earth continues its rapid decline. We continue to lose forests in Africa, Asia, and Latin America. There are so few wild tigers and apes that they will be lost forever if current trends continue. Simply put, we are losing many more special places and species than we're saving.[10]

Neoprotectionists agree with this, but are generally more apocalyptic, arguing that the entire planet will literally be lost unless something drastic is done. Yet, new conservation and neoprotectionism respond very differently to this overwhelming situation. The former embrace the Anthropocene and try to give it a positive spin. The latter denounce the concept and want to reconstruct, reinforce and return to the fortress.

But, while we may disagree with the prescriptions on both sides, it is important to analyze and understand why so many conservationists respond the way they do. So, even if we have thoroughly criticized the half earth plan for being extreme, and for having potentially extreme costs if ever implemented (which would be impossible), we still need to understand why people like E.O. Wilson feel the need to come up with ideas like this in the first place. Why, in other words, he believes that 'only by setting aside half the planet in reserve, or more, can we save the living part of the environment and achieve the stabilization required for our own survival'.[11] Or why Kareiva et al. believe that unless radical change happens, 'conservation will fail, clinging to its old myths'?[12] This is what we call the 'lived reality' of the Anthropocene conservation debate, which corresponds with the overwhelming 'lived reality' of the Anthropocene era more broadly.[13]

The challenge, then, is how to get the Anthropocene back down to earth – so to speak – so that we can discuss conservation in its

10    Kareiva et al., 'Conservation'.

11    Wilson, Half-Earth, 3.

12    Kareiva et al., 'Conservation'.

13    This is also a central theme in Thomas Hylland Eriksen's book *Overheating*, in which he argues that 'the big story about the overheated world is one of large scale imping-ing on and dominating small scale', particularly by bringing more 'intensified competition', often leading, literally and figuratively, to 'burn-outs'. Thomas Hylland Eriksen, *Overheating: An Anthropology of Accelerated Change* (London: Pluto Press, 2016), 31, 150–1.

rightful proportions, rather than under the unbearable weight of the 'great acceleration'. Fortunately, several scholars have already provided the handles to do exactly this. They do so by questioning the term Anthropocene itself.

## FROM ANTHROPOCENE TO CAPITALOCENE

The term 'Anthropocene' is profoundly unsatisfying. As many scholars have by now argued, it treats 'humanity' as a single entity that somehow dominates the entire planet. It obscures and depoliticizes profound differences between (groups of) people with vastly different impacts and claims.[14] As argued by Lesley Head, the Anthropocene narrative also suffers deeply from deterministic, linear, even teleological thinking, as though history simply *had* to lead us to this moment of 'the great acceleration'. And, importantly for this book, Head also shows that the nature–culture dualism is part and parcel of the Anthropocene narrative. In fact, she argues that:

> It is not surprising that the human–nature dualism is so deeply embedded in the narrative, given its deep historical roots in Western thought . . . embedding of the associated concept of nature in contemporary life . . . and the fact that industrial capitalism is itself partly constitutive of both the dualisms that we now wrestle with and the Anthropocene itself.[15]

This sounds familiar. It is, again, the political economy that connects the nature–culture dualism and the evidently dualistic Anthropocene. Indeed, the Anthropocene concept seems to have brought the dualism to new heights (or depths) by elevating one part of the equation to the driving seat of all contemporary change, including that of the

---

14    Malm and Hornborg, 'The Geology of Mankind'; Davies, *The Birth*; Jason Moore, 'The Rise of Cheap Nature'. In *Anthropocene or Capitalocene? Nature, History, and the Crisis of Capitalism*, Jason Moore, ed. (Oakland: PM Press, 2016), 78–115.
15    Lesley Head, 'Contingencies of the Anthropocene: Lessons from the "Neolithic"', *The Anthropocene Review* 1, 2 (2016), 117.

geological record. No wonder, then, that some scholars contend that our current era should more properly be termed the 'Capitalocene'. Yes, they say, a pervasive human influence over nonhuman systems can be seen to characterize this epoch. But this has been most centrally produced by the globalization of capitalist production over the past five hundred years, not by some general 'anthropos'. Moreover, this dynamic of capitalist production is, by definition, always already both 'human' and 'natural', something that Jason Moore conceptualizes as 'world ecology'. How, then, will the analysis change if we switch from the Anthropocene to the Capitalocene? Let us start answering this question by following Moore a bit further.[16]

There are two basic and integrated elements that we draw from Moore's work to aid our purposes. The first is historical, the second political. Historically, Moore criticizes what he calls 'the Anthropocene's love affair with the Two Century Model of modernity: *industrial* society, *industrial* civilization, *industrial* capitalism'.[17] Basically, much historiography around the Anthropocene, Moore asserts, revolves around eighteenth and nineteenth-century industrialization and, in particular, the harnessing of coal and steam power to ignite modern, capitalist development.[18] The solution to the ecological crisis, from this perspective, is to curb and limit the use of fossil fuels with the resultant carbon dioxide ($CO_2$) along with other emissions – something clearly visible in the 2015 United Nations Framework Convention on Climate Change (UNFCCC) Paris Agreement, which was widely acknowledged as an attempt to end the 'fossil fuel era'.[19]

---

16  Swyngedouw and Ernstson argue that perhaps we should get rid of all the 'ocenes', as each of these foreground certain issues and actors and hide others. This is an important point, but not a reason to dismiss *Capitalocene*, we argue, precisely since we wish to foreground the contradictions of capitalism. Swyngendouw and Ernston, 'Interrupting'.

17  Moore, 'The Rise', 94–5, emphasis in original.

18  One could argue that this type of 'short' historiography is now again repeated with the focus on the 'great acceleration' after World War II; see McNeill and Engelke, *The Great Acceleration*.

19  See 'The Paris Agreement', United Nations Climate Change, 22 October 2018, unfccc.int and Suzanne Goldenberg and Arthur Neslen, 'World governments vow to end fossil fuel era at UN climate signing ceremony', *Guardian*, 22 April 2016, theguardian.com, accessed 9 December 2016.

Moore, in contrast, emphasizes a different historical origin of the current crisis: 'the remarkable remaking of land and labor beginning in the long sixteenth century, ca. 1450–1640'. This era, he argues, is the beginning of the 'capitalist world-ecology', which 'marked a turning point in the history of humanity's relation with the rest of nature'. The turning point is not just that early capitalism 'marked an epochal shift in the scale, speed, and scope of landscape transformation' across swiftly expanding capitalist geographical terrains, but that this led to a lasting bifurcation in the way humans saw themselves in relation to the rest of nature – the dramatic reinforcement and globalization of the nature–culture dualism.[20]

This brings us to the political implications of Moore's intervention, poignantly summed up as follows:

> To locate modernity's origins through the steam engine and the coal pit is to prioritize shutting down the steam engines and the coal pits, and their twenty-first century incarnations. To locate the origins of the modern world with the rise of capitalism after 1450, with its audacious strategies of global conquest, endless commodification, and relentless rationalization, is to prioritize a much different politics – one that pursues the fundamental transformation of the relations of power, knowledge, and capital that have made the modern world. Shut down a coal plant, and you can slow global warming for a day; shut down the relations that made the coal plant, and you can stop it for good.[21]

---

20   Moore, 'The Rise', 94, 96. See also Andreas Malm, who argues that 'either the Anthropocene narrative is a form of tacit social Darwinism, or it is founded on a category mistake, ascribing actions to an entity that could not have performed them. The choice of a prime mover in commodity production could not have been the prerogative of the human species, since it presupposed, for a start, the institution of wage labour. Capitalists in a small corner of the Western world invested in steam, laying the foundation of the fossil economy; at no moment did the species vote for it either with feet or ballots, or march in mechanical unison, or exercise any sort of shared authority over its own destiny and that of the earth system. *It did not figure as an actor on the historical stage.*' Andreas Malm, *Fossil Capital: The Rise of Steam Power and the Roots of Global Warming* (London: Verso, 2016), 267, emphasis in original; see also Elmar Altvater, 'The Capitalocene, or, Geoengineering against Capitalism's Planetary Boundaries'. In Jason Moore, ed., *Anthropocene or Capitalocene?*

21   Moore, 'The Rise', 94.

Moore's politics is not focused on how one part of the dualism, 'humanity' or 'anthropos', has used or transformed specific elements of the other part of the dualism, 'nature' or, more specifically, fossil resources. Rather, it is – overtly so – focused on the inherently and historically integrated capitalist 'world ecology', which brings together 'the accumulation of capital, the pursuit of power, and the production of nature as an organic whole'. Simply put, the focus for Moore must be on the historic and contemporary relations between power and politics, and for him these are always at the same time 'human' and 'nature'.[22]

Conservation, as we have shown in previous chapters, has been an inherent part of the historical equations that have led to the rise of the Capitalocene. This means, on the most basic level, that the Anthropocene conservation debate should more accurately be termed the 'Capitalocene conservation debate'. If we rename it this way, it is clear that the debate opens questions and issues far beyond conservation, nature or the overwhelming grandness of the 'great acceleration'. Instead, it opens up potential for radically rethinking conservation within and through historical political economies writ large, as well as radically challenging and transforming them towards something new, something infinitely more liveable and positive than the problematic Anthropocene outlook. At the same time, this also means we should not get ourselves stuck in the Capitalocene. The point in highlighting the term should be to move beyond it. The specific reasons for doing so, however, are important.

## BEYOND THE CAPITALOCENE?

In highlighting the Capitalocene label, we get closer to doing empirical and analytical justice to historical political economy and to recognizing how it evolved up to this moment. In so doing, moreover, we also have a better frame for understanding the current juncture in the 'great conservation debate'. But how do we move beyond the Capitalocene

---

22    Moore, 'The Rise', 97.

(in a dual sense of moving beyond the term as well as beyond the historical period) and hence move the debate forward? Here, recent discussions in relation to Moore's central concern of moving resolutely beyond the nature–culture dichotomy may help. Two strands of recent thinking on the Anthropocene are especially important for us here: work that, like Moore, aims to employ the Anthropocene discussion to resolutely do away with the nature–culture dichotomy and recent critiques of some of the theoretical predilections this has led to.

In the first strand, two major creative statements responding to the Anthropocene discussions that aim to move beyond the nature–culture dichotomy are Anna Tsing's *The Mushroom at the End of the World* and Donna Haraway's *Staying with the Trouble*. Both books build on the by now familiar critiques of the Anthropocene concept. In Tsing's words: 'although some interpreters see the name as implying the triumph of humans, the opposite seems more accurate: without planning or intention, humans have made a mess of our planet'. Starting from the premise that 'precarity *is* the condition of our time', Tsing argues that the disasters expected to emerge from the great acceleration are already here and that we need to accept this. At the same time, she directs our attention to the 'possibilities of life in capitalist ruins', especially that which grows on the 'edges' of the system. Tsing focuses on mushrooms as one key example of life springing up in edgy places and traces their 'cultural-and-natural histories' through 'entanglements' and 'ephemeral assemblages'.[23] This resonates with new conservation's focus on 'new natures', for example by paying attention to the importance and *possibilities* of alien and invasive species. While his subtitle 'why invasive species will be nature's salvation' is overstated, Fred Pearce's basic point, like Tsing's, that we need to pay heed to the promise of unexpected reinvigorations of nonhuman life is important.

Like Tsing, Haraway challenges us to accept a basic reality of capitalist ruins while simultaneously encouraging us not to leave it at that. She even conceived the awkward term *Chthulucene* to make her

---

23   Tsing, *The Mushroom*, 19, 20, 52, 61.

point. This term, according to Haraway, is meant to 'name a kind of timeplace for learning to stay with the trouble of living and dying in response-ability on a damaged earth'. What she means by this is that 'there is a fine line between acknowledging the extent and seriousness of the troubles and succumbing to abstract futurism and its affects of sublime despair and its politics of sublime indifference'. Her term *Chthulucene* is thus an act of alternative realism, a deliberate attempt 'to cut the bonds of the Anthropocene and Capitalocene'. Our project, and especially our attempt to develop an alternative conservation paradigm, shares this objective of trying to encourage acts of alternative realism. At the same time, the Chthulucene, Haraway emphasizes, is a project for imagining different 'pasts, presents, and futures' *while* we 'stay with the trouble' of the Capitalocene.[24]

In interventions such as these, Tsing, Haraway and many others open space to think, sense and act differently – potentially outside or on the edge of 'capitalist ruins'. This is important for understanding the Anthropocene conservation debate since it too provides space to think and act outside or on the edge of the capitalist ruins of lost or degraded biodiversity, ecosystems and landscapes.[25] Yet, the terms with which we think through the debate matter, and here we need to distance ourselves from one of the main theoretical foci of Tsing, Haraway and Moore (as well as many others): their creative yet ultimately unconvincing attempts to move beyond the nature–culture dichotomy. The core of the problem we believe is simple: as these authors – and many others in a variety of theoretical 'turns' from new materialism and actor–network to the 'more–than' or 'post'-human – attempt to move beyond the dichotomy in order to show that nature and society are deeply integrated and related, they often push too far. In the process, they erase (too) many critical distinctions, with dangerous consequences. Two are particularly important: the lapse into radical monism and the infinite extension of agency.

---

24   Donna Haraway, *Staying with the Trouble: Making Kin in the Chthulucene* (Durham: Duke University Press, 2016), 2, 4–5, 37, 57.

25   Cf. Lorimer, *Wildlife*.

The philosophical alternative to dualism is monism: regarding everything in the world as ultimately one, whereby any demarcation or distinction is seen as suspicious. In John Bellamy Foster's words,

> The new left hybrid theories are fond of references to cyborgs, quasi-objects, bundles, and imbroglios: anything that suggests the blurring of boundaries between humans, animals, and machines . . . In the Anthropocene, however, such a perspective easily takes on a reactionary frame insofar as it removes sharp contradictions, replacing them with nebulous imbroglios.[26]

And precisely this – removing contradictions, based on actual and meaningful distinctions – is dangerous. Erik Swyngedouw and Henrik Ernstson, basing their arguments on work by Frédéric Neyrat, write that 'the effort to contain and transcend the nature–society split or dualism through ontologies of internal relationality disavows the separation upon which relationality is necessarily constituted'.[27] Or as Michael Carolan phrases it, 'once we begin to see these two realms as being ontologically inseparable . . . we lose analytic force to distinguish between different *types* of hybridity'.[28] In our words: especially because nature and society are inherently interrelated do we need to distinguish between their different elements; only in this way can we *meaningfully* understand the relations that constitute their inter-relation. If everything is ultimately and *only* one and the same, then we can neither understand the whole nor the parts.

Consequently, and precisely because nature and society are so deeply integrated, we cannot dissolve the nature–society dualism, according to Foster and others. They contend that we need to see both integration and separation to be able to identify the problems caused

---

26   John Bellamy Foster, 'Marxism in the Anthropocene: Dialectical Rifts on the Left', *International Critical Thought* 6 (2016), 409.

27   Swyngedouw and Ernstson, 'Interrupting', 17.

28   Michael Carolan, 'Society, Biology, and Ecology: Bringing Nature Back into Sociology's Disciplinary Narrative Through Critical Realism', *Organization & Environment* 18 (2005), 394.

by human-induced environmental change. As Andreas Malm phrases it, 'the very notion of anthropogenic causation requires one of independent nature.' As such, he asserts, 'It seems to follow that some sort of distinction between "society" and "nature" remains indispensable' for both research and activism concerning environmental politics.[29]

But the problem goes further. As Andreas Malm shows, much contemporary theory believes not only in hybrids and imbroglios, but also decentres agency away from humans to encompass everything, including animals and matter itself.[30] This is often framed as radically 'distributing' or even 'democratizing' agency.[31] And, while animals indeed have agency,[32] there is something disturbing about removing a unique form of *political* agency from humans, as this 'evacuates the world of recklessness, improvidence, liability, responsibility and a whole range of other moral parameters'. If coal itself becomes co-responsible for climate change, as some argue, we can no longer hold anybody or anything accountable for (continued) global warming.[33] Even worse, the result could be 'to undermine all genuine radical praxis, implicitly supporting the status quo'.[34] Thus, while we should aim to overcome the nature–culture dichotomy by recognizing the inherent interrelations between nature and culture–society, we should not lapse into monism and in the process extend agency to a degree that attributing causality to human action becomes meaningless and completely depoliticized. Rather, as Hornborg asserts, 'we need to retain the capacity to distinguish between sentient actors pursuing their purposes, on the one hand, and objects that simply have consequences, on the other.'[35]

---

29    Malm, *The Progress*, 30.

30    Malm, *The Progress*.

31    See for example Karen Bakker and Gavin Bridge, 'Material worlds? Resource geographies and the matter of nature', *Progress in Human Geography* 30 (2006), 5–27; Sarah Whatmore, 'Materialist returns: Practising cultural geography in and for a more-than-human world', *Cultural Geographies* 13 (2006), 600–9;

32    Frans de Waal, *Are We Smart Enough to Know How Smart Animals Are?* (New York: WW Norton & Company, 2016).

33    Malm, *The Progress*, 93, 95. Swyngedouw and Ernstson, 'Interrupting', 19.

34    Foster, 'Marxism in the Anthropocene', 409.

35    Alf Hornborg, 'The political economy of technofetishism: Agency, Amazonian ontologies, and global magic', *HAU: Journal of Ethnographic Theory* 5 (2015), 46.

The way out of this conundrum is an emphasis on critical realist dialectics, where 'parts and wholes are mutually constitutive of each other'.[36] Yet, while Malm, Foster and others provide a critical corrective to much current theory that seems to have lost itself in hybrids and imbroglios, we need to be careful that we do not go back to wholly separating nature and culture afresh, including the disturbing racial, colonial, gender and other consequences that this often entails.[37] Instead, we must place ourselves firmly within the tension that the co-constitution of nature and society represents, which is always a political balancing act that responds to forces of power and other relationships. The term 'Capitalocene', for us, helps to highlight those relationships that are crucial to comprehend the contemporary moment in which conservation finds itself. And hence we need to take these relations seriously – as we tried to do in previous chapters – in order to move beyond them.

Yet stating this and actually stimulating concomitant action are different things, the latter being overambitious for any text like the present one. That is why, in the next sections, we have more modest – though still rather ambitious – goals: first, to explore the potential for radical connections between different 'environmental studies' literatures in more generic terms, along with the ability to overcome these radical differences without depoliticizing them; and, second, to distil from this and the previous discussions in this book several key principles that inform our own radical alternative proposal of convivial conservation.

---

36   David Harvey, *Justice, Nature & the Geography of Difference* (Oxford: Blackwell, 1996), 53. See more generally chapter three of this book as a useful guide to a 'balanced' dialectics.

37   Harvey, based on the work of Bertell Ollman, argues that: 'Marx was in general highly critical of the "common sense" view which whenever "it succeeds in seeing a distinction it fails to see a unity, and where it sees a unity it fails to see a distinction" and so "surreptitiously petrifies" distinctions to the point where they become incapable of generating new ideas let alone new insights into how the world works.' Harvey, *Justice*, 61.

## RADICAL CONNECTIONS

So far, in this chapter, we have focused on understanding the radical possibilities in what we should now be calling the 'Capitalocene conservation debate', while (hopefully) doing justice to the 'lived' *and* political economic realities underpinning the 'great acceleration' of the Capitalocene. But to perceive and locate radical possibilities and to act on them are two different things entirely. We believe that one basic starting point for the latter would help significantly: deeper, more numerous and more radical connections between the sciences, particularly those natural and social sciences dedicated to the big environmental questions of our time. This call is not new. Several others have made similar calls recently.[38] We want to build on and reinforce these, focusing in particular on generating engaged and effective *political* alliances.

Basically, what these authors are saying is that the full breadth and depth of the environmental social sciences and humanities (ESSH) is often not appreciated by the physical sciences, including those focused on conservation. Geographer Noel Castree and colleagues, for example, argue that 'a particular framing of "human dimensions"' research on the environment has 'become normalized in those places where leading researchers are, today, discussing the future of GEC [global environmental change] inquiry'. They continue:

The frame's major presumption is that people and the biophysical world can best be analysed and modified using similar concepts and protocols (for example, agent-based models). A single, seamless concept of integrated knowledge is thereby posited as both possible and desirable, one focused on complex 'systems'. The frame positions researchers as metaphorical engineers whose job it is to help people cope with, or diminish, the Earth system perturbations unintentionally caused by their collective actions.

---

38   See also Malm, who argues that 'surviving the warming condition requires full alignment with cutting-edge science'. Malm, *The Progress*, 132.

Castree et al. believe that global environmental scientific inquiry should instead be connected to 'a wider body of ESSH scholarship according to a model of "plural, deep and wide interdisciplinarity"', which can 'serve a representative function by making visible several actual, probable and possible realities that are relevant to different constituencies' and which consequently 'will serve a deliberative function by encouraging decision-makers and other stakeholders to make what some have, affirmatively, called "clumsy" choices among substantive options for change'.[39]

Following Castree et al.'s lead, we have also developed and now offer our argument (and, indeed, our book) in relation to this same model, which we believe should be the basis for engaged, fractious-yet-positive, meaningful interdisciplinary politics. And, we believe, the time seems right for such radical connections.[40] As political ecologist Hannes Bergthaller, and colleagues, also argue:

> The emergence of the environmental humanities presents a unique opportunity for scholarship to tackle the human dimensions of the environmental crisis. It might finally allow such work to attain the critical mass it needs to break out of customary disciplinary confines and reach a wider public, at a time when natural scientists have begun to acknowledge that an understanding of the environmental crisis must include insights from the humanities and social sciences. In order to realize this potential, scholars in the environmental humanities need to map the common ground on which close interdisciplinary cooperation will be possible.[41]

39   Castree et al., *Challenging*, 764, 766.

40   Indeed, many universities have already been experimenting with these connections, such as the Environmental Humanities South programme at the University of Cape Town in South Africa, where the first author was fortunate to spend several months in 2017. See envhumsouth.uct.ac.za.

41   Hannes Bergthaller et al., 'Mapping Common Ground: Ecocriticism, Environmental History, and the Environmental Humanities', *Environmental Humanities* 5 (2014), 261.

In conservation, too, there have been serious attempts to analyse and bridge the social and natural sciences.[42] Most recently, Nathan Bennett and colleagues have started mapping 'common ground' for conservation. They provide a thorough overview of the 'conservation social sciences' and argue that these 'can be valuable to conservation for descriptive, diagnostic, disruptive, reflexive, generative, innovative, or instrumental reasons'. Yet, while their overview and aim is instructive and important, their conclusion that conservation social sciences should be a 'vital component, along with the natural sciences, for effective conservation decision-making during planning, implementation and management' remains too instrumental for our taste.

In their acknowledgement that 'designing and implementing conservation social science projects and communications strategies that will enable real improvements in conservation practices or outcomes is not a straightforward task', we believe that they do not emphasize nearly enough that conservation is not just about effective 'planning, implementation and management'.[43] Rather and mostly, it is about politics. For us, making radical connections is about much more than planning, implementation and management. It is, most importantly, about creating (more) effective political alliances that challenge vested (capitalist) power structures and interests.[44]

The goal, then, is to not only stimulate more debate across the sciences, but to actively create networks and alliances across disciplines for taking political action. We do not expect all conservation biologists to become social scientists or vice versa. But we do expect many conservationists *and* social scientists who want to change the

---

42    Michael Mascia et al., 'Conservation and the social sciences', *Conservation Biology* 17 (2003), 649–50; Arun Agrawal and Elinor Ostrom, 'Political Science and Conservation Biology: a Dialog of the Deaf', *Conservation Biology* 20, 3 (2006), 681–2; Pete Brosius, 'Common Ground Between Anthropology and Conservation Biology', *Conservation Biology* 20, 3 (2006), 683–5; Bram Büscher and William Wolmer, 'Introduction'. In 'The Politics of Engagement Between Biodiversity Conservation and the Social Sciences', *Conservation and Society* 5, 1 (2007), 1–21; William Adams, 'Thinking like a Human: Social science and the two cultures problem', *Oryx* 41, 3 (2008), 275–6.

43    Bennett et al., 'Conservation social science', 93.

44    Cf Bonneuil and Fressoz, *The Shock of the Anthropocene*, 44.

current situation to become much more openly and brazenly political. Here is where we draw inspiration from neoprotectionism. Many working in this paradigm have understood this point and have become 'bold' and more politically active. As Reed Noss and colleagues phrase it: 'our task is not to be beaten down by political reality, but to help change it.'[45]

Now, this might seem to create some problems, as we are not saying that simply *any* political action is what is needed. Our analysis makes it quite clear that we fundamentally differ from neoprotectionists concerning where political action should lead. The question is whether *certain* fundamental differences should stop political alliances altogether. We think not. As long as there are *also* certain fundamental agreements on issues, they might be linked strategically in the political arena.[46] And, here, we might actually see more opportunities to liaise with neoprotectionists than with new conservationists, since the former do increasingly want to radically challenge the political economic roots of our current environmental problems. Above and beyond that, fundamental differences and even antagonisms should be vigorously, openly and respectfully debated, as it should ideally be in a democratic dispensation.[47] This book is our attempt to be part of this type of democratic politics. But the point about differences and its relation to political action goes much further.

## RADICAL DIFFERENCES?

One crucial point about dealing with 'radical differences' is that in doing so, we are taken far beyond (already complex) differences between scientific traditions and disciplines. Perhaps, even more importantly, we arrive at different ways of understanding, seeing and

---

45   Noss et al., 'Bolder Thinking', 20.

46   We are here thinking about older debates about the balance of class forces and how this translates politically in terms of power that can be wielded. Part of political action is always to create alliances across differences (though, of course, certain differences are unbridgeable).

47   Matulis and Moyer, 'Beyond Inclusive'.

knowing the world around us. This, in turn, leads to different visions for political action and how to understand, deal with and confront entrenched power – a point that we will come back to in the next chapter. Hence, underlying the three radical proposals – those of neoprotectionists, the new conservationists, and our convivial conservation proposal – are fundamental, radical differences on conceptual and other levels. And these radical differences are, to make matters even more complicated, based on and steeped in academic traditions and fields with their own radical differences.

Take our own main field of academic inquiry, that of political ecology, which has turned into a thriving field with many fundamentally different interests, ideas and political, social and academic viewpoints. How can we point towards so many different voices, opinions and ideas about the world and say that this will help us further? Yet, this is exactly the argument we want to make! We need to make explicit and be open about these differences, and debate them scientifically *and* politically. Or, phrased from a negative angle, by *not* acknowledging or accepting (fundamental or other) differences, one hides the politics associated with them – a strategy that is *anti-political* and a dynamic that is in itself a major interest of many political ecologists.[48] The key, therefore, is to open up politics; to *be* open about politics, about differences of interest and power, and from there build a political platform which will allow us to move beyond these differences. So, how then do we deal with radical differences and on what basis can we move forward in building this platform? Our strategy is to render explicit the set of principles upon which we base our alternative of convivial conservation.

---

48  See Bram Büscher, 'Anti-Politics as Political Strategy: Neoliberalism and Transfrontier Conservation in Southern Africa', *Development and Change* 41, 1 (2010), 29–51; Megan Youdelis, '"They could take you out for coffee and call it consultation!": The Colonial Antipolitics of Indigenous Consultation in Jasper National Park', *Environment and Planning A* 48, 7 (2016), 1374–92; Erik Swyngedouw and Japhy Wilson, eds, *The Post-Political and its Discontents: Spaces of Depoliticization, Specters of Radical Politics* (Edinburgh: Edinburgh University Press, 2014).

Our proposal of convivial conservation is erected on four key statements that form the pillars of our framework. They are not meant
as exhaustive. Rather, they are offered to clarify and render explicit
the theoretical underpinnings of the book's two main objectives: an
evaluation of the Anthropocene conservation debate and the development of a creative alternative to the radical proposals currently on
the table. The following discussions will therefore explicitly refer back
to the earlier discussions *and* look forward to chapter five on convivial conservation.

### 1. Reality is constructed, but this does not mean that 'everything is relative'

This statement is derived from the influential discussions concerning
the construction of nature that raged in political ecology and conservation studies in the 1990s and 2000s. The social construction of reality thesis was then – and still often is now – regarded as heresy in the
conservation and wilderness communities.[49] Yet the debate has not
gone away, and, indeed, it should not. For us, the way we understand
and act upon socio-ecological realities is that they are constructed
by myriad individual and collective social, political, economic,
cultural and other configurations. It follows from this that the scientific endeavour to understand and interpret reality is also always
constructed and political and therefore subject to different power and
interest positions.[50]

At the same time, we do not want to fall into the trap of (absolute)
relativism. The point that reality (along with nature, science, and so
on) is socially constructed does not mean that some things are not

---

49    James Proctor, 'The Social Construction of Nature: Relativist Accusations,
Pragmatist and Critical Realist Responses', *Annals of the Association of American
Geographers* 88, 3 (1998), 352–76.

50    See, for example Sheila Jasanoff, ed., *States of Knowledge: The Co-production of
Science and Social Order* (London: Routledge, 2004).

more truthful than others. They certainly are, including with good science at its basis. As Michael Carolan contends, 'although we may never be able to know reality as it is, we can say that because reality is real, some approximations of it can be better than others. Indeed, if the Green critique is to possess any force we must be able to say this, for without being able to make some reference to an objective reality "out there," such a critique is greatly undermined'.[51] Conservation is and always has been a construction in the context of different histories, forces and dynamics, most notably the long and uneven rise of global capitalist development. But this does not mean that the problems conservationists respond to are not real. They are. Yet placing them in context might suggest different ways forward, as we will show in the coming chapter.

It is interesting to note that in discussions on the Anthropocene, several scholars are again starting to press home the 'reality' of the current era more forcefully. Interestingly, this includes people like Donna Haraway, Noel Castree and many others who have been frequently placed within the social constructivist camp.[52] Important *politically* is that in this shift different 'sides' come out of their comfort zones: from the social sciences, there has to be a commitment to let go of those destructive forms of constructionism and hybridism that leave (any) 'reality' hanging or dissolve any meaningful distinction and so disable more effective political action; while from the natural sciences, there has to be a commitment to accept that science and reality are always constructed and political. Or to put it more bluntly: natural scientists should start acknowledging and dealing with the fact that reality is always constructed, while social scientists should start dealing with the fact that reality is not *only* constructed. James Proctor thus enjoins us to

---

51   Carolan, 'Society, Biology', 411.

52   Haraway, *Staying with the Trouble*, 35; Noel Castree, 'Geography and the Anthropocene II: Current Contributions', *Geography Compass* 8, 7 (2014), 450–63; See Foster, 'Marxism in the Anthropocene', and Malm, *The Progress*, which makes a similar argument for Actor-Network scholar Bruno Latour on pages 123–7.

accept the paradoxical truths that nature is, so to speak, *both* autonomous and socially constructed, that our knowledge of nature speaks
to *both* secure objectivity and slippery subjectivity, that our caring for
nature is based on values fully arising from our particular and hence
limited perspectives yet also fully aspiring to some claim of universality – that, in short, we must all found our environmental ethics in a
dual spirit of confidence and humility, with one leg standing surely
on solid rock and the other perched tentatively on shifting sands.[53]

This will be difficult. But we are committed to the conviction that long-
standing dynamics of mistrust, tension and misunderstanding among
the sciences concerning how to view reality should be confronted head-
on. From this position, one thing we can do is first look at ourselves
and be frank about where many social scientists have failed, something
poignantly summarized by John McNeill and Peter Engelke:

> Strangely enough, just as the Great Acceleration was shifting into
> high gear, academic social scientists and humanists chose to retreat
> from grimy and greasy realities into various never-never lands.
> They found all manner of discourses worthy of their studied atten-
> tion, revelling in the linguistic and cultural 'turns.' But the extinc-
> tion of species, the incineration of forests, the concentration of $CO_2$
> in the atmosphere – all this seemed unworthy of their power, inter-
> esting only for the discourses it aroused. Meanwhile, one species
> of social scientists, economists, jilted reality in favour of a different
> fantasy, one of ever-more-abstract modelling based on universaliz-
> ing assumptions of individual behaviour and state conduct, casually
> ripped from all historical and cultural, not to mention ecological,
> context. Social sciences and the humanities, especially in their most
> prestigious bastions, showed themselves scarcely more attuned to
> the advent of the Anthropocene than governments floundering with

---

53   James Proctor, 'Solid Rock and Shifting Sands: The Moral Paradox of Saving a
Socially Constructed Nature'. In *Social Nature: Theory, Practice and Politics*, Noel Castree
and Bruce Braun, eds (Oxford: Blackwell, 2001), 226, emphasis in original.

energy policy and climate politics. The intellectual flight from reality made it slightly easier for those in positions of power to avoid facing up to it.[54]

While some elements here may be overstated, the sentiment and political implications of this statement are clear and we support these wholeheartedly.

## 2. 'Nature' and 'society' are dialectically integrated

This sentiment and its implications logically lead to a particular perspective on the nature–society dualism so central to this book. In the face of social constructivist critiques, Michael Carolan, Kate Soper, John Bellamy Foster, Andreas Malm and others assert that we must retain the sense of a realm of nature independent of human perception as the basis for political analysis and action. After all, as the preceding quotation makes clear, it is precisely activity in this natural realm that is currently confounding convictions on both left and right that we can and do control this realm in both discourse and practice. Richard Lewontin, similarly, describes of the history of plant science:

> In an attempt to increase the productivity of crops, plant engineers make detailed measurements of microclimate around the plant and then redesign the pattern of leaves to increase the light falling on the photosynthetic surfaces and the available carbon dioxides. But when these redesigned plants, produced by selective breeding, are tested it turns out that the microclimatic conditions for which they were designed have now changed as a consequence of the new design. So the process must be carried out again, and again the redesign changes the conditions. The plant engineers are chasing not only a moving target but a target whose motion is impelled by their own activities.[55]

---

54    McNeill and Engelke, *The Great Acceleration*, 209–10.
55    Richard Lewontin, *The Triple Helix: Gene, Organism, Environment* (Cambridge, MA: Harvard University Press, 2000), 57.

It is this type of conflict between human representations and the workings of some reality non-reducible to (though not wholly separate from) such representations that the concept of an external nature seeks to capture. This is important for political action, for as Carolan asserts, 'by neglecting biophysical variables we risk undermining our ability – and ultimately our legitimacy in the eyes of the public – to inform public policy.'[56]

But an important caveat is in order: we need to be careful when we generically refer to this biophysical reality as 'nature' tout court. By doing so, we risk reinstating a false sense of distinction between it and 'society'. Both categories, after all, are homogenizing abstractions concealing great diversity among and within the entities they designate. Moreover, as we emphasized above, they are *co-constituted every step of the way*. Hence, we somehow need to preserve a sense of an independent reality without equating this with nature, while at the same time describing the relationship between this reality and human thought and action not as dualistic but as dialectical.[57] Simply put, in a dialectic, things, processes and systems are never just what they seem; they are always part of broader sets of relationships whereby patterns of unification and differentiation are bound in perpetual struggle. Hence, to do justice to the two radical conservation proposals emanating from the Anthropocene conservation debate, we needed to take some time – in chapters two and three – to reinsert and clarify the sets of relationships that conservation is part and parcel of, and how these have changed and continue to do so over time.

A corollary of this statement is that it renders any theoretical or scientific act political, as biologists Levins and Lewontin proclaimed

---

56   Carolan, 'Society, Biology', 411.

57   As Harvey describes in *Justice* (page 48), the dialectic is 'a process in which the Cartesian separations between mind and matter, between thought and action, between consciousness and materiality, between theory and practice have no purchase'. Rather, he stresses that it is a methodological and *logical* practice that focuses on the 'relationships between processes, things, and systems (page 57) in order to 'try to identify a restricted number of very general underlying processes which simultaneously *unify and differentiate* the phenomena we see in the world around us' (page 58).

in their 1985 book *The Dialectical Biologist*.[58] It also reinforces the point we made earlier that science can never be the sole arbiter over conflicts concerning what needs to be done, where, how and by whom. Instead, this premise, more positively, opens up *the promise of politics*, as philosopher Hannah Arendt stated: the promise of political connections and (ensuing) political action to change the way we see, view and act on reality.[59] Clearly, this is the basis of our own radical proposal in the next chapter.

## 3. Conservation is an element within a broader process of 'uneven geographical development'

Conservation is not the opposite of development. Rather, as argued in chapter three, it is a form of development – not simply of 'people' but of dialectically integrated natures and societies. This, however, as we also showed, did not hinder conservation from being frequently posited as separate from, and indeed, *against* development. The way we resolved this paradox in the book is by understanding (dominant forms of) development explicitly as *capitalist* development. From this perspective, we argued that conservation has historically experienced various relations to development, including: (1) as *a bulwark to* development; (2) *to safeguard* development; (3) *for* development; and (4) that it *is* synonymous with development. The current premise extends this argument into the recognition that conservation is one particular element within a broader process of 'uneven geographical development'. Conservation, in other words, has always been part of, and indeed contributed to 'the extreme volatility in contemporary political economic fortunes across and between spaces of the world economy (at all manner of different scales)'.[60]

This statement also implies, as we have insisted throughout, that conservation and capitalism are historically intertwined. Therefore,

---

58   Richard Levins and Richard Lewontin, *The Dialectical Biologist* (Cambridge, MA: Harvard University Press, 1985).

59   Hannah Arendt, *The Promise of Politics* (New York: Schocken, 2005).

60   Harvey, *Spaces of Global Capitalism*, 71.

making sense of key elements of contemporary neoliberal capitalism is crucial to understanding conservation and its challenges and prospects.[61] At the same time, this statement also means that we must be critical of contemporary capitalism, as capitalism values nature and conservation in particular ways that undermine the objectives of the conservation movement. Conservation must therefore start 'developing' differently, based on alternative values. This point is so important that it is at the centre of our fourth and final statement.

### 4. Value matters

Value in conservation is not just about the worth of natural resources, but also about systems of valuation. A key question thus becomes: How should we 'value' nature within a global context dominated by neoliberal capitalism and how can we build systems of conservation in relation to this? Many in the conservation community, as we have shown, are content to move along with the capitalist valuation of nature in order to supposedly render nature 'visible' to economists, CEOs and governments. Many are also highly sceptical of such valuation, such as a majority within the neoprotectionist camp but also others, including in mainstream conservation. But what are we talking about precisely when we talk about value and valuation? A key issue in this debate relates to whether we should prioritize intrinsic or extrinsic values; whether nature should be appreciated for its inherent 'existence value' or rather for its utility to humans. This, however, is a false dichotomy. Instead of prioritizing one or the other, we should see differential values as dialectically integrated as per statement two above.

But what do we mean by 'value'? We see value as 'assigned worth', which is a politically constructed process subject to power, context and interests. If value, then, is only seen within one set of power relations, hence narrowed to what it should mean under and within capitalism,

---

61    And, we would argue, vice versa: interrogating conservation is important for understanding contemporary capitalism.

we get to the fundamental problems noted above with respect to capitalist conservation and the nature–culture dichotomy. After all, value under capitalism should always be 'in motion'; seeking yet more value, as an endless process of accumulation. This, not coincidentally, is the very definition of 'capital'. In turn, assigning worth by turning nature's value into 'value in motion' – or *natural capital* – entails not merely describing 'what is already there' but rather prescribing a radical transformation of the meaning of nature and our relation to it.[62] This is, ultimately, what continues to increase pressure on people and nature, through processes of intensification, and what is increasingly sparking new waves of 'green wars'.[63]

What the radical conservation alternatives offer us is the potential to radically rethink the possibilities of value in relation to conservation. The key, moving forward, is to build different value systems, away from capital as 'value in motion'.[64] Part of our proposal in the next chapter, therefore, is to reinterpret and reclaim the notion of *value* away from capital towards what we call *embedded value*.

## CONCLUSION

This chapter is entitled 'radical possibilities', which we believe are amply present in the time we live in. While this may seem contradictory to some, it is especially true after the 2016 election of Donald Trump as US President (as we discuss further in the conclusion). What we mean here is that the radical conservation alternatives and some of the issues they put on the table provide important new space in the great conservation debate to discuss issues that could not really be discussed – *openly* and *politically* – under the hegemony of mainstream conservation and its 'let's-just-get-on-with-it' attitude and urgency. With the onset of the Anthropocene debate they now can,

---

62   Sullivan, 'Green Capitalism'.
63   Jeffrey Nealon, *Foucault Beyond Foucault: Power and its Intensification Since 1984* (Stanford, CA: Stanford University Press, 2008); Büscher and Fletcher, 'Under pressure'.
64   Brian Massumi, *99 Theses on the Revaluation of Value: A Postcapitalist Manifesto* (Minneapolis: University of Minnesota Press, 2018).

and we have sought to take advantage of this new space in order to significantly enlarge it. In this chapter, then, we have further conceptualized and analysed this space, in order to transition from a space of radical possibility to the formulation of a viable alternative.

Two key elements and related arguments stand out here. First: the need to acknowledge both the lived reality *and* the political economy of the contemporary Anthropocene/Capitalocene/great acceleration moment. Second, the need to lay out differences on the table and openly discuss them. It is important to note that in being open about differences we also highlighted several aspects that are clearly shared across the sciences concerned with human–nonhuman relations. The most important of these *is* the fact of difference and that the only way to deal with this – above and beyond doing good science – is through acknowledging, engaging with and even celebrating politics. Based on these deliberations and observations, as well as the analysis presented in earlier chapters, we posited several principles that serve as a prism for 'alternative realism'. So, what if we peek through this prism? What could we see? This is the subject of the next and final chapter. However, before we move there, a short 'intermezzo' is necessary; one that helps lay out the 'sea of alternatives' alongside which we present our proposal.

# Intermezzo: The Sea of Alternatives

This short intermezzo aims to provide some context for our convivial conservation proposal. We believe this is important to show that convivial conservation does not come out of the blue or could ever function in isolation from other struggles. Our proposal should be seen as one of many confluent streams contributing to a much larger river of what Arturo Escobar calls 'transition discourses' and what McKenzie Wark refers to as acts of 'alternative realism'.[1] Both of these deliberately construct different worlds beyond the boundaries of neoliberal capitalism. Both authors (along with many others) also emphasize that there are already a great number of these around the world, in on-the-ground practice as well as in more general conceptualizations. It is beyond the scope of this book to describe all or even a number of them. Yet it is crucial to emphasize that they are out there, and that they already contain most of the elements we need to build the kind of world that we want.

We are inspired by the many transformative movements, initiatives, actions and engagements that have streamed into being over the last decades, including (but not limited to) those around 'buen vivir', 'radical ecological democracy', 'the right to the city', reinvigoration of the commons, 'diverse economies', ecosocialism, economic 'degrowth', 'steady state economics', the 'wellbeing economy', doughnut economics, 'bioregional' economies and youth movements demanding an

---

1    Arturo Escobar, 'Degrowth, Postdevelopment, and Transitions: A Preliminary Conversation', *Sustainability Science* 10, 3 (2015), 451–62; Wark, *Molecular Red*.

earth uprising.² We see these – and many others – as confluent streams that play an important role in the current historical moment. Hence, they will infuse our discussions at every step of the way; often implicitly so, sometimes more explicitly; occasionally because we agree with them and cannot say it any better, but also because we may disagree with aspects of their arguments and build on them to make our point.

Importantly, these confluent streams are just a small sample of the myriad alternative ideas, discussions or 'hope movements' in circulation.³ Indeed: there is such an 'embarrassment of riches' in

---

2   Eduardo Gudynas, 'Buen Vivir: Today's Tomorrow', *Development*, 54, 4 (2011), 441–7; Eija Maria Ranta, 'Toward a Decolonial Alternative to Development? The Emergence and Shortcomings of *Vivir Bien* as State Policy in Bolivia in the Era of Globalization', *Globalizations* 13, 4 (2016), 425–39; Roger Merino, 'An alternative to "alternative development"?: *Buen vivir* and human development in Andean countries', *Oxford Development Studies* 44, 3 (2016), 271–86; Ashish Kothari, 'Radical Ecological Democracy: A Path Forward for India and Beyond', *Development* 57, 1 (2014), 36–45; David Harvey, *Rebel Cities: From the Right to the City to the Urban Revolution* (London: Verso, 2012); Martijn Koster and Monique Nuijten, 'Coproducing urban space: Rethinking the formal/informal dichotomy', *Singapore Journal of Tropical Geography* 37, 3 (2016), 282–94; Michael Hardt and Antonio Negri, *Commonwealth* (Cambridge, MA: Harvard University Press, 2009); J.K. Gibson-Graham, Jenny Cameron and Stephen Healy, *Take Back the Economy: An Ethical Guide for Transforming Our Communities* (Minneapolis: University of Minnesota Press, 2013); Chris Williams, *Ecology and Socialism: Solutions to Capitalist Ecological Crisis* (Chicago: Haymarket Books, 2010); Magdoff and Foster, *What Every Environmentalist*; Giacomo D'Alisa, Federico Demaria and Giorgos Kallis, eds, *Degrowth: A Vocabulary for a New Era* (Abington: Routledge, 2015); Giorgos Kallis, 'In Defence of Degrowth', *Ecological Economics* 70, 5 (2011), 873–80; Rob Dietz and Daniel O'Neill, *Enough is Enough: Building a Sustainable Economy in a World of Finite Resources* (San Francisco: Berret-Koehler, 2013); Brian Czech, *Supply Shock: Economic Growth at the Crossroads and the Steady State Solution* (Gabriola Island: New Society Publishers, 2013); Lorenzo Fioramonti, *The World after GDP: Politics, Business and Society in the Post Growth Era* (London: Polity Press, 2017); Kate Raworth, *Doughnut Economics: Seven Ways to Think like a 21st-Century Economist* (London: Penguin, 2017); Molly Scott Cato, *The Bioregional Economy: Land, Liberty and the Pursuit of Happiness* (London: Routledge, 2012); see earthuprising.org. See also Rebecca Hollender, 'Post-Growth in the Global South: The Emergence of Alternatives to Development in Latin America', *Socialism and Democracy* 29, 1 (2015), 73–101; Charles Masquelier and Matt Dawson, 'Beyond capitalism and liberal democracy: On the relevance of GDH Cole's sociological critique and alternative', *Current Sociology* 64, 1 (2016), 3–21, the various articles in the special issue of the *Annals of the Association of American Geographers* on 'socio-ecological transformations' (volume 105, 1) and the articles in the special issue of *Antipode* on 'The point is to change it' (volume 41, 1), for broader discussions on alternatives.

3   Ana Dinerstein and Séverine Deneulin, 'Hope Movements: Naming Mobilization

terms of the sheer number of possible alternatives that to assume that neoliberal capitalism is the 'only game in town' is patently absurd.[4] At the same time, these alternatives are themselves heavily interrogated, debated and contested (as they should be) and they exist in a context wherein neoliberal capitalism is materially dominant. Hence, we do not present our alternative in the naïve presumption that it is easy to realize – quite to the contrary.[5] We are realistic about the strength and force of contemporary capitalism, even though it is intellectually, inspirationally and spiritually moribund.[6]

But this does not mean that we revert to *capitalist realism*, which, to go back to Wark again, is about seeing the world through capitalist eyes. This would be disastrous, as capitalist realism would rather let the planet go to waste than to think of attempting the difficult yet vital task of changing entrenched power structures, something that some new conservationists seem content to facilitate in their embrace of capitalist mechanisms. Many neoprotectionists, as we have seen, are no longer buying into this. We have long felt the same and are inspired by this. Hence our goal is to present a liberating, positive vision, in conjunction, connection and spirit with the many proposed alternatives out there. A key element in all of these, we argue, concerns the need to seriously engage with degrowth.

---

in a Post-Development World', *Development and Change* 43, 2 (2012), 585-602.

4    This also makes any attempt to summarize or do justice to them in one chapter unrealistic.

5    Bram Büscher, Wolfram Dressler and Robert Fletcher, 'Nature™ Inc Redux: Towards a dialectic of logics and excess', *Environment and Planning A* 47, 11 (2015), 2404–08.

6    Neil Smith referred to neoliberalism as 'dead yet still dominant', while others like Jamie Peck (2010) and Kojin Karatani (2014) provide further variations on this theme. Smith, 'The Revolutionary Imperative'; Jamie Peck, *Constructions of Neoliberal Reason* (Oxford: Oxford University Press, 2010); Kojin Karatani, *Structures of World History: From Modes of Production to Modes of Exchange* (Durham: Duke University Press, 2014). At the same time, this does not mean that capitalism is some distanced 'cold monster', without emotion, morality or faith as Martijn Konings has argued; Martijn Konings, *The Emotional Logic of Capitalism: What Progressives have Missed* (Stanford: Stanford University Press, 2015). Hence the reason we prefer the term 'moribund' over 'dead'.

### DEGROWTH AND POSTCAPITALIST CONSERVATION

As we see convivial conservation as one stream in a broader post-capitalist river, it is important that we encourage this stream to flow with others so it can stand a chance of gaining ground. Most fundamentally, we argue, convivial conservation must be grounded in an overarching society-wide programme of 'degrowth'.[7] A key issue that has arisen in recent years is the contention that our measurements of GDP and growth warrant rethinking in order to do justice to social and environmental issues.[8] Indeed, in order to achieve a more sustainable planetary trajectory, analysts have recently argued that a strategy of managed degrowth of the economy is necessary, pointing at the fact that the only time when global environmental impacts seemed to be decreasing was during the 2007–2008 global economic crisis and related dip in global growth levels.

Developed through social activism since the turn of the century and elaborated on through a series of international conferences over the past several years, degrowth implies a period of 'planned economic contraction'[9] leading eventually to the type of steady-state economy at a sustainable level of aggregate, which has long been advocated by Herman Daly and others.[10] Kallis and colleagues present a list of policy proposals commonly championed in degrowth discussions.[11] These include 'resource and $CO_2$ caps; extraction limits; new social security guarantees and work-sharing (reduced work hours); basic income and income caps; consumption and resource taxes with affordability

---

7    See, especially, Kallis, 'In Defense'; D'Alisa et al., *Degrowth*.

8    Lorenzo Fioramonti, *Gross Domestic Problem: The Politics Behind the World's Most Powerful Number* (London: Zed Books, 2013).

9    Samuel Alexander, 'Planned economic contraction: The emerging case for degrowth', *Environmental Politics* 21 (2012), 349–68.

10    Herman E. Daly, 'A Steady-State Economy: A Failed Growth Economy and a Steady-State Economy are Not the Same Thing; They are the Very Different Alternatives we Face', Presentation for the UK Sustainable Development Commission, London, UK, 24 April 2008; Rob Dietz and Dan O'Neill, *Enough is Enough: Building a Sustainable Economy in a World of Finite Resources* (San Francisco: Berrett-Koehler Publishers, 2013).

11    Giorgos Kallis, Christian Kerschner, and Joan Martinez-Alier, 'The economics of degrowth', *Ecological Economics* 84 (2012), 172–180.

safeguards; support of innovative models of "local living"; commercial and commerce free zones; new forms of money; high reserve requirements for banks; ethical banking; green investments; cooperative property and cooperative firms'.[12] Meanwhile, degrowth activism occurs at the grassroots level, entailing organization and mobilization by community groups promoting diverse initiatives including 'cycling, car-sharing, reuse, vegetarianism or veganism, co-housing, agro-ecology, eco-villages, solidarity economy, consumer cooperatives, alternative (so-called ethical) banks or credit cooperatives as well as decentralized renewable energy cooperatives'.[13]

Links between such initiatives have facilitated their scaling up into national and transnational networks. D'Alisa and colleagues summarize, 'Explicit degrowth networks have also emerged nationally and regionally since 2000 in France, Italy, and Spain, with also an informal international academic network consolidating around degrowth conferences. The movement is now spreading to Belgium, Switzerland, Finland, Poland, Greece, Germany, Portugal, Norway, Denmark, Czech Republic, Mexico, Brazil, Puerto Rico, and Canada; more than 50 groups from around the world organized simultaneous "picnics" for degrowth in 2010 and 2011'.[14]

Yet, as Kallis and coauthors point out, degrowth advocacy often 'fails to explain how a capitalist economy would work without a positive profit rate, a positive interest rate or discounting'. After all, 'capitalist economies can ... either grow or collapse: they can never degrow voluntarily'.[15] Hence, Foster contends that widespread degrowth must properly entail 'deaccumulation'.[16] Particularly within a neoliberal regime, growth is imperative as the basis of social policy.[17] More

---

12   Kallis et al., 'The economics of degrowth', 175.

13   Giacomo D'Alisa, Federico Demaria and Claudio Cattaneo, 'Civil and uncivil actors for a degrowth society', *Journal of Civil Society* 9 (2013), 212–24, 218.

14   D'Alisa et al., 'Civil and uncivil actors', 217.

15   Kallis et al., 'The economics of degrowth', 177.

16   John Bellamy Foster, 'Capitalism and degrowth: An impossibility theorem', *Monthly Review* 62 (2011), 26–33; see also George Liodakis, 'Capital, economic growth, and socio-ecological crisis: A critique of de-growth', *International Critical Thought* 8 (2018), 46–65.

17   Fletcher, 'Neoliberal environmentality: Towards a poststructuralist political

mainstream commentators tend to evade this issue. In his call for 'prosperity without growth', for instance, the economist Tim Jackson contends that whether we call his envisioned society capitalist or otherwise is irrelevant.[18] Yet the policy revisions he advocates imply a fairly radical movement away from the neoliberal capitalist system as we know it. On the other hand, some degrowth proponents are more forthright in their acknowledgment of capitalism's essential incompatibility with even a steady-state economy. For example, Kallis asserts that implementing degrowth would require 'such a radical change in the basic institutions of property, work, credit and allocation, that the system that will result will no longer be identifiable as capitalism'.[19]

From this perspective, serious degrowth is an essentially postcapitalist platform, and we approach it as such in this book. The consequences are important: if conservation is tied to capitalism and capitalism necessitates growth, then degrowth, in its more radical incarnation, means moving beyond capitalism and hence should have profound consequences for conservation. Vital questions arise: if exploitative pressures on ecosystems and natural resources diminish due to managed degrowth, does this 'automatically' mean that there is more space for biodiversity and ecosystems to develop and thrive? Would people have more time to pay attention to nature in their daily lives and hence become less alienated from the rest of nature? How would conservation organizations, policies and practices – now increasingly geared and attuned to fitting conservation in capitalist growth strategies – need to adapt and transform in order to support a degrowth political economy?

These are critical questions that are rarely discussed openly in policy, academic or other discussions. Indeed, capitalist mainstream conservation is at present fundamentally concerned with harnessing increased economic growth as the basis for the substantial revenue generation it views as necessary for the maintenance of a global protected area estate and related activities.

---

ecology of the conservation debate', *Conservation & Society* 8, 3 (2010), 171–81.

18    Tim Jackson, *Prosperity without Growth: Economics for a Finite Planet* (London: Routledge, 2009).

19    Kallis, 'In Defense', 875.

## SHARING THE WEALTH

Achieving degrowth, by contrast, would necessitate strong mechanisms for redistribution if it is also to redress currently extreme levels of inequality. Herman Daly states unequivocally, 'without aggregate growth, poverty reduction requires redistribution'.[20] In chapter four, we went even further to argue that capitalist growth is the cause rather than the cure for poverty, which provides an additional reason to move decisively beyond (capitalist, GDP-oriented) growth. Rather than seeking to generate additional finance through spurring further economic growth, therefore, we will argue that convivial conservation must seek to redirect resources from other arenas to support both biodiversity protection and the livelihoods of local people who depend on them. This does not mean courting multinational extractives to try to direct a portion of their proceeds into conservation as offsets for ecological damage, as capitalist conservation seeks to do, but rather to reign in these extractives altogether so that their activities do not need to be offset at all. In place of the potential revenue lost in this approach (as well as through other activities like ecotourism that must also be curtailed), resources must be generated by mobilizing forms of redistribution that harness available wealth, in various forms including money but also the sharing of labour and other collective activities.[21]

Conservationists on all sides of the great debate commonly claim that we face 'hard choices', essential tradeoffs in our efforts to support both economic and ecological thriving.[22] But in fact this may be an inaccurate characterization of our situation once the dynamics of

---

20    Daly, 'A Steady-State', 12.

21    Neera Singh, 'The affective labor of growing forests and the becoming of environmental subjects: Rethinking environmentality in Odisha, India', *Geoforum* 47 (2013), 189–98; Neera Singh, 'Payments for ecosystem services and the gift paradigm: Sharing the burden and joy of environmental care', *Ecological Economics* 117 (2015), 53–61.

22    See, for instance, Thomas O. McShane et al., 'Hard choices: Making trade-offs between biodiversity conservation and human well-being', *Biological Conservation* 144 (2011), 966–72; George Wuerthner et al., eds, *Protecting the Wild*; Dieter Helm, *Natural Capital: Valuing our Planet* (New Haven, CT: Yale University Press, 2015).

capitalism are brought into the picture.[23] André Gorz, for instance, argued some time ago that:

> Nothing – other than the logic of capitalism – prevents us from manufacturing and making available to everyone adequate accommodation, clothing, household equipment, and forms of transportation which are energy-conserving, simple to repair, and longlasting, while simultaneously increasing the amount of free time and the amount of truly useful products available to the population.[24]

It is precisely this type of programme that degrowth pursues, and our proposal of convivial conservation fits right into this vision.

### RECLAIMING THE COMMONS

At the same time as 'degrowing' the global economy and de-accumulating the political economy, we must redevelop communal forms of resource governance based on egalitarian, democratic decision-making and resource allocation – what Ashish Kothari calls radical ecological democracy.[25] In doing this, convivial conservation must build on and at the same time transcend existing models of common pool resource (CPR) management. Another element of this discussion relates to the surviving commons. This is not only the commons that survive despite forces of privatization highlighted by Nobel Prize winner Elinor Ostrom and her school of thought, but also the focus of more recent research showing that autonomous spaces can work positively for common resource management as well.[26] As Prakash Kashwan explains, 'recognizing the agency of rural residents in the process of adjudication of land use conflicts and providing

---

23    Fletcher, 'Using the Master's Tools?'

24    André Gorz, *Ecology as Politics* (New York: Black Rose Books, 1980), 28.

25    See radicalecologicaldemocracy.org for further information and discussions on radical ecological democracy.

26    Elinor Ostrom, *Governing the Commons: The Evolution of Institutions for Collective Action* (Cambridge, UK: Cambridge University Press, 1990).

them with autonomous spaces for management of local resources is likely to significantly boost the local demand for environmental stewardship.'[27]

As copious research shows, common property regimes are commonly limited by the fact that they do not act in a vacuum but are in reality encroached upon by numerous external forces, not least of which are powerful industrial enterprises with claims upon the same resources that common pool resources manage.[28] Hence, finding ways to limit this influence while building more conducive global and higher-scale regimes is essential to effective commons management. Also essential is finding new sources of revenue to support this management that do not entail further commodification of the resources to be conserved or offsetting of increased extraction elsewhere, which merely displaces ecological damage rather than reducing it in aggregate. In turn, this requires moving from the 'Anthropocene' to a politics where 'taking responsibility for nature and taking responsibility for democracy come together' whereby 'the democratic responsibility is the responsibility of making a world'.[29]

### RECLAIMING REVOLUTION

The logical conclusion becomes inevitable: reclaiming revolution. The very fact of thinking and imagining beyond capitalism is already a revolutionary step, as argued by Neil Smith:

> One of the greatest violences of the neoliberal era was the closure of the political imagination. Even on the left, perhaps especially so,

---

27  Kashwan, 'What explains', 657.

28  See Fikret Berkes, 'Community-based conservation in a globalized world', *Proceedings of the National Academy of Sciences* 104 (2007), 15188–93; Dressler et al., 'From hope'; Elinor Ostrom and Michael Cox, 'Moving beyond panaceas: A multi-tiered diagnostic approach for social-ecological analysis', *Environmental Conservation* 37 (2011), 451–63.

29  Jedediah Purdy, *After Nature: A Politics for the Anthropocene* (Cambridge, MA: Harvard University Press, 2015), 286.

the sense became pervasive that there was no alternative to capital-ism. Revolutionary possibility was generally confused with utopian-ism, the history of revolutions notwithstanding, and revolution was collapsed into a caricature of inevitable failure.[30]

The Anthropocene conservation debate has shown that positing radi-cal ideas for conservation can be done, that big thinking is impor-tant and that *it works*. It works to open up space and political possi-bilities. Whether these lead to actual revolution, and in what form, cannot be predicted. But we can no longer let fear of failure hinder us from trying. The failures of contemporary capitalism are simply too devastating to not try. And besides: trying, imagining and opening up space for doing and thinking differently is fun and energizing! If this sounds amateurish rather than 'professional' or 'serious', then this may be precisely the point.[31] The revolution certainly needs serious 'social and political organisation for a more humane future'. But not at the cost of losing 'the radical and liberating pleasure of doing things we love'.[32]

## ERGO

Let us wrap up this intermezzo in straightforward terms. Convivial conservation must be pursued within a broader *revolutionary* context of degrowth and sharing the wealth that promotes mixed land-scapes in which humans and nonhumans coexist rather than being separated by promoting radical redistribution of resource owner-ship and control through reining in the power of global corpora-tions (and their capitalist ways of producing 'value in motion') rather than appealing to them for leadership and funding. All this, in turn, must be grounded not in monetary valuation or even more general benefit–cost calculation but in an ethic of reciprocity, care and gifting

---

30   Smith, 'The Revolutionary Imperative', 56.
31   Andy Merrifield, *The Amateur: The Pleasures of Doing What you Love* (London: Verso, 2017), especially chapter nine: 'The Amateur Revolution'.
32   Smith, 'The Revolutionary Imperative', 64; Merrifield, *The Amateur*.

supported by pursuing financing not from the private sector but from collective pooling of resources in whatever form, from state taxation through crowdsourcing. It is in this context that we believe our proposal for convivial conservation must be pursued and to which it should always be connected.

# 5

# Towards Convivial Conservation

Mainstream conservation as currently practised is not adequate to save nature in the Anthropocene, the Capitalocene, or simply the twenty-first century. This is why we have witnessed the dramatic and rapid rise of radical proposals away from foundational aspects of this approach. At the same time, we have shown that these radical proposals are highly contradictory and therefore unable to provide a logical, coherent or practicable alternative to mainstream conservation. In fact, our contention is that the current radical proposals are not nearly radical enough. This is because they continue to sustain elements of contemporary mainstream conservation that stand in the way of a truly productive, positive and realistic way forward. Neoprotectionists try to sustain a problematic nature–culture dichotomy while new conservationists defend an unsustainable capitalist economy that reinforces this same dichotomy.

Both proposals consequently fall short in two ways: they fail to transcend the limitations of contemporary conservation in pursuit of a genuinely radical position capable of providing an adequate response to the grave threats to sustain biodiversity within the Capitalocene; they also fail to fully recognize and hence do justice to both the lived realities and the political economic context that contemporary conservation comes out of, is part of, and needs to take into account in moving forward.

Having said this, we do not throw the baby out with the bathwater. There are important positive aspects in both radical proposals that need to be nurtured and brought together into a more coherent alternative.

This chapter aims to develop this alternative, which we call convivial conservation. Inevitably, this will be an exercise with many loose ends. The chapter is therefore as much a call for further development of alternative radical proposals to conserve nature beyond the Capitalocene as a proposal in itself. Yet, even with these necessary disclaimers, we will conclude that this proposal, however nascent, is already a more realistic and positive way forward for conservation than those currently dominating the Anthropocene conservation debate.

The statements posited towards the end of chapter four help to provide a logical and coherent frame to develop an alternative radical yet realistic proposal. In the following chapter we build on these to outline the core principles of our convivial conservation position. Our aim in doing so is decidedly not to present a fully worked out or foolproof plan, let alone a magic bullet solution. One simple reason for this is that real-world historical change does not work like that; actual change only happens through social, political and other types of struggle. This is why we will present a theory of change that integrates short and long-term actions as co-constitutive steps that acknowledge, break down and transform institutionalized forms of power and politics geared towards the status quo.

A second reason why we do not present a fully worked out proposal relates to the intermezzo which argued that convivial conservation should be seen as one of many confluent streams contributing to a much larger sea of alternatives. This makes our effort here somewhat easier, as we need only focus on one stream – the one concerned explicitly with conservation. Hence, our discussion in this chapter will address how *conservation* can become but one part of and contribute to a broader postcapitalist movement.

A third and final reason for deliberate partiality is that many of the ideas in our convivial conservation alternative are not wholly new. While we do not know of a comprehensive proposal that sets out a postcapitalist conservation under an overarching banner, there are many attempts, in practice and research, towards the same overall goal. From the various consortia supporting 'indigenous and community conservation areas' known as ICCAs and several International Union

of Conservation of Nature (IUCN) committees to academic contributions like Ashley Dawson's attempt to imagine a 'radical anti-capitalist
conservation movement',[1] there are alternatives and novel ideas out
there, and we build upon them.

Yet, at this point, these proposals lack an overarching frame which
could be used to unite them and contrast them with the other radical
proposals that are being aggressively promoted with pithy titles and
slogans (Nature Needs Half, Natural Capital Coalition, and so on).
Our aim here is thus, in part, to bring together the progressive forms
of conservation already in development, describe the key principles
towards which we believe they (can) collectively build, and place all
of this within the context of an overarching societal transformation
that is ultimately needed to move us beyond the Capitalocene and its
degrading impulses. Hence, we present the following in the hope that
numerous streams together will lead to something powerful enough
to challenge vested, institutionalized and vicious capitalist interests,
cultures and habits.

We start with a more detailed conceptualization of convivial
conservation, followed by our overarching vision. After that, we will
render the vision increasingly pragmatic by discussing how to get
'from here to there', including our theory of change. We end the chapter by proposing several short-term propositions and actions.

## CONVIVIAL CONSERVATION

In its core, our conceptualization of conviviality is necessarily postcapitalist and non-dualist. Regarding dualisms, our understanding of
'convivial' is meant to build on its etymological roots of 'con' (with)
and 'vivire' (living) or 'living with'. Hence, it is in line with our second
theoretical principle, which fundamentally envisions a conservation
that does not separate humans and nature – as the mainstay of conservation through protected areas has long done and continues to do

---

1   Ashley Dawson, *Extinction: A Radical History* (New York: OR Books, 2016),
83–94.

– but instead rejects this false dichotomy. It focuses on a conservation that, inspired by Esther Turnhout et al., enables humans to truly 'live with' biodiversity.[2] This is in line with the spirit of the new conservation position. In contrast with this position, however, convivial conservation emphasizes not economic cost–benefit calculation but affective affinity and other ways of relating with nonhumans irreducible to destructive capitalist ratio.[3]

Regarding the question of postcapitalism, we build explicitly on Illich's conceptualization of conviviality. In 1973 he argued that 'a convivial society would be the result of social arrangements that guarantee for each member the most ample and free access to the tools of the community and limit this freedom only in favour of another member's equal freedom'.[4] More concretely, Illich argues that he chose

the term 'conviviality' to designate the opposite of industrial productivity. I intend it to mean autonomous and creative intercourse among persons, and the intercourse of persons with their environment; and this in contrast with the conditioned response of persons to the demands made upon them by others, and by a man-made environment. I consider conviviality to be individual freedom realized in personal interdependence and, as such, an intrinsic ethical value. I believe that, in any society, as conviviality is reduced below a certain level, no amount of industrial productivity can effectively satisfy the needs it creates among society's members.[5]

Some of the wording Illich employs now sounds slightly archaic, like the ways that (industrial) 'tools' 'degrade' modern people. But what Illich points to is the turning around of the 'deadening' forces

---

2    Esther Turnhout et al., 'Rethinking biodiversity: From goods and services to "living with"', *Conservation Letters* 6 (2013), 154–61.

3    In so doing, our proposal also builds on and extends Tim Ingold's critique about the 'grand narrative of the human transcendence of nature' produced by 'the self-domestication of humanity in the process of civilisation'. Tim Ingold, *The Perception of the Environment: Essays on Livelihood, Dwelling and Skill* (London: Routledge, 2000), 61, 77.

4    Illich, *Tools*, 12.

5    Illich, *Tools*, 11.

of industrial capitalism and the ways in which it stifles creativity, imagination, judgement and 'the right to the fundamental physical structure of the environment with which man has evolved'.[6] Indeed, he very explicitly refers to 'biological degradation' as the first of 'five dimensions on which the balance of life depends'.[7] This balance, he argues, has been thoroughly upset by the tools designed by industrial capitalism. This is not to say that Illich believes that life is a balanced affair. What he is after is a balance between the tools and possibilities that we use and an idea of the good life that these may both enable and threaten. In his own words: 'a tool can grow out of man's [sic] control, first to become his master and finally to become his executioner'.[8] He provides the following examples to illustrate:

> An increase in social mobility can render society more human, but only if at the same time there is a narrowing of the difference in power which separates the few from the many. Finally, an increase in the rate of innovation is of value only when with its rootedness in tradition, fullness of meaning, and security are also strengthened.[9]

To extrapolate this logic: the use of modern tools of conservation – including technologies, finance, 'smart' systems, governance and management – is of value only to the extent that they allow for more conviviality between humans and between humans and the rest of nature. Mainstream conservation and its tools do not provide this value anymore, nor do the dominant radical alternatives. A new vision is needed.

---

6   Illich, *Tools*, 47–8. Or, perhaps more aptly, the way in which capitalism enables creativity, imagination and judgement to function in the pursuit of endless accumulation.

7   Illich, *Tools*, 84. Although for our liking he places too much emphasis on the early arguments for population control, especially by Paul Ehrlich. For more on this, see Robert Fletcher, Jan Breitling, and Valerie Puleo, 'Barbarian hordes: The overpopulation scapegoat in international development discourse', *Third World Quarterly* 35 (2014), 1195–1215.

8   Illich, *Tools*, 84.

9   Illich, *Tools*, 84.

## ELEMENTS OF A VISION

Ivan Illich saw his broader project as one of 'convivial reconstruction'; the reconstruction of society so as to enable humans to lead good, frugal lives. The convivial reconstruction of conservation depends on and aids this broader project currently (and historically) pushed and supported by many post-colonial, indigenous, emancipatory, youth, progressive and other movements, organizations and individuals around the world.[10] For this we need to allow ourselves to envision several major, progressive transformations that might characterize postcapitalist convivial conservation. We propose five key elements of a convivial conservation vision.

### 1. From protected to promoted areas

The default mode of conservation has commonly been about protecting nature *from* people, particularly through protected areas. Elaborate systems have been set up to govern who has access to (parts of) protected areas and how these (parts) ought to be used (see the IUCN classification system). This is about putting the focus on continuously marking and emphasizing the boundaries between human and nonhuman nature rather than celebrating the many inherent links between them.[11] Under convivial conservation, this would be reversed. The principal goal of special conservation areas should not be to protect nature from humans but to promote nature for, to and by humans.[12] They should transition from protected to 'promoted areas',

---

10  Xavier Albó, '*Suma Qamaña* or Living Well Together: A Contribution to Biocultural Conservation'. In: Ricardo Rozzi et al., eds, *Biocultural Homogenization to Biocultural Conservation* (Springer, 2018) 333–42; Berch Berberoglu, ed., *The Palgrave Handbook of Social Movements, Revolution, and Social Transformation* (London: Palgrave Macmillan, 2019).

11  Chris Sandbrook, 'Separate yet connected: The spatial paradox of conservation'. Retrieved from thinkinglikeahuman.com; Fletcher, 'Connection with Nature'.

12  To a degree, it could be argued that this process had already started in the 1970s with the then radical critique of protected areas and top-down, colonial conservation. However, as the history in chapter one showed, this process which led to manifold forms of community-based conservation was effectively cut short by a neoprotectionist revival and neoliberal restructuring.

although not in capitalist terms whereby they are marketed on the basis of capital accumulation and are hence exploited via (eco)tourism and so forth (see below). Rather, promoted areas are conceptualized as fundamentally encouraging places where people are considered welcome visitors, dwellers or travellers rather than temporary alien invaders upon a nonhuman landscape. This can only take place within an overall context focused not on exploitation or productivity but on conviviality: the building of long-lasting, engaging and open-ended relationships with nonhumans and ecologies.

This proposition includes an important discursive shift. 'Protected from' sounds negative,[13] while promoted by and for is positive, and democratic.[14] Some positive steps in this regard have been made, all around the world, including, especially, by the ICCA coalition of indigenous and local peoples. But more is needed, especially seeing how some hard-won democratic experiments have recently been turned back in the fight against poaching and the broader militarization of protected areas.[15]

It is also important to continue to emphasize, along with many neoprotectionists and other conservationists, all that is incredibly valuable in and about current protected areas. This cannot be lost as the discussion progresses, and hence 'promotion' does not mean that every action is possible or desirable.[16] The value of biodiversity requires promotion, too, especially vis-à-vis values linked to (unnecessary or excessive) extractive and destructive types of enterprise. But unlike neoprotectionists, we do not think this value will survive by positing it *against* humanity and 'population growth', as it frequently is.[17] The

---

13   We are not arguing here that 'protection' is *only* negative, as obviously protecting that which we love or care about is not a negative pursuit; our reason for moving away from the term 'protected areas' is a deliberate *political* move within the context of the political economic history and the present state of conservation.

14   Purdy, *After Nature*.

15   See Duffy, 'Waging a war'; Lunstrum, 'Green Militarization'; Büscher and Ramutsindela, 'Green Violence'.

16   Cf. Locke, 'Green Postmodernism'.

17   This also does not mean that population (growth) is not important and should not be addressed. Yet, we believe, the only way to respectfully address the issue is by doing so in its multiple political, economic and historical contexts, with a special emphasis on the historical colonial burden still deeply affecting non-western societies and people (see

deep value of nature for humans only makes sense through and by humans.[18] Hence, the only solution to protecting nature's value is to build an integrated (economic, social, political, ecological, cultural) value system that does not depend on the destruction of nature but on 'living with' nature.[19] Under such a value system, debate will continue to centre on which activities are permissible in 'promoted' areas, and which must of necessity remain excluded in the interest of sustainable democratic development. But these different activities will not be seen as trade-offs or opposites but the logical extension of a broader mindset that recognizes the need for the promotion of conviviality.

### 2. From saving nature to celebrating human and nonhuman nature

The next element follows logically: we must move away from the idea that conservation is about 'saving' only nonhuman nature. The main actors that humans save nonhuman natures from are other humans.[20] Yet since humans are part of a larger 'natural' whole that contains nonhumans as well, we get into tricky territory when speaking about 'saving' nature from humans, reinforcing the very nature–society dichotomy we seek to dismantle. In fact, we have long suspected that something must be terribly wrong if we have to put boundaries between ourselves and nonhuman nature; it means, essentially, that we have to protect ourselves from ourselves. This contradiction can only be overcome by challenging the idea that conservation is ultimately and only about saving *nonhuman* nature.

We need to start focusing on saving and celebrating both human *and* nonhuman nature equally. This may sound strange, even wrong, to many conservationists and political ecologists alike. Indeed, in the social sciences, there are strong tendencies and 'turns' towards

---

Dawson, *Extinction*).

18   Something that the discussion on the Anthropocene has helped to clarify. See Davies, *The Birth*.

19   Turnhout et al., 'Rethinking biodiversity'.

20   Obviously, desired natures, species or ecosystem traits are also protected from other, non-desired natures, species or ecosystem traits.

decentring the human and putting human and 'more-than-human' on an equal footing.[21] While we certainly see reasons to take the 'more-than-human' much more seriously, this does not necessitate that the human and 'more-than-human' must therefore be given wholly equal standing. In line with our first theoretical principle and following David Harvey we need a 'broad agreement on how we are both individually and collectively going to construct and exercise our responsibilities to nature in general and towards our own human nature in particular'.[22] Harvey, following legal scholar James White, refers to this as 'learning to be distinctively ourselves in a world of others'.[23]

Opening up the question of 'human nature' may be somewhat ambitious. But it is necessary, even if only briefly. As Marshall Sahlins 'modestly' concluded: 'Western civilization has been constructed on a perverse and mistaken idea of human nature. Sorry, beg your pardon; it was all a mistake. It is probably true, however, that this perverse idea of human nature endangers our existence'.[24] Sahlins refers to the idea of human nature as competitive, self-interested and rational, the stereotypical 'homo economicus' underlying neoliberal forms of governance that even '21st century economists' do not believe in anymore.[25] This reductionist idea of human nature has been responsible for creating needs, wants and actions that 'endanger our existence' and are most certainly not convivial. Opening up the question of human nature, therefore, means asserting that there are 'various ways in which we

21   See, especially, Donna Haraway, *When Species Meet* (Minneapolis: University of Minnesota Press, 2008); Rosi Braidotti, *The Posthuman* (Cambridge, MA: Polity Press, 2013); Juanita Sundberg, 'Decolonizing posthumanist geographies', *Cultural Geographies* 21 (2013), 33–47. Some authors even argue that labour is not distinctly human, but that animals labour as humans do (for example Maan Barua, 'Nonhuman labour, encounter value, spectacular accumulation: The geographies of a lively commodity', *Transactions of the Institute of British Geographers* 42 (2017), 274–88). We believe this argument is a mistake.

22   David Harvey, *Spaces of Hope* (Berkeley: University of California Press, 2000), 223.

23   Ibid.

24   Marshall Sahlins, *The Western Illusion of Human Nature* (Chicago: Prickly Paradigm Press, 2008).

25   Raworth, *Doughnut Economics*, 94. Raworth goes on to argue that we need to 'nurture human nature' by moving 'from rational economic man to social adaptable humans', 94.

can "be ourselves"';[26] that we can construct needs, wants and actions differently, in line with sustainable conviviality. It means, fundamentally, challenging the 'dangerous' processes of capitalist alienation that change and go against human nature.[27]

The fact that these distinctively relate to *human nature* does not mean it excludes nonhumans. A certain form of human exceptionalism, in other words, can be entirely convivial. Indeed, a certain form of human exceptionalism appears necessary if we are to retain a focus on the particular threats posed by human action to nonhuman survival at all rather than merely attributing this to the workings of a diffuse 'assemblage'. As Kate Soper asserts, 'Unless human beings are differentiated from other organic and inorganic forms of being, they can be made no more liable for the effects of their occupancy of the ecosystem than can any other species, and it would make no more sense to call upon them to desist from destroying nature than to call upon cats to stop killing birds.'[28]

While a 'posthuman' perspective seeks to challenge human 'exceptionalism', consequently, an alternative perspective – again in line with our first theoretical principle – would assert that humans (both as a species and as individuals) are in fact exceptional and unique; but that all other species and organisms are, in their own way, special and unique as well.[29] Decentring the human, in other words, may be best accomplished not by homogenizing and levelling all forms of life but on the contrary by insisting on the unique nature possessed by each of these myriad forms. The key, then, would be to highlight those characteristics unique to humans, or at least that humans possess in unique quantities, that have facilitated the devastation we have wrought upon the rest of the planet (while also avoiding the pitfall of homogenizing a highly variegated humanity). Chief among these must be our capacity to function as intentional, *political* actors.[30] Convivial conserva-

---

26  Harvey, *Spaces of Hope*, 223.
27  Harvey, *Seventeen*.
28  Soper, *What is Nature*, 160.
29  De Waal, *Are We Smart*.
30  Malm, *The Progress*.

tion allows for celebration of this diversity while the 'saving' of this diversity is in recognition of how differential needs, wants and actions of humans and nonhumans are always related and tied to broader political economic trends and dynamics.[31]

### 3. From touristic voyeurism to engaged visitation

As the way we promote and save nonhuman and human nature changes under convivial conservation, so the way we engage, see and experience nonhuman nature must also change. Increasingly, we engage 'wild' nature, and especially parks, through commodified tourism experiences. As we now know, tourism, as one of the largest *capitalist* industries in the world, is not the great saviour of nature it is often made out to be. It is both indirectly and often even directly responsible for the destruction of nature.[32] But capitalist tourism is about more than just the destruction or conservation of nature. It is also a way of seeing and understanding nature, one that can be shorthanded as a type of voyeurism: peeking 'at' nature through commodified tours, spaces, sites and other experiences; often more with the aim of ticking boxes and fulfilling 'bucket lists' (been there, done that, seen the 'big five', Niagara Falls, or whatever else) then of creating meaningful long-term engagement.

This is not to say that the latter does not exist. But the problem with a focus on 'conservation-funded-through-tourism' is that meaningful long-term engagement with nature seems to increasingly become an elite privilege rather than a democratic possibility. Visiting

---

31   Some might point out that we are using dualist language ('between') yet we hold that even as we move beyond dualism we should analytically talk about relations between two entities, namely humans (or 'human nature') and extra-human nature. Clearly, we here depart from Jason Moore's discursive strategy to embrace a more straightforward mode of Marxian dialectics.

32   Freya Higgins-Desbiolles, *Capitalist Globalisation, Corporatised Tourism and their Alternatives* (New York: Nova Science, 2009); Robert Fletcher, 'Sustaining tourism, sustaining capitalism? The tourism industry's role in global capitalist expansion', *Tourism Geographies* 13 (2011), 443–61; Bram Büscher and Robert Fletcher, 'Destructive creation: Capital accumulation and the structural violence of tourism', *Journal of Sustainable Tourism* 25 (2017), 651–67.

or owning 'pristine' nature is very often (and has long been) an elite activity, imbued with problematic racial, gender and class divisions.[33] And even if capitalist tourism enables or leads to long-term deep engagement with species or ecosystems, this is all too often used as escape from, not confrontation with or developing alternatives to the destructive dynamics of global capitalism.[34]

Under convivial conservation, the emphasis will be on long-term *democratic* engagement[35] rather than on short-term voyeuristic tourism or elite access and privilege. Does that mean that short-term tours or trips will become impossible? We do not know. But it has become patently clear that we simply cannot afford to continue to fly around the world in climate-changing airplanes in order to 'contribute' to conservation through (eco)tourism. The alternative is to encourage long-term visitation focused on social and ecological justice,[36] preferably in relation to the natures closer to where we live.

Not all of this is new, and some of it was foreseen by Illich:

The richer we get in a consumer society, the more acutely we become aware of how many grades of value – of both leisure and labor – we have climbed. The higher we are on the pyramid, the less likely we are to give up time to simple idleness and to apparently nonproductive pursuits. The joy of listening to the neighborhood finch is easily overshadowed by stereophonic recordings of "Bird Songs of the

---

33  See George Holmes, 'The rich, the powerful and the endangered: Conservation elites, networks and the Dominican Republic', *Antipode* 42 (2010), 624–46; George Holmes, 'Biodiversity for billionaires: Capitalism, conservation and the role of philanthropy in saving/selling nature', *Development and Change* 43 (2012), 185–203; Fletcher, *Romancing the Wild*; Bram Büscher, 'Reassessing fortress conservation: New media and the politics of distinction in Kruger National Park', *Annals of the Association of American Geographers* 106 (2016), 114–29.

34  Bunn, *An Unnatural*.

35  Based on principles outlined by Aseem Shrivastava and Ashish Kothari, *Churning the Earth: The Making of Global India* (New York: Penguin, 2012) and Scott Cato, *The Bioregional Economy*. These include, amongst others, bioregional economic development, sharing of state functions with civil society, new indicators of well-being, degrowth and a devolution of powers.

36  Freya Higgins-Desbiolles, 'Justice tourism and alternative globalization', *Journal of Sustainable Tourism* 16 (2008), 345–64.

World", the walk through the park downgraded by preparations for a packaged bird-watching tour into the jungle.³⁷

The emergence of the Anthropocene has brought these issues into stark relief. As a growing discussion of 'Anthropocene tourism' asserts,

> tourism policy and practice in the Anthropocene . . . implies that tourism needs to be measured up in specific relation to the boundaries and limits vis-à-vis the Earth and humanity at the global scale . . . [It is] necessary to deepen the debate on sustainability in and of tourism by addressing the existing problems from the perspective of the geophysical forces of humanity and the Earth in the Anthropocene.³⁸

Hence, Higgins-Desbiolles, amongst others, insists that achieving a truly 'sustainable tourism necessitates a clear-eyed engagement with notions of limits that the current culture of consumerism and pro-growth ideology precludes'.³⁹ It is just this sort of engagement that we endorse here.

## 4. From spectacular to everyday environmentalisms

Capitalist conservation interactions with nature, including but not limited to tourism, are focused on what Jim Igoe calls the spectacle of nature.⁴⁰ Inspired by Guy Debord, the 'spectacle of nature' means that 'images become commodities alienated from the relationships that produced them and consumed in ignorance of the

---

37    Illich, *Tools*, 80.

38    Martin Gren and Edward H. Huijbens, 'Tourism and the Anthropocene', *Scandinavian Journal of Hospitality and Tourism* 14 (2014), 6–22, 12–13.

39    Freya Higgins-Desbiolles, 'The elusiveness of sustainability in tourism: The culture-ideology of consumerism and its implications', *Tourism and Hospitality Research* 10 (2010), 116–129, 125.

40    Jim Igoe, 'The spectacle of nature in the global economy of appearances: Anthropological engagements with the images of transnational conservation', *Critique of Anthropology* 30 (2010), 375–97; Jim Igoe, *The Nature of Spectacle: On Images, Money, and Conserving Capitalism*. (Tucson, AZ: University of Arizona Press, 2017).

same'.[41] Conservation, in other words, is increasingly communicated and consumed through images of the very idealized, spectacular natures that are increasingly disappearing in reality. This, however, is also increasingly more difficult to see due to what Igoe refers to as a 'double act of fetishization':

> The conjuring of possibilities undertaken in these spectacular productions requires a double act of fetishization . . . First the relationships and connections that they present are themselves fetishized, since their larger historical, social and ecological contexts are hidden from view. Next, and more fundamentally, the connections and relationships that allowed for the selective concealment of these larger contexts are also hidden from view. These spectacular productions thus become their own evidence, continuously referring back to themselves in affirmation of the realness of the world(s) that they show their viewers.[42]

Capitalist conservation depends on particular forms of communication that often centre on the 'spectacle of nature'.[43] These types of communication are often (necessarily) superficial, anti-political and devoid of context and, despite many promises to the contrary, new media in practice often reinforces this dynamic.[44] Under convivial conservation we need to move away from the spectacle of nature, and instead focus on 'everyday nature', in all its splendour *and* mundaneness.[45] Indeed, we argue that it is in mundaneness rather than spectacle that we can find the most meaningful engagement with nature.

---

41   Igoe, 'The spectacle of nature', 375.

42   Igoe, 'The spectacle of nature', 389–90,

43   One of the major current empirical manifestations of this can be found in the BBC's *Planet Earth* series, which is, interestingly, criticized on exactly this point. See: Martin Hughes-Games, 'The BBC's Planet Earth II did not help the natural world', 1 January, 2017, theguardian.com, accessed 2 January 2017.

44   Büscher, 'Reassessing fortress conservation'; Robert Fletcher, 'Gaming conservation: Nature 2.0 confronts nature-deficit disorder', *Geoforum* 79 (2017), 153–62.

45   Cronon, 'The trouble with wilderness'.

Living with nature means appreciating nature on an everyday level,[46] including all the manifold material and discursive implications that arise from this statement.

### 5. From privatized expert technocracy to common democratic engagement

The fifth element of our vision is that convivial conservation means that *all* people have to be able to (potentially) live with *all* nature.[47] Hence, the way significant nature is often managed, namely in a top-down fashion based on technocratic expert opinions, is inherently alienating for most of us (which comes through in its most extreme form in E.O. Wilson's vision of allowing most humans to only peer at the 'other' side of earth – nature's half – through micro-cameras).[48] This, again, implies a need for a much more democratic management of nature, focused on nature-as-commons and nature-in-context rather than nature-as-capital. This point is important for conservation generally, and perhaps especially in relation to the extinction crisis. As authors such as Tracey Heatherington, Genese Sodikoff and Ashley Dawson argue, technoscience may save some species from extinction, but will not save them as part of a broader amalgam of 'living land-scapes' that do long-term socio-ecological justice to both humans and nonhumans.[49] 'Saving' species, they all emphasize, is only meaningful

---

46    Alex Loftus, *Everyday Environmentalism: Creating an Urban Political Ecology* (Minneapolis: University of Minnesota Press, 2012).

47    While this aim is admirable, it must be acknowledged that in practice, any conservation policy will inevitably entail making 'political choices between this rather than that nature' (Swyngedouw and Ernstson, 'Interrupting', 20), as not all organisms are symbiotic. And while the interests of nonhumans must be considered in these delib-erations, it must also be acknowledged that it is ultimately humans that must make these political choices (rather than seeking to evade this responsibility by attributing political agency to the nonhumans who cannot actually participate as equals in fora that have been designed in relation to uniquely human forms of interaction); see Fayaz Chagani, 'Critical political ecology and the seductions of posthumanism', *Journal of Political Ecology* 21 (2014), 424–36.

48    Wilson, *Half-Earth*, 192.

49    Tracey Heatherington, 'From ecocide to genetic rescue: Can technoscience save

within manifold broader social, cultural and environmental contexts.

Following our theoretical principle that 'value matters', a key issue here concerns the operationalization of 'value'. Convivial conservation grounded in radical ecological democracy would require that the value of natural resources be determined locally rather than in abstract global (and increasingly algorithm-based, computerized) markets. This value would then need to be realized in ways that do not promote the commodification of resources but rather provide autonomous funding streams that allow qualitative, multidimensional values to be preserved and promoted. As we have argued at length, capitalism cannot mediate interests and values in a transition towards a more sustainable society. This is, fundamentally, because it ultimately prioritizes one type of value above all others: 'value in motion', that is, 'capital'. By contrast, convivial conservation cannot and will not prioritize capital in making decisions about resource allocations, how to manage promoted areas, how to celebrate nature or how to organize engaged visitation.

So, instead of asking how conservation can lead to more (necessarily monetized) 'value' in the future, we should start by asking how a (necessarily non-monetized) value is embedded in the here and now and in which contexts this value receives local and extra-local meaning. In short, we need to refocus from value in motion, or capital, to what we could call 'embedded value'. The latter's logic is not based in market-based commodity exchange whereby nature has to 'provide services' to humans to be protected, but receives its worth from and through humans and nonhumans 'living with', understanding, appreciating but also politically confronting and agonistically struggling with each other (through cultural, artistic, experiential, affective or other non-commodified or non-monetized forms). This requires, quite simply, that all conservation decisions are taken in terms not of their contribution to (global) capital (value in motion, and ultimately economic

---

the wild?' In Genese Marie Sodikoff, ed., *The Anthropology of Extinction: Essays on Culture and Species Death* (Bloomington: Indiana University Press, 2012); Genese Marie Sodikoff, ed., *The Anthropology of Exinction*; Dawson, *Extinction*.

growth, GDP and monetized well-being) but in terms of value embedded in daily life and non-capitalist needs, wants and actions.

ICCAs are a good example here. According to Grazia Borrini-Feyerabend and Jessica Campese, 'ICCAs embody many material and non-material values. Specific relationships and values should be identified by their custodian communities, not by outsiders,' and may include: 'secured livelihood', 'social resilience', 'cultural identity', 'spiritual significance', 'pride and community spirit', 'sovereignty', 'links to community history', and 'continuance' for the host community as the 'custodians of bio-cultural diversity'.[50] This, of course, is not to say that all is good and well with all ICCAs – as Borrini-Feyerabend and Campese also emphasize.[51] But the challenges and political nature of ICCAs are recognized by the consortium, and this, together with their convivial vision, is crucial for moving conservation forward.

#### FROM NATURAL CAPITAL TO EMBEDDED VALUE(S)

These five elements of a convivial conservation vision enable what would still be a form of *conservation* but one very different from current practice, namely a use of some parts of nature that is sustainable (that is, *not* geared towards eternal quantitative growth and accumulation), whilst being part and parcel *of* nature. It would entail *living with* other aspects of nature rather than physically or discursively being alienated from it. Indeed, conservation itself would be integrated and (re)embedded into daily life and all other domains of policy and action rather than something we do only in protected areas or when donating to an NGO.[52]

---

50   Grazia Borrini-Feyerabend and Jessica Campese, *Self-Strengthening ICCAs – Guidance on a Process and Resources for Custodian Indigenous Peoples and Local Communities* – draft for use by GSI partners, The ICCA Consortium, March 2017. Online at: iccaconsortium.org.

51   Borrini-Feyerabend and Campese, *Self-Strengthening*, 14.

52   In practice, this does actually occur to a significant degree, in the sense that environmental regulations and norms influencing everyday activities but not explicitly directed at protected areas (e.g. pollution control, vehicle emissions regulations, recycling, and so on) do often have the effect of supporting conservation in the latter. Convivial conservation would build on this to make such connections explicit and work to integrate them into a

Moreover, convivial conservation moves away from capital-inspired ways of rendering visible the value of nature, and instead become a part of broader structures of sharing the wealth that nature provides. As has been emphasized by non-Western, indigenous and other communities and scholars for centuries already, the wealth of nature does not lie in how it enables the accumulation and privatization of capital; it lies in the manifold ways in which it allows all humans to live convivial lives. Sharing this wealth must therefore always trump its privatization and subsequent accumulation.

How to do this will always be political, subject to interests, needs, histories and power dynamics. It will not lead to equilibrium or perfect sharing, including in a postcapitalist world. But it will allow *better* sharing, certainly if human natures over time grow accustomed to different systems of needs, wants and actions. In the process, we need to start 'seeing' nature differently. Nature, under conviviality, is always already visible. To 'render nature's values visible', as the capitalist TEEB project – The Economics of Ecosystems and Biodiversity – aims to do, would thus be unthinkable. The importance of nature – the web of life, the basis of all life – should never have to be 'made' visible. Living with nature means that it is visible by definition. 'Money' – the universal equivalent that is supposedly the tool to make nature 'visible' under capitalism – only renders nature visible on spreadsheets and through necessarily simplistic, technocratic decision-making models outside of relevant contexts. This renders nature unidimensional – solely what it is worth to humans-as-investors.[53] It does not – cannot – provide the kind of lived relationship to *multidimensional* (human *and* nonhuman) natures that convivial conservation foresees.

But 'visible' is not the right word for conviviality, as we are focused here on the levels of *being* and *becoming*. As humans are, so nature is – and vice versa. As humans become, so does nature – and vice versa. Living with nature, in many ways, is acute: it directly triggers or

---

cohesive policy package.

53   Ironically, this occurs even in effort to take into account those 'intrinsic' values that money can indeed never accurately represent – including 'spiritual' ones – as projects like the Natural Capital Protocol claim to do.

stimulates the senses – positively and negatively – and as such enables a continuous, direct feedback loop (we might call this metabolism!) between humans and the rest of nature. Convivial conservation is therefore about different *uses*, *frames* and forms of *embeddedness* of multiple natures. It is about *not* setting nature apart but integrating the uses of (nonhuman) natures into social, cultural, and ecological contexts and systems (i.e., re-embedding).

In each of the five elements of the vision, important practical steps can immediately be taken that help to bring a world of convivial conservation into being. But before we get there, let us reflect on the process of transition itself.

### FROM HERE TO THERE

So how do we get to convivial conservation? This is the next major element to be discussed: our theory of change, or how we view the process of transition from here to there. We highlight three important elements: how to deal with *power*, with *time* and with *actors*.

### DEALING WITH POWER

In the previous chapter, we already alluded to the radical differences that exist with respect to the question of power. How should we pursue social change and what should our politics and struggles be aimed at? On these questions, progressive critical theorists differ fundamentally, as illustrated by the contrasting positions of Rosi Braidotti and David Harvey. Braidotti sees 'unopposed' capitalism as the biggest problem we face: 'the "new" ideology of the free market economy has steam-rolled all oppositions, in spite of massive protest from many sectors of society, imposing anti-intellectualism as a salient feature of our times.'[54] Harvey agrees and argues that 'something different in the way of investigative methods and mental conceptions is plainly needed in these barren intellectual times if we are to escape the current hiatus in

---

54   Braidotti, *Posthumanism*, 4.

economic thinking, policies and politics'.[55] Yet the two differ greatly in their responses to these issues. Braidotti asserts:

> The awareness of the instability and the lack of coherence of the narratives that compose the social structures and relations, far from resulting in the suspension of political and moral action, become the starting point to elaborate new forms of resistance suited to the polycentric and dynamic structure of contemporary power. This engenders a pragmatic form of micro-politics that reflects the complex and nomadic nature of contemporary social systems and of the subjects that inhabit them. If power is complex, scattered and productive, so must be our resistance to it.[56]

This is precisely what Harvey argues against when he writes:

> What remains of the radical left now operates largely outside of any institutional or organized oppositional channels, in the hope that small-scale actions and local activism can ultimately add up to some kind of satisfactory macro alternative. This left, which strangely echoes a libertarian and even neoliberal ethic of anti-statism, is nurtured intellectually by such thinkers as Michel Foucault and all those who have reassembled postmodern fragmentations under the banner of a largely incomprehensible post-structuralism that favour identity politics and eschews class analysis. Autonomist, anarchist and localist perspectives and actions are everywhere in evidence. But to the degree that this left seeks to change the world without taking power, so an increasingly consolidated plutocratic capitalist class remains unchallenged in its ability to dominate the world without constraint.[57]

A central problematic – at least in leftist academic writing – thus concerns how to build resistance to the power of capitalism and its

---

55    Harvey, *Seventeen*, xiii.
56    Braidotti, *Posthumanism*, 26–7.
57    Harvey, *Seventeen*, xii-xii.

'commodification of everything'. Is it about micro-politics or about 'taking (structural) power'? Power, as conceptualized in this book, is *both* structural and dispersed in micro-settings. Hence, we agree with Braidotti that power is 'complex, scattered and productive', but to leave it at that, which she and many poststructuralists do, is a fundamental mistake that indeed plays in the hands of structural capitalist power itself.[58] Slavoj Žižek rightfully notes that a focus on an 'irreducible plurality of struggles' runs the risk of renouncing 'any real attempt to overcome the existing capitalist liberal regime'.[59]

In our writing, we have consistently argued for a co-constitutive understanding of structural and post-structural understandings of reality, as well as the co-constitution of structural power and the power of agency.[60] Hence dispersed forms of resistance matter, but these alone will never achieve our aims. Naomi Klein reinforced this position when she recently acknowledged that her own earlier celebration of the 'movement of movements' comprising the alterglobalization protests at the turn of the century was problematic in not also calling for the organization of these movements into a cohesive overarching platform. This she now argues is badly needed, particularly if we want to deal with the global threat of climate change.[61] Again, this is not to dismiss the importance and potential of micro-political struggles, which are essential to effecting change on the ground. The point is that these must be accompanied and inspired by more organized efforts to effect large-scale structural change as well for them not to be undermined by these same forces. Whether this 'organised effort' must be through the state, as Harvey asserts, is uncertain (although

---

58   Harvey, *Seventeen*.

59   Judith Butler, Ernesto Laclau and Slavoj Žižek, *Contingency, Hegemony, Universality* (London: Verso, 2000), 95.

60   See, especially, Robert Fletcher and Bram Büscher, 'The PES conceit: Revisiting the relationship between payments for environmental services and neoliberal conservation', *Ecological Economics* 132 (2017), 224–31; Robert Fletcher and Bram Büscher, 'Neoliberalism in denial in actor-oriented PES research? A rejoinder to Van Hecken et al. (2018) and a call for justice', *Ecological Economics* 156 (2019), 420–23.

61   Naomi Klein, *This Changes Everything: Capitalism vs. the Climate* (London: Penguin, 2014).

certainly not the contemporary capitalist state), but, certainly, power
needs to be organized across different levels of governance.[62]

## DEALING WITH TIME: A TWO-STEP STRATEGY OF CHANGE

Any act of change must – whatever else it is – be a political struggle and a strategy to deal with institutionalized forms of accumulated
power across both material and discursive domains. As Peck shows,
this was actually a core component of neoliberals' own theory of
change in the tireless promotion of their perspective over the course
of many decades.[63] Milton Friedman famously proclaimed,

> Only a crisis – actual or perceived – produces real change. When
> that crisis occurs, the actions that are taken depend on the ideas that
> are lying around. That, I believe, is our basic function: to develop
> alternatives to existing policies, to keep them alive and available
> until the politically impossible becomes the politically inevitable.[64]

The remarkable prescience of this statement implies that change
requires both promotion of a coherent conceptual structure vis-à-vis
the status quo and transformation in the underlying material structures able to create a new opening for this promotion.

This is no different in conservation. Despite neoprotectionists'
occasional and implicit assertions to the contrary, conservation is
not somehow separate from the broader capitalist world order but
is integral to it. This is why we believe a two-step strategy for dealing
with change over time is most realistic, one that does not separate
but rather combines (radical) reformism and radical, systemic change
away from capitalist modes of production, valuation, exchange
and living. Hence, we are talking about a short(er) term and a

---

62   See Harvey, *Spaces of Hope*, for a proposal on how to organize power and livelihoods across scale in a postcapitalist society.

63   Peck, *Constructions*.

64   Milton Friedman, *Capitalism and Freedom: Fortieth Anniversary Edition*
(Chicago: University of Chicago Press, 2002), xiv.

medium-to-long(er) term strategy enacted *at the same time*. One part of the change strategy must always be accompanied by the other, as the one needs to lead to, and be inspired by, the other. Obviously, this is anything but easy, as Aili Pyhälä and colleagues along with many others show, but it is necessary nonetheless.[65]

In the short term, we must do what we can to subvert the logic of capital in micro, meso, and macro-political practice, through state, non-state and individual action simultaneously. In this, we take inspiration from the community economies perspective pioneered by Gibson-Graham, which points to the ways that postcapital-ist practice can be effected in myriad forms within the overarching capitalist order.[66] In the medium to longer term, immediate actions must be accompanied by larger-scale efforts to conceptualize and build 'alternative economic spaces', based not on the logics of capital and economic growth but on those of equality and radical ecologi-cal democracy. Likewise, for conservation, the short-term actions described below always need to be inspired by and work towards the convivial conservation vision outlined above.

The actual outcomes of these interlinked strategies of change (for nature and conservation) depend on complex, contrived and contra-dictory processes that no one can foresee. Hence, this will require political expediency, shrewdness, organization and persistence. But we do believe that this two-part strategy is the most realistic to start building an appropriate context for a productive future for global conservation.

---

65   Aili Pyhälä et al., 'Global environmental change: Local perceptions, understand-ings, and explanations', *Ecology and Society* 21 (2016), 25.

66   Gibson-Graham, *A Postcapitalist Politics*. Key practices to promote include the key degrowth proposals detailed earlier: truly 'green' production; elimination of perverse subsidies for unsustainable production; augmenting and redirecting public spending to support green production and community-based conservation; taxing $CO_2$ and financial transactions to generate the finance needed to do this; defusing competitive pressure; slow-ing down international trade; reducing advertising; promoting alternative cosmological visions and values; myriad household changes in terms of consumption, energy use, build-ing materials, and so forth.

### DEALING WITH ACTORS

Within structures of power across space and time, different actors take different positions. These cannot be homogenized or generalized easily (if at all). And yet, it is important that we try to do so. Following our theoretical principle that conservation is an element within a broader process of 'uneven geographical development', we need to acknowledge the variegated political positions of different actors within a fundamentally 'uneven' conservation politics. This will allow us to *politically* account for the relation between local actors who live in or near conservation spaces or spaces of conservation interest, and the actors who in terms of their position in the global capitalist system live far from these but put much pressure on them – and on biodiversity *in toto* – nonetheless. After all, a major contradiction of conservation has long been that the focus of interventions is commonly on local actors ('community based') because they have a *direct* link to certain species or ecosystems.[67] Conservation interventions focus much less often on extra-local actors responsible for adding to the general pressure on biodiversity. This needs redressing.

To start doing so, distinguishing four different categories of global conservation actors is a useful starting point (see figure 4).[68] Actors within these four categories have different (historical and contemporary) types of responsibilities and roles within and related to conservation. The local residents who often live in or with biodiversity and who (still) depend on the land for subsistence comprise category 4: the rural lower classes. They are often (seen as) poor and the ones who have least contributed to global problems of biodiversity loss (historically and contemporarily). Yet they are most often targeted in conservation interventions and forced or 'incentivized' to change their livelihoods to meet biodiversity targets.

---

67    Michael P. Wells and Thomas O. McShane, 'Integrating protected area management with local needs and aspirations', *AMBIO: A Journal of the Human Environment* 33 (2004), 513–19.

68    Crucially, this categorization (in figure 4) is meant as a heuristic, not to provide an adequate reflection of empirical reality in actual places.

Figure 4. Generic categorization of classes important for conservation.

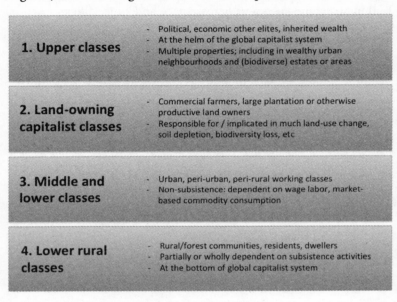

| 1. Upper classes | - Political, economic other elites, inherited wealth<br>- At the helm of the global capitalist system<br>- Multiple properties; including in wealthy urban neighbourhoods and (biodiverse) estates or areas |
| --- | --- |
| 2. Land-owning capitalist classes | - Commercial farmers, large plantation or otherwise productive land owners<br>- Responsible for / implicated in much land-use change, soil depletion, biodiversity loss, etc |
| 3. Middle and lower classes | - Urban, peri-urban, peri-rural working classes<br>- Non-subsistence: dependent on wage labor, market-based commodity consumption |
| 4. Lower rural classes | - Rural/forest communities, residents, dwellers<br>- Partially or wholly dependent on subsistence activities<br>- At the bottom of global capitalist system |

Category 3 consists of the general urban, semi-urban or semi-rural middle and lower classes throughout the world, who do not depend directly on the land for subsistence and are mostly involved in global labour and consumer markets that they participate in but have little control over save for their consumption choices. Via this consumption they do heavily influence biodiversity in many places. But they are often not part of or specifically targeted by conservation interventions, except as potential donors. When they are actively targeted by conservation organizations, they are mostly considered consumers rather than political agents.

Next, we distinguish land-owning capitalist classes such as major capitalist farmers and/or landholders for large agro-industry. They are often targeted by conservation, not as part of community-based interventions, but as partners in the conservation effort or as targets of (so-called) activist interventions or forms of resistance. In many places (Indonesia, Brazil, Central Africa and so forth) these classes are also part of violent frontiers of land conversion, and hence difficult to target and engage with.[69]

Then there are the global upper classes that are, politically, economically or otherwise, at the helm of the global capitalist system.[70] Interestingly, these elites are often both urban and rural – owning multiple properties, including in rich residential areas in cities to be close to elite political–economic circles, but also with second, third or even more properties in rural, semi-rural and biodiversity-rich spaces, including large estates and private reserves.[71] Upper class elites are often recruited as funders or included on boards of conservation organizations, but rarely targeted as part of conservation initiatives aiming at behavioural or livelihood change, as they are often either seen as unreachable (they live behind walls, security systems, or simply remotely) or as doing good for the environment through their philanthrocapitalism or other forms of conservation related charity (including through the privatization of nature and parks and so on). Hence the upper classes have a contradictory double role as they are at the helm of the system that keeps the pressure on biodiversity intense and high, while considered either untouchable or even seen as championing conservation through their large donations to conservation causes, NGOs and similar organizations.

Lastly, we consider the role of state actors, who historically have been among the most important players in enforcing conservation in most places, particularly through fortress strategies that have commonly relied on state financing and direction. A key question for leftists has long been the role of the state in progressive politics. While many Marxists have viewed the modern state as primarily a

---

69   See Jeremy Campbell, *Conjuring Property: Speculation and Environmental Futures in the Brazilian Amazon* (Seattle: University of Washington Press, 2015) for an astute analysis of this frontier in the Brazilian Amazon.

70   Often referred to as the 'transnational capitalist class' (see Sklair, *The Transnational*).

71   Holmes, 'The rich'; Holmes, 'Biodiversity for'.

tool of elite capitalist interests,[72] others take a more nuanced view of the relationship between state actors and capitalist processes.[73] There is also the issue of whether political action should engage or attempt to wholly evade the state. Addressing both issues, Foucault famously argued that 'the state, no more probably today than at any other time in its history, does not have this unity, this individuality, this rigorous functionality, nor, to speak frankly, this importance,'[74] and anarchists tend to follow this view in seeking to avoid state-centred politics entirely.[75] Marxists, by contrast, have always understood the state as a vital target of revolutionary action, a perspective reiterated by Harvey in stating, 'There is also a big problem on the left that many think the capturing of state power has no role to play in political transformations and I think they're crazy. Incredible power is located there and you can't walk away from it as though it doesn't matter.'[76]

The history of conservation shows that different states have performed in dramatically different ways, with some effectively nurturing biodiversity, others also working to combat poverty in relation to this, and still others acting ineffectually or even counterproductively with respect to either or both aims. The state must therefore be approached not as a homogenous monolith but rather, following Foucault, as a complex entity that 'does not have an essence'.[77] Yet we also agree with Harvey that tremendous power remains concentrated in state agencies; hence convivial conservation must engage with, enlist or emanate from these agencies as important potential mediators among the various actors previously discussed when this can support its goals. How this can best proceed – or whether convivial

---

72   For example, Louis Althusser, *Lenin and Philosophy and Other Essays* (New York: Monthly Review Press, 1972).

73   For example, see Arrighi, *The Long*.

74   Michel Foucault, *Power* (New York: The New Press, 1994), 220.

75   See, for instance, David Graeber, *Fragments of an Anarchist Anthropology* (Chicago: Prickly Paradigm Press, 2004); Simon Critchley, *Infinitely Demanding: Ethics of Commitment, Politics of Resistance* (London: Verso Books, 2014).

76   David Harvey, 'Is this really the end of neoliberalism?' *Counterpunch*, counterpunch.org, 13 April 2009.

77   Michel Foucault, The *Birth of Biopolitics* (New York: Palgrave MacMillan, 2008), 90.

conservation can be pursued more effectively independent of the state apparatus – will depend on the particular state in question and broader struggles in relation to changing the politics and organization of particular states.

While empirical reality is much more complex than our figure can depict, its broader point is that convivial conservation should not aim only or even mostly at category 4 actors, as it tends to do at present. Rather, it should target actors according to their differential responsibilities and accountabilities in relation to both the direct and indirect impacts their actions have on biodiversity, as well as the relative power these actors possess within broader structures of capitalist accumulation. Paraphrasing Jason Moore, it is about identifying, targeting and 'shutting down the relations' that produce biodiversity loss.[78]

In this way, we might reverse the model of 'polycentric' governance proposed by Ostrom and others.[79] In this standard model, governance is seen to start with local people and then must consider their embeddedness within overarching structures of governance with which they must contend to assert their space for self-governance. In our vision, by contrast, effective conservation governance would start by addressing actors in these superordinate levels in order to first target their actions, then work down towards the local people in direct contact with the biodiversity in question. In this way, the pressures exerted on local conservation initiatives can be proactively addressed at their source rather than merely retrospectively in relation to their impacts.

We should clarify that this governance model pertains only to the ways that conservationists frame and confront threats to conservation, not to how decision-making regarding effective conservation should proceed. As previously stated, the latter must embody deeply democratic forms of engagement in which local actors are placed at centre stage. A comprehensive conservation politics, therefore, must

---

78 Moore, 'The Rise', 94.
79 For example, see Ostrom and Cox, 'Moving beyond'.

simultaneously centre local people as key decision-makers in conservation planning and decentre them as the central targets of interventions aimed at fostering behavioural change.

This, we believe, is the only way to do democracy and history justice: to place the possibility for democratic arrangements in larger structures of power that highly influence whether and how these will succeed (or not) in practice. Phrased differently: merely focusing on local democracy without taking into account the power of 'outside' actors is naïve. The difficult tension between centring and decentring local people is therefore the right place to situate the democratic politics of convivial conservation.

## FROM THE LONG TERM TO THE SHORT TERM: CONCRETE ACTIONS

Convivial conservation calls for consideration of new ways to transform mainstream forms of economic development as neoprotectionists contend, while at the same time transcending human–nature divides as promoted by new conservationists. What types of concrete, short-term actions befit this approach and might enable us to move closer to the broad vision outlined earlier? We suggest several actions, with different registers and foci. These derive logically from the foregoing but are anything but exhaustive (and indeed not intended to be, as argued above).

### 1. Historic reparations

Convivial conservation needs to start by doing justice to conservation's history, especially the dynamics of dispossession and displacement that long characterized protected area formation and are still ongoing today in many places. *Historic reparations* – mainly directed at category 4 actors – are thus in order, which we believe need to be focused on the relations between people and their land, the biodiversity conserved on or through this land and the benefits communities do or do not derive from these. Importantly, these benefits, and the reparations, are material and non-material: acknowledgement of past injustices and the (re)distribution of resources need to go hand-in-hand.

Ideally, reparations mean that local communities receive their land back or at the very least get co-ownership of or co-management responsibilities over it. We recognize that these are anything but straightforward issues, especially since the land, the dispossessed peoples and the contexts in which these function have changed over time, and often drastically so.[80] Moreover, the value and needs of the biodiversity itself also need to be taken into account. These considerations can lead to myriad outcomes that must be worked out in context-specific ways. Regardless of the contextual specificities, however, a concern with historical justice and thorough decolonization needs to pervade convivial conservation moving forward, with special attention for the ways in which indigenous and other (previously) marginalized peoples themselves lead and inspire different forms of resistance to the violence brought about by the sixth extinction crisis.[81]

## 2. Conservation basic income

Above and beyond historic reparations through repossession of land and resources we advocate a *'conservation basic income'* for all communities living in or next to important conservation areas. A conservation basic income (CBI) is a monetary payment to individual community members living in or around promoted areas that allows them to lead a (locally defined) decent life. We consider this the conservation equivalent of a 'basic income grant' that is the hallmark of the new 'politics of redistribution' within international development circles.[82] This should be aimed at allowing people to

80    Stasja Koot and Bram Büscher, 'Giving land (back)? The meaning of land in the indigenous politics of the South Kalahari Bushmen land claim in South Africa', *Journal of Southern African Studies* (2019).

81    Audra Mitchell, 'Revitalizing laws, (re)-making treaties, dismantling violence: Indigenous resurgence against "the sixth mass extinction"', *Social & Cultural Geography* (2018).

82    See James Ferguson, *Give a Man a Fish: Reflections on the New Politics of Distribution* (Durham: Duke University Press, 2015). Basic income grants can be structured

(hopefully) sustain biodiversity-friendly livelihood pursuits without having to compete within a ruthless global marketplace in ways that undermine the sustainability to which these pursuits aim. CBI should be provided to communities by coalitions of resourceful conservation actors, especially large and small NGOs, states and the private sector. They can be combined with or used to supplement the society-wide basic income schemes that should be implemented more generally. To ensure that enough funds are available for this scheme, these actors should lobby governments to implement a conservation variant of the Tobin or 'Robin Hood' tax that seeks to redistribute resources from category 1 and 2 to category 4 actors.

Clearly, there are challenges determining who should receive such a grant, but we believe the policy should be substantial and include both communities of place (residing close to the conservation area of concern) and communities of use (those who have been making regular use of the area). Moreover, these payments are not meant to 'bribe' or incentivize communities away from their resources. In this sense, payments must be 'unconditional', that is, not tied to fulfilment of certain actions as in conditional cash transfer programmes.[83] They are meant to provide rural residents with options for livelihoods that will always need to include use of and interaction with biodiversity and resources (hopefully in a way similar to ICCAs). If any distancing should take place, it should not be between local people and their natural resources, but between local people and other, more powerful actors, so as to provide the former with more autonomy and options for democratic resource control.

---

in various ways, not all of them progressive. As Clark cautions, 'The hope of a social policy solution to the problems created by neoliberalism and the attacks associated with it is profoundly dangerous because that very "solution" can so readily assume a form that furthers the very agenda that left BI-advocates hope to escape. The institutions of global capitalism are taking an interest in Basic Income and the Davos crowd are even considering it.' See socialistproject.ca, accessed 11 November 2017. The key, then, is to combine CBI with the other elements of convivial conservation to ensure that it functions as a transformative form of resource redistribution rather than a bulwark of the current social order.

83   See Jamie Peck and Nik Theodore, *Fast Policy: Experimental Statecraft at the Threshold of Neoliberalisms* (Minneapolis: University of Minnesota Press, 2015).

To enable these two actions, we suggest that all conservation NGOs set up convivial conservation departments, which could replace or be merged with their current business or private sector liaison departments. This institutional innovation solves two important issues: first, it enables a shift in stakeholders considered most important for conservation NGOs. These should be local people living in or around, or making use of conservation areas, not wealthy companies as it seems is often the case today. Second, it enables a shift in the terms of engagement between corporations and conservation NGOs.

## 3. Rethinking (Relations with) Corporations

Clearly, the policy of trying to 'engage business' on the latter's terms (by making nature profitable and turning it into natural capital) has failed; hence this relationship needs drastic rethinking. Does this mean that conservation NGOs should no longer work with corporations? Not necessarily, but such engagement should proceed under stricter conditions. One of these is that conservation NGOs should only work with companies if the latter pledge to move towards a different economic model beyond capitalist accumulation and GDP-based economic growth. Ideally, and for the longer term, this should be focused on degrowth, but for the short term this could be towards a circular or doughnut economy.[84] If they are not willing to do so, then the NGO should not waste energy on 'engagement' as this too often leads to a problematic position of dependency and allows for green washing. Rather, NGOs should spend their energy on building countervailing power from an independent position.

After all, major conservation BINGOs such as WWF, CI, TNC and many others often collude with actors in category 1, while targeting actors in category 3 merely for modest consumption changes and donations and directly targeting category 4 for livelihood restrictions – sometimes even to enable category 1 actors to buy nice biodiversity-rich properties! This is not just historically unjust but does little, in

84   Raworth, *Doughnut Economics*.

the end, to help solve the problem. Hence conservationists' relations with corporations, and the global upper classes more generally, need to be drastically reconsidered.

We understand that this would inevitably exclude many large corporations that are not (yet) willing to consider the necessity for more radical change towards an alternative economic model.[85] But even many corporations and their CEOs should and do realize that their future, as well as that of their children, depends on a healthy planet, which should provide more than enough reason to come on board with convivial conservation. We also realize that this means that many conservation NGOs, especially the large BINGOs, may lose out on currently essential sources of income. But if their main goal is maximum income instead of maximum (or even minimum) benefit for nature, then clearly their priorities are distorted and not deserving of support.

Foregoing such revenue will indeed be a hard choice, as less income would also mean a more limited ability to pay historic reparations and provide for CBIs. But at least in this way NGOs become part of the solution again, rather than being part of the problem. And as a convivial conservation approach takes hold, new sources of funding would likely become available as states and international financial institutions (IFIs) refocus towards supporting CBIs and other forms of redistributive remuneration.

## 4. Convivial Conservation Coalition

All this should lead to a different global coalition – not a natural capital coalition, but a convivial conservation coalition (CCC) that focuses on the transition towards convivial conservation. The work of the CCC would focus on gaining power not to get money and a small seat at the global table but rather to hold other powerful actors accountable for their actions and to transform them from within. This coalition can help local, place-based actors to diffuse attention away

---

85   Itself the partial outcome of structural power relations developed over time.

from only category 4 actors to include the others as well. For example, this can be done by mapping reverse 'commodity chains' to identify the broader actors responsible for putting pressures on specific areas. An important example here is the Rainforest Action Network,[86] which does exactly this, but also others such as Greenpeace.[87]

As more and more groups and organizations come on board, the coalition can become increasingly influential in shaping global conservation policy and consequently its materialization within local spaces around the world. Yet convivial redirection can never be just top-down. It requires redirection in and rethinking concrete conservation spaces as well.

## 5. Redirection: Landscape, Governance and Finance

Finally, convivial conservation needs to be translated into concrete pathways for transformation in the governing of space, which we believe entails building: a) conservation landscapes that do not strictly separate humans and other species but promote coexistence; b) different modes of governing conservation in these spaces; and c) alternative funding arrangements that do not rely on market expansion and can – at least initially until redistributive mechanisms start gaining critical mass – work under conditions of austerity. Under convivial conservation, we envision change agents bringing together conceptual innovations from sustainability research and practical experiences from concrete case studies throughout the world to develop, evaluate and strengthen the transformative potential of these three pathways in pursuit of convivial conservation.[88]

---

86   See for example this recent pamphlet: 'Every Investor has a Responsibility', *A Forests and Finance Dossier*, forestsandfinance.org, accessed 25 February 2018.

87   See Jonathan Hari, 'The Wrong Kind of Green', *The Nation* 22 (2010).

88   Which means that there is also a research element to our programme, namely to study real-world cases that exhibit elements of convivial conservation in practice, and to see how these function in context, and whether these could, potentially, be transferred or upscaled. Or, if not, how they could network with like-minded initiatives to create political energy and inspiration. See convivialconservation.com.

## 5a. Integrated Conservation Landscapes

Developing conservation spaces that do not strictly separate humans and other species demands a landscape vision wherein we 'learn to accept both nature that looks a little more lived-in than we are used to and working spaces that look a little more wild than we are used to'.[89] Convivial conservation could operationalize this vision in multiple ways and here we provide just two possible examples focusing on human–animal cohabitation, especially when this leads to conflicts, and the relations between humans and larger ecosystems. In both examples, inspired by Molly Scott Cato's ideas about broader bioregional economies, the *production of space* will be critical: the ways in which socio-natural spatial designs are related to a complex socio-ecological variety of needs and interests.[90]

Regarding human–animal cohabitation, we envision a landscape – urban or rural – wherein important species could live, and start by identifying and studying economic and political impediments and opportunities related to potential spatial implications of solving human–animal conflicts in these spaces. This entails two steps. First, the examination of the spatiality of human–environment conflicts and tensions across the landscape and the identification of potential landscape modifications that could aid in solving these. Second, based on this, and through participatory mapping with local and certain extra-stakeholders, conceptualization of various landscape development trajectories that take human-environment conviviality as the central objective. Crucially, these will be based on the fact that many interactions between environments and people already happen in shared, fragmented spaces. Hence, we advocate turning habitat fragmentation into a spatial opportunity for convivial landscape planning.[91]

---

89  Marris, *Rambunctious Garden*, 151.

90  Scott Cato, *The Bioregional Economy*.

91  This is, obviously, not to say that fragmentation is a good thing, or that all ecological problems can be sorted by seeing fragmentation as a spatial opportunity. We fully realize certain species need large contiguous spaces to survive and hence we do not advocate fragmentation. Rather, this point is meant to emphasize that we need to start from the

Regarding the relation between humans and larger ecosystems, we imagine a similar process but one that focuses on a more detailed planning of how production and consumption activities in particular bioregions (again, *both* urban and rural, and everything in between) relate to specific ecosystems that provide the (raw) materials for these activities. This, of course, has become so complex in contemporary times, especially in large urban areas, that to try and do everything would be impossible. That is why we advocate starting with specific ecosystems wherein this dependency can be most directly established. These could include (fresh) water, as the distances between water and their use – although they can be large – are often local or regional. As the case of the drought of Cape Town shows – the first major global city that faced an acute water crisis[92] – the conservation of water sources is critically important, and depends on complex political–ecological factors, some of which can be directly controlled and some not (such as climate change). But once the availability and sustainable supply of water is more-or-less known, needs and interests can be renegotiated accordingly.[93] Another example could be locally specific biodiversity and their needs vis-à-vis inhabited (urban or rural) landscapes.

Importantly, the tools for this planning in both examples should be less important than the socio-cultural and political-economic process that accompanies it. This process maps the needs and interests of stakeholders in the short-term but also how these might change as the overall economy shifts to emphasize degrowth and sharing the wealth. Or, vice versa, as the planning process starts creating awareness of and promoting action on how people in bioregions can

---

reality of currently fragmented landscapes and make these part of a political process of convivial (landscape) reconstruction. The hope is that this will also lead to the restoration of larger, contiguous ecosystems fit for large predators (amongst others).

92   See capetowndrought.com for more information. Accessed 25 February 2018, two months before alleged 'day zero' was projected, the day that water will no longer come from Cape Town taps.

93   As is, indeed, happening in Cape Town, see 'City continues proactive water demand management and medium-to-long term planning', capetown.gov.za, 27 February 2017, accessed 25 February 2018.

contribute to degrowth and sharing the wealth. This is how an active process of changing needs and interests (and hence, human nature), while also challenging the vested interests associated with the creation of capitalist needs and interests, might start.

## 5b. Democratic Governance Arrangements

Following our landscape approach, governance focuses on three integrated dimensions: economics, politics and scale. Our most basic assumption is that taking into account political and economic histories, dynamics and trends is critical for any transformation to sustainability.[94] Convivial conservation in specific landscapes therefore not only studies the political and economic context within which integrated landscape development must function, but also builds convivial conservation into and through local and regional political and economic alliances. This helps to render transformations towards convivial conservation more locally legitimate, sensitive to situated knowledge and hence more socially sustainable. The local, however, is always co-constituted with larger (regional, national, global) dynamics (and vice versa), which necessitates governing *scale*. Focusing on integrated landscape development with a focus on human-more-than-human conviviality entails identifying those critical links between landscape and 'higher' governance scales that (positively or negatively) impact on the former. Convivial conservation thus asks what will be necessary for effective polycentric governance across scale and how actors in categories 1, 2 and 3 need to be engaged.

Following the preceding theory of change, one of these links may entail a reassessment and broader application of community-based conservation (CBC): with flexibility and decentralization focused on social re-embedding instead of (neoliberal) market engagement; with a deliberate change in the meaning of 'community' to also *include* (the rights of) nature (meaning: 'more-than-human' forms of affect,

---

94   Scott Cato, *Bioregional Economy*.

companionship and responsibility).[95] Researchers have increasingly highlighted the ways that nonhumans help to shape how they are understood and treated by humans.[96] This 'more-than-human' focus on nonhumans as 'actants' has important implications for conservation practice, pointing toward the need for much more sensitivity in terms of how nonhumans are studied and managed in protected areas and other conservation spaces.[97] The needs and rights of nonhumans in shaping the conservation practice to which they are subject is an issue that neoprotectionists emphasize,[98] as well as a concern in terms of an expansive understanding of democratization in conservation politics. This must be a central focus of attention in convivial conservation, while again recognizing that it is ultimately humans who will have to accept and exercise their unique and unequal agency in deciding how to treat nonhumans who cannot actually participate in democratic deliberations as equivalent subjects.

Living with biodiversity and ecosystems within manifold contexts would entail the deliberate construction of a new form of CBC. This is not a neoliberalized, interventionist type of community-based natural resources management (CBNRM). It is one where 'some of the core values of CBNRM [are] brought back to the fore in both discourse and action: ensuring social justice, supporting material wellbeing and stimulating environmental integrity relative to local conditions and context'.[99]

It would also require developing deeper forms of participatory democracy in conservation decision-making. While ensuring the 'participation' of local 'stakeholders' has become a stock requirement of most conservation planning these days, how this is understood varies greatly among projects,[100] and is usually implemented only

---

95    Lorimer, *Wildlife*; Haraway, *Staying with the Trouble*.

96    Key references include Donna Haraway, *When Species Meet*; Haraway, *Staying with the Trouble*; Lorimer, *Wildlife*; Tsing, *The Mushroom*.

97    Lorimer, *Wildlife*.

98    See Wuerthner et al., *Against the*; Wuerthner et al., *Protecting the*.

99    Dressler et al., 'From hope', 13.

100    Bina Agarwal, 'Participatory exclusions, community forestry, and gender: An analysis for South Asia and a conceptual framework', *World Development* 29 (2001),

superficially in most.[101] Convivial conservation, by contrast, would require that relevant local residents be integrated into planning and decision-making as central voices from start to finish.

## 5c. Alternative Funding Mechanisms

Critical for convivial landscape development is the generation of funding mechanisms beyond tourism and other market-based instruments (MBIs). This, as mentioned, is in line with a growing critique of market-led approaches and calls for creative new forms of (re) distribution within international development.[102] Convivial conservation builds on these by studying the potential for (at least) three interrelated forms of conservation finance that promote redistribution above and beyond the suggestions above. First, we ask how we can cut conservation operating costs. 'Living with' nature through the above landscape and governance arrangements requires less funding since it aims to reduce human–animal conflicts.

The transformation to get there, however, takes time. Therefore, a second convivial conservation explores the possibilities of adapting existing conservation and development funding schemes, particularly payments for environmental services (PES) and cash transfer programmes, towards newly envisioned, convivial ends. While conceived as MBIs, many such mechanisms in reality function as forms of redistribution,[103] and this dynamic may be built upon in developing the CBI mechanism outlined earlier. These may be supplemented by acquiring investment funds through public bonds or 'Robin Hood' taxes which provide capital required to shift systems from high to low costs, with the principal and any interest payments – if necessary – being met by long-term savings of cheaper management regimes.

Third, we envision development of local conservation insurance schemes, particularly when it comes to dealing with more dangerous

---

1623–48.
101   Wells and McShane, 'Integrating protected'.
102   Ferguson, *Give a Man a Fish*.
103   Fletcher and Büscher, 'The PES conceit'.

fauna, funded via preceding and local mechanisms, aimed at generating a further investment pool. Many of these are already in existence or development in various places, and hence should be studied in terms of both their potential and pitfalls. Beyond reparations from human–animal conflicts, this funding can be invested to further stimulate integrated landscape development. Ultimately, to fund convivial conservation we envision a diverse set of revenue sources combining state-based taxation (including public bonds), grants from international donors and individual patrons, insurance schemes, long-term engagement fees, sale of sustainable products, crowdsourcing campaigns, new blockchain technologies, and whatever else can be harnessed in the interest of a broader convivial conservation platform.

## CONCLUSION

In this chapter, we have developed our alternative proposal for saving nature in the Capitalocene called convivial conservation. Or rather, we started to develop this proposal, as one chapter could never do justice to all the intricacies, issues and dynamics that need to be taken into account in such a proposal. One issue that we have, for example, not touched upon is the role of the Internet and online (social) media in enabling (or disabling) transformative change. These have obviously become critical in influencing actual politics and governance dynamics and hence need to be seriously considered and studied as part of the above proposals and reflections. Yet, rather than attempting to do all this and more here, we believe the further development of convivial conservation necessarily needs to become part of a broader collective effort.

In other words, a proposal presented in this form could never be more than a set of loose and incomplete guiding principles whose concrete form would need to be worked out in practice through processes of participatory co-creation. What matters most to us, however, is how the logic informing our proposal has been developed over the course of the book. This logic – steeped in political ecology and the principles outlined in chapter four – helped us to evaluate existing radical conservation proposals while also imagining a more promising alternative. This type of logic and reasoning is inspired by many others and will, we hope, be taken further by others still, in actual conservation spaces, practices and conversations. In fact, this is already happening to some degree, as the various illustrations throughout the book have emphasized.

So, even as we are sensitive to Foucault's caution that formulating proposals of this sort risks replicating the same hierarchal relations of power one seeks to subvert, we agree with a growing chorus of voices that scholarly engagement can no longer be merely about critique.[104] Grounded in a thorough analysis of the problem in question, such engagement must begin to construct or at least envision practicable alternatives as well. In this sense, the proposal outlined here is an act of imaginative 'alternative realism' serving to transcend the status quo. What this means will be explicated in our final, concluding chapter.

---

104   Michel Foucault, *Remarks on Marx: Conversations with Duccio Trombadori* (New York: Semiotext(e), 1991).

# Conclusion: Revolution!

In this book we have presented and evaluated several radical ideas for saving nature in the Anthropocene. But we never really defined what we mean by 'radical'. Radical comes from 'radix' or 'radic', which means 'roots' in Latin. Being radical in the original etymological sense of the word therefore has nothing to do with 'extremes'. It rather means going to the roots. Anyone can understand that the only real solution to the conjoined environmental and development problems of our time must address the root causes of these problems. This meaning of radical entails attaining a coherent and logical understanding of what the roots of our problems are and how they manifest in practical reality. This is why, in chapters two and three, we spent quite some time on theoretical questions raised by the debate on how to save nature in the Anthropocene. This is also why we spent a good deal of space, in the previous chapter, developing our own proposal for 'convivial conservation'.

But, even if we follow the popular connotation of the term as meaning 'extreme', we think that our convivial conservation proposal is actually not that radical. Yes, our proposal goes to the roots of the problem and, from there, tries to build up a constructive alternative, taking into account current material and political realities through our strategy for change in relation to power, time and various actors. Going against the capitalist grain always invites the same type of response, namely that the thinking we have displayed in the last chapters of the book is 'unrealistic', fanciful or simply incorrect – that the kind of radical proposal we put forward will never work because, indeed, it is *too* 'radical'. Our response is that this is exactly the point: it *should* be 'unrealistic' if realism means 'capitalist realism'. After all, ideological hegemony functions precisely to 'define . . . what is realistic and what is not realistic, and to drive certain aspirations and grievances into the realm of the impossible, of idle dreams'.[1] Challenging capitalist hegemony, therefore, entails challenging its definition of what is 'realistic' or 'possible' as well.

What is truly radical, in an extremely negative way, is to continue down a status quo path knowing it will lead to disaster for most of earth's inhabitants. Or put differently: a capitalist political economy hell-bent on continuing destructive 'business as usual' at all cost – is this *not* radical?[2] Yet if we understand radical as going to the roots in trying to attend to, nurture and care for the roots of life, then current capitalist conservation is not truly radical, but merely extreme. Its proposals for reform do not go to the roots but remain shockingly superficial.

In refusing to confront a capitalist economy that will inexorably diminish the resources it seeks to defend, mainstream conservation is far more radical or extreme than our proposal. It systemically colludes in destroying the radix of life rather than working to nurture it (a point nicely captured by Zapiro in figure 5). And since we have shown that the radical alternatives now on the table – new conservation and

---

1   James C. Scott, *Domination and the Arts of Resistance* (New Haven, CT: Yale University Press, 1990), 73.
2   Here, however, we have to be careful, because many rather conservative or 'business-as-usual' approaches, such as the Natural Capital Accounting platform also position themselves as a radical challenge to business as usual (see Robert Fletcher, 'Orchestrating consent: Post-politics and intensification of Nature™ Inc. at the 2012 World Conservation Congress', *Conservation and Society* 12 (2014), 329–42). As Dan Brockington ('A radically conservative vision? The challenge of UNEP's towards a green economy', *Development and Change* 43 (2012), 409–22) points out, such positions are actually 'radically conservative' in asserting that 'we have to change radically, but within the contours of the existing state of the situation . . . so that nothing really has to change'. (Erik Swyngedouw, 'Apocalypse forever? Post-political populism and the spectre of climate change', *Theory, Culture & Society* 27 (2010), 219.) Truly transformative change means moving away from capital and general ideas about growth, including GDP. Anything else risks contributing to worsening the situation.

Figure 5. Debating how to destroy earth more slowly.

Source: Zapiro.

new back-to-the-barriers – cannot provide a credible way out of this conundrum, we believe that our radical alternative of convivial conservation is the most optimistic, equitable and, importantly, the most *realistic* model for conservation for the future. This final concluding chapter serves to elaborate on this argument – not by trying to convince readers that our alternative knows or resolves everything, but that it is part of a broader stream of generative, radical and inspiring ideas, proposals, dynamics and practices that work to build a constructive alternative realism.

### ALTERNATIVE REALISM AND RADICAL CHOICES

We began this book by stating that conservation is at a crossroads, and that the emergence of the Anthropocene has made the choices that are facing conservation even more difficult than they already were. This, then, is the basic reality facing conservation: radical choices *have* to be made. The time is over for incorporating all manners of finding a way forward (through 'integrated conservation and development projects', 'peace parks', or the like) or for simply seeing 'what works' regardless of political context or commitment, although perhaps not in many policy circles or neoliberal, social democratic communities. But even these spheres should (and increasingly do) accept that we can no longer afford to not think about the radical choices we confront. This is not to say that we should not look for complementarities and things that unite. Yet we must always do this in pursuit of the broader systemic change that will be needed to confront entrenched and institutionalized power.

The alternative radical proposals we have discussed go some way towards accepting and accomplishing this. Driven by the credo 'desperate times call for desperate measures', they have led an increasing number of conservationists to propose radical changes to our society and economy to halt the current social and ecological crisis. But as we have shown, the full implications of their calls are deeply concerning, both for the changes that they portend and because they do not get to the roots of the problems they address. New conservation points to the limits of a nature–culture dichotomy and the need to address poverty in cultivating effective conservation while neoprotectionists point to the problematic promotion of capitalist conservation. In so doing, however, both positions overlook essential elements of the problems they identify. New conservationists fail to connect their critique of the nature–society dualism with a capitalism that perpetuates both the dualisms and the poverty they wish to address, while neoprotectionists fail to explain how an autonomous nature could possibly be defended from this same capitalism that is grounded upon cannibalizing nature in its quest for continual growth, nor how issues of poverty or social development could be addressed within their nature-needs-half platform.

We thus believe that our convivial conservation alternative is more realistic, simply because it is more logical and consistent with empirical reality than these other two radical alternatives. Following McKenzie Wark, we propose this as a deliberate act of *alternative realism* that imagines conservation outside of the capitalist box. This we find a liberating exercise that allows for harnessing necessary anxieties triggered by the devastating implications of our contemporary crises in order to unleash positive energy and anti-catastrophic prospects. It is also truly necessary given the political economic context we are in, both in terms of the directions that contemporary capitalism is taking generally, and very specifically with regard to several massive political developments that occurred in 2016, culminating in the election of Donald Trump as president of the United States. If our point was not already clear by analysing the general and dangerous directions that contemporary capitalism is taking, then we believe they should become especially clear with what we refer to as the 'Trump moment in conservation'.[3]

## THE TRUMP MOMENT IN CONSERVATION

We had hoped it could not be possible but it did happen during the writing of this book: Donald Trump was elected and installed as US President. And while the full environmental consequences of his presidency remain to be seen, they clearly do not look good. From his appointments of a climate change denier as head of the Environmental Protection Agency and ExxonMobile CEO as (erstwhile) Secretary of State to the immediate dismantling of environmental regulations and reinstating of major oil pipelines in his first days in office, Trump has set back an already beleaguered environmental movement quite some way, both in the US and globally. In this way, he demonstrates our earlier point that capitalism can persevere in the short term even as it exacerbates ecological crisis in the long term. Biodiversity is equally likely to suffer under a Trump presidency, but this is not the only reason why his election is significant for conservation. Following from the analysis presented in this book, we argue that conservation faces a much bigger challenge; one that we believe should be referred to as the 'Trump moment in Conservation'.

---

3    Earlier published as a blog post on the Entitle blog site: Bram Büscher and Robert Fletcher, 'The Trump moment in environmental conservation', entitleblog.org, 2 February 2017.

Basically, the Trump moment means that mainstream conservation refuses – at its peril and that of the biodiversity it aims to conserve
– to properly acknowledge the root causes of biodiversity loss and to
support the radical types of responses necessary to halt and reverse
this trend. Instead, as we have shown, many conservationists are
content – often proudly or 'pragmatically' so – to join forces with the
economic logics and institutions of destruction behind such terms as
'natural capital' or 'ecosystem services'. In doing so, they might occasionally slow down some biodiversity loss in some places. But at the
very same time they strengthen the broader drivers of biodiversity
destruction that completely undermine the small gains that might be
made (again, see figure 5). This is the conservation equivalent of the
'Trump' moment, which can only be tackled by taking and supporting
much more radical action. It is on this point that we have, in chapter four, insisted that we not only look at different positions in the
Anthropocene conservation debate in terms of their logical contradictions, but also in terms of their importance in demonstrating that
discontent with mainstream conservation is growing rapidly. We
argue that the time is now to push this movement much further.

Despite their differences, proponents of both the new conservation and neoprotectionist positions agree that the increasingly desperate state of the entire planet's environment calls for radical new forms
of action to defend it from destruction. Trump's election makes this
acknowledgement even more acute. For his election is in fact itself a
radical – extreme – response to the increasingly desperate situation
in which we find ourselves, environmentally, economically and politically. As part of a disturbing rise of reactionary politics in many places
– the election of Jair Bolsonaro in Brazil in 2018 comes to mind – it
can be seen as an intensification (prompted by the ongoing fallout
from the 2008 global economic crisis) of the intimate links between
financialization and militarization that capitalism – and particularly
its neoliberal variant – has always displayed. And what this signals
is that opposition to this type of radical right politics can no longer
be content to pursue the conciliatory 'Third Way' or more general
consensus politics institutionalized by Bill Clinton and Tony Blair,

either in the overarching political realm or in conservation politics in particular. If we do not become more radical and politically astute, more positive, equal and sustainable futures will be overwhelmed and emptied by the radical groundswell from populist right-wing movements on the ascent in many places.

In terms of conservation, this means that the two radical proposals currently on the table are not nearly radical enough. Indeed, both positions are self-defeating in failing to adopt a consistent, new position that would transcend the limitations of current, mainstream conservation efforts and provide the basis for a truly radical new politics capable of providing an effective counterbalance to the inertia on the (populist) right.

What the Trump moment tells us, most fundamentally, is that the era of moderate, compromise politics, both in the environmental realm and more generally, is over. We cannot appeal to the corporate social responsibility of Coca Cola, Shell, Rio Tinto or other members of the World Business Council for Sustainable Development. Nor can we turn half the earth into a fortress and expect this to be appropriate defence against them. Instead, we must develop and vigorously champion a critical-constructive position that directly challenges the integrated social and environmental consequences of capitalist production and the human alienation from nonhuman processes that this same production promotes.

Fortunately, there are already some insightful models for how to do this that have been marginalized by the polarization between the so-called radical positions currently dominating the conservation debate.[4] A movement towards convivial conservation must proceed in lockstep with other burgeoning degrowth, climate justice, slow food, housing, peasant, labour and other movements that – although not perfect – show us the right way forward, both in content and increasingly in terms of the kind of radical politics we believe is necessary.

---

4   Matulis and Moyer, 'Beyond Inclusive'.

## SIMPLE CHOICES?

In this Trumpian moment, therefore, our choices may actually have become rather simple: only by promoting a massive redistribution in control of the earth's remaining natural resources and occupation of its natural spaces, while transitioning to an economic system that strives for equitable sufficiency rather than ever-increasing profit-seeking growth, can we possibly hope to redress the mounting crisis we are facing. This is very far from where we are right now, but is it any less realistic a vision than herding half the world's human population onto half of the earth's surface? Or allowing profit-driven corporations to turn global conservation into a profitable endeavour by, quite literally, turning all of life on earth into accounting sheets?

Whichever stance one takes, it is time for critical conservation scholars to clearly stake out our own position vis-à-vis those outlined above. Indeed, we would argue that we do not have the luxury to *not* do so, given that our research, which we have inserted into the public sphere, has already been appropriated to stake out positions in the debate with which many of us likely disagree. As anthropologists Henrik Vigh and David Sausdal point out, 'the knowledge we ... produce ... enters into our world(s) in unintended and uncontrollable ways',[5] sometimes causing us, as Bruno Latour laments, 'to be considered as friends by the wrong sort of allies'.[6] Yet this uptake may be rendered (slightly) more intended and controllable by more clearly explaining how we envision our work to be understood and utilized. Thus far, critical conservation scholars have been principally concerned with criticizing and deconstructing the perspectives and actions of those we find objectionable on conceptual, ethical, as well as practical grounds. While this remains important, it is also crucial to now respond to this reception and uptake of our work and to more actively shape its future use.

---

5   Henrik E. Vigh and David B. Sausdal,' From essence back to existence: Anthropology beyond the ontological turn', *Anthropological Theory* 14 (2014), 49–73, 64.

6   Bruno Latour, 'Why has critique run out of steam? From matters of fact to matters of concern', *Critical Inquiry* 30 (2004), 231. In Latour's case, these 'wrong allies' should perhaps not be surprising considering the direction of his work, cf. Malm, *The Progress*.

## CODA: WELCOME TO THE CONSERVATION REVOLUTION!

If the point of critical scholarship is, ultimately, to change the world in which we live, then we need to ensure that the change we promote is just: one that champions neither the commodification nor the militarization of conservation spaces.[7] By more clearly understanding the central terms of debate and the different positions and disputes concerning them we can be clearer about our own positions vis-à-vis others. Our hope is that the analysis offered here has clarified where the conservation debate currently stands while pointing to productive avenues for moving it forward beyond the present standoff.[8] Our proposal for convivial conservation is but one stream in a broader river of movements, struggles and ideas that seek to transcend the capitalist status quo. Convivial conservationists – whether social scientists, practitioners, rangers or otherwise – must therefore ally themselves with, learn from and contribute to these broader rivers

---

7  Noel Castree et al., eds, *The Point is to Change it: Geographies of Hope and Survival in an Age of Crisis* (New York: John Wiley & Sons, 2010).

8  In doing so, we are acutely aware that we need to move beyond familiar circles. In fact, in this we may find heretofore unlikely allies among conservation practitioners themselves. Sandbrook et al., ('Social Research and Biodiversity Conservation') have begun to study views among 'actual existing conservationists' whose voices do not necessarily register within the public debate outlined above. Their initial findings suggest that employees of major conservation organizations may be broadly divided into three main camps. The first two comprise forms of 'cautious pragmatism'. While these positions are largely rhetorical, they are to some degree both reflective of and reflected in 'real world' conservation practice, which is today becoming increasingly polarized between distinct yet intersecting trends towards neoliberalization, reflecting the Anthropocenists, on the one hand, and militarization, reflecting the neoprotectionists, on the other. A third position, however, appears to be critical of both of these positions, namely those who are more sceptical of market mechanisms than critical social science often gives them credit for. It is therefore important to emphasize that many conservationists feel uneasy about markets and the neoliberalization of conservation as well (Sandbrook et al., 'Social Research and Biodiversity Conservation'; George Holmes et al., 'Understanding conservationists' perspectives', 353–63) and that several conservationists have written expressly and critically about the links between neoliberal capitalism and conservation, including species extinction. This, then, provides a potentially fertile ground for enlarging the collective of actors *within* conservation (-minded) circles to pursue convivial conservation.

of change. This is a massive challenge. It is, in fact, a revolutionary challenge; one already tackled by many people around the world. Through this book, we join them with hope.

# Index